4-77

D0975723

SCHOOL OF

CALIFORNIA PROFESSIONAL

PSYCHOLOGY

San Francisco Campus

Gift of

James Vaughan

BEHAVIORAL SCIENCE
AND MODERN PENOLOGY

BEHAVIORAL SCIENCE AND MODERN PENOLOGY

A Book of Readings

Edited by

WILLIAM H. LYLE, JR., Ph.D.

Scientist Director
United States Public Service
Washington, D.C.
Formerly Chief Psychologist
Federal Penitentiary
Marion, Illinois

and

Thetus W. Horner

Inmate
Tennessee State Penitentiary
Nashville, Tennessee

CHARLES C THOMAS · PUBLISHER
Springfield · *Illinois* · *U.S.A.*

Published and Distributed Throughout the World by

CHARLES C THOMAS • PUBLISHER

BANNERSTONE HOUSE

301-327 East Lawrence Avenue, Springfield, Illinois, U.S.A.

© *1973, by* CHARLES C THOMAS • PUBLISHER

ISBN 0-398-02677-7

Library of Congress Catalog Card Number: 72-88450

With **THOMAS BOOKS** *careful attention is given to all details of manufacturing and design. It is the Publisher's desire to present books that are satisfactory as to their physical qualities and artistic possibilities and appropriate for their particular use. THOMAS BOOKS will be true to those laws of quality that assure a good name and good will.*

Printed in the United States of America

C-1

CONTRIBUTORS

Myrl E. Alexander, Professor, Center for the Study of Crime, Delinquency and Correction, Southern Illinois University, Carbondale, Illinois.

F. Lovell Bixby, Senior Adviser, Asia and Far East Institute for the Prevention of Crime and Treatment of Delinquency, Tokyo, Japan.

John C. Burke, Formerly Warden, Wisconsin State Prison, Waupun, Wisconsin.

William R. Cozart, Assistant Professor, California Institute of Technology, Pasadena, California.

Donald R. Cressey, Professor of Sociology, University of California, Santa Barbara, California.

Arthur E. Fink, Professor, School of Social Work, University of North Carolina, Chapel Hill, North Carolina.

Howard B. Gill, Director, Institute of Correctional Administration, Washington, D.C.

Daniel Glaser, Professor, Department of Sociology and Anthropology, University of Southern California, Los Angeles, California.

Jack Hedblom, Assistant Professor, State University of Wichita, Wichita, Kansas; Formerly Staff Sociologist, Pennsylvania Prison Society, Philadelphia, Pennsylvania.

Garrett Heyns, Formerly Executive Director, Joint Commission on Correctional Manpower and Training, Washington, D.C.

Raymond C. Hodge

Richard Jessor, Professor of Psychology, University of Colorado, Boulder, Colorado.

O. G. Johnson, Associate Professor, Southern Illinois University, Edwardsville, Illinois.

A. M. Kirkpatrick, Executive Director, John Howard Society of Ontario, Toronto, Ontario.

Richard R. Korn, Assistant Professor, School of Criminology, University of California, Berkeley, California.

Rabbi William J. Leffler, Chaplain, Clinical Research Center, Lexington, Kentucky.

Edward B. Lewis

Louis Lipschitz, Member of Philadelphia Bar, Philadelphia, Pennsylvania.

Manuel Lopez-Rey, Director, Program of Criminological Research, Social Science Research Center, University of Puerto Rico, Rio Piedras, Puerto Rico.

Lewis Merklin, Research Fellow, Tavistock Centre, London, England.

Norval Morris, Julius Kreeger Professor of Law and Criminology and Director of the Center for Studies in Criminal Justice, University of Chicago, Chicago, Illinois.

Elmer K. Nelson, Jr., Professor of Public Administration, University of Southern California, Los Angeles, California.

Sheldon B. Peizer, Associate Professor of Psychology, Florida State University, Tallahassee, Florida.

Austin L. Porterfield, Emeritus Professor of Sociology, Texas Christian University, Fort Worth, Texas.

Alfred C. Schnur, Professor, Department of Sociology and Anthropology, Kansas State University, Manhattan, Kansas.

Robert W. Scollon, Professor of Psychology and Director of the Mental Health Counselor Training Program, Gannon College, Erie, Pennsylvania.

Saleem A. Shah, Chief, Center for Studies of Crime and Delinquency, National Institute of Mental Health, Washington, D.C.

Paul S. Spitzer, Director, Psychological Services and Research, Friends Hospital, Philadelphia, Pennsylvania.

John Stratton, Associate Professor, Department of Sociology and Anthropology, University of Iowa, Iowa City, Iowa.

A. J. W. Taylor, Professor of Clinical Psychology, Victoria University of Wellington, New Zealand.

Walter M. Wallack, Formerly Warden, Wallkill Prison, Wallkill, New York.

Lewis Yablonsky, Professor of Sociology, San Fernando Valley State College, Northridge, California.

INTRODUCTION

THE greatest interface between the free world and inmates of correctional institutions occurs between line correctional officers and those whom they directly supervise. At precisely this level, most complaints regarding treatment occur. Institutional policy rarely can specify interpersonal relations between the officer and the inmate in sufficient detail to take the subtler issues involved in the use of power into consideration. Policy is general; its implementation is specific, and its intent is not self-evident. It is generally considered that institutionalization purely for punishment is not sufficient, and goals beyond punishment are widely accepted by the administrative staff of correctional facilities. Communicating these broader goals is particularly difficult, since educational levels of line staff are rarely on a par with the levels of administrative personnel. Thus, closing this communication gap is a critical task. The present set of papers is intended to assist in resolution of this problem.

The authors of this collection of articles are or were intimately involved in the correctional process. Their accumulated years of direct experience in corrections is impressive; on the whole they represent the most informed application of concepts from the behavioral sciences to the correctional situation. They include criminologists, directors of state and federal correctional programs, former wardens, prison psychologists and sociologists, institutional chaplains, officers of the American Correctional Association, attorneys, psychiatrists, and probation and parole personnel. Representing a broad spectrum of the criminal justice system, they are not armchair theorists; their experience with legal offenders is firsthand. Further, their viewpoints have been hammered out on the anvil of correctional history. In American corrections, they represent those persons in the forefront of the field. They can in no sense be regarded as "bleeding hearts"; their viewpoint is unemotional. Their interest is solely in im-

provement of the efforts and realization of the economic investment which this nation makes in penal facilities. All of the articles are not of this decade, but those that are not are still
timely. Institutional change is tortuously slow in the most enlightened systems, and corrections in general lags substantially
behind the most innovative penologists. The perspective is not
limited to American corrections; while we have made no effort
to provide a vista that is international in the sense of constitut-
ing a comparative penology, a brief consideration of other national penal systems is included.

An acknowledgment of the conflicting issues in penology has
been sought. Even those persons who concentrate most heavily
on custody and discipline do so from a reasoned and humanitarian point of view, keeping in mind the ultimate goal of corrections, i.e. the return of the offender to society under conditions
which leave him certainly no further handicapped than on his
entry and, hopefully, better prepared to cope with the problems
which led to his original confinement. Also, the stigma which attaches to legal confinement must be outweighed by gains. The
contributors keep this added pro-social deterrent to the forefront of their thinking.

The overriding view of the editors has been that the correctional process must encompass the conception of the inmate as
a rational human being worthy of restoration to society. At the
same time, an attempt has been made to represent differing
viewpoints as to how this may be accomplished and how the efforts of our own correctional system compares with those of selected others. The resultant groupings were not predetermined;
rather, they developed naturally in the process of selection.
Other groupings are, of course, possible. The present one, however, does represent some of the major confrontations extant
in the correctional process. There is plenty of room for con-
troversy; thus we have attempted to provide material to encourage constructive dialogue, since it is our hope that this selection shall be useful in in-service training programs in correctional facilities, as well as elsewhere.

The initial section provides an overview of the task of corrections, broadly conceived. The facts of institutional life and

the manner in which they bear on the task is viewed from the perspective of those whose experience and knowledge transcend national boundaries. The variance between theory and application and some of the reasons for this are outlined. The inclusion of material largely descriptive of other national penal systems may seem strange; however, need for an awareness of the extent to which the very existence of the institution as a separate social system impairs its effectiveness is particularly considered.

The complexity of the line officer's role as one which requires a professional point of view, emphasizing his point of contact not merely as the guardian of society, but as society's agent of change, is an important part of this section. The importance of this conjunctive role is stressed by some authorities as central and critical, if not indispensable. The need for more intensive training of line staff, the nature of the content of such training, and the quality of personnel employed are discussed. A historical perspective on training of correctional personnel calls attention to some of the early training efforts.

Section Three, in general, deals with the inmate and his attempts to come to grips with the hazards of confinement. It reproaches the tendency of some representatives in the correctional process to treat the inmate as a totally different breed of animal—a wolf howling in the wilderness, rather than a sheep strayed from the fold. The manner in which this fallacy develops, the effect it has on management of inmates, and how it may be overcome are described. The degrading and dehumanizing effects of imprisonment are not required to achieve correctional goals but are side effects of institutionalization. Positive suggestions for systematic program endeavors to cope with these unnecessary adjuncts to the prison experience are presented.

The fourth grouping zeroes in on the social lag extant in the field of corrections. To reiterate a proposition that is itself advanced far toward cliché, theory is miles in advance of practice; and, unless the gap is closed, those from outside the system may in haste abandon it, in ignorance of the abysmally limited extent to which theory in penology has been the backbone of institutional programming. The contributors in this section look at the institution as a backdrop for the implementation of penological theory. Essentially, they view institutions as nineteenth-century social organisms, arthritically operant, in a twentieth-century context. The numerous conflicts which exist and the limited effort being made to resolve them restrain fulfillment of penological goals.

The awareness of authority and the imposition of discipline as integral to the management of institutions are discussed in Section Five. There is general recognition of the necessity of setting limits; the confusion between limit-setting and punishment, however, leads to destruction of the possible rewards of effective discipline. Punishment is accorded on imposition of sentence; control is a necessary tool of the penal process. No one denies that limits are necessary. It is the imposition of limits that is too often not constructive but provocative of a contest of wills which confirms criminality. The authors of this section make recommendations for the most meaningful and humane use of institutional authority.

The final section presents treatment as the focal part of institutionalization. A variety of perspectives is offered. The contribution of inmates to the treatment effort is theoretically justified, as is the necessity of opening the process to the purview of the "correctional consumer," who pays for the service of the system. The tendency to repeat the mistakes of past generations of correctional workers is forcefully presented. No attempt has been made to deal with the specifics of treatment; rather, a treatment rationale is presented which must form the major vantage point of effective corrections.

ACKNOWLEDGMENTS

I WOULD like to gratefully acknowledge the assistance of the Research and Projects Office, Southern Illinois University, Carbondale, Illinois, in preparation of the manuscript.

CONTENTS

xv

BEHAVIORAL SCIENCE
AND MODERN PENOLOGY

SECTION I

THE CULTURAL BACKGROUND OF PENOLOGY

IN general, this group of articles stresses the deleterious effects of generating pressures which strengthen and maintain the inmate code. These pressures conspire to make the inmate an "organization man," in a manner which requires that he give his allegiance to the system opposed to official authority in order to render an otherwise intolerable existence barely tolerable.

The impossibility of divorcing "discussion about the rehabilitation of the offender from examination of the prisons and the process of punishment" is forcefully noted by Kirkpatrick. His capacity of working with men who have survived the imprisonment experience has permitted him first-hand awareness of the effects of "punitive deterrence." He shows the manner in which this approach tends to polarize the inmate-staff relationship, thus imposing barriers within the rehabilitative process. Destruction of this polarization is essential if line officers are to fulfill their role in its most therapeutic manner. Handicaps to restoration are noted, and some suggestions for aiding reentry into the community are discussed.

Limitations imposed on the treatment procedure by depersonalizing processes is Bixby's focal theme. The European approach to penology is described. Efforts made within the European system to minimize polarization and to reduce isolation from the outside world are noted, as is the positive regard for correctional workers, the great care exercised in their selection, and their resultant loftier status in European society. There is nothing basically wrong with the ideas we have developed, Bixby demonstrates, with particular emphasis in his description of the Danish prison system based almost wholly on ideas generated from within the American system of criminal justice; they have simply been so much more effectively implemented elsewhere.

An additional comparison of the American system is furnished by Morris. In his view, the Swedish correctional system ranks among the world's most humane. He points up the value of comparative study of penal systems with a focus that is "candidly reformist." It is instructive to note that ninety percent of Swedish sentences are of less than one year. In highlighting the most prominent features of the Swedish system, Morris includes a description of the features of that system which reduce social isolation, such as furloughs, institution size, staff-inmate ratio, employment of women throughout adult corrections, and provision of normal sexual satisfaction even for those with maximum sentences. Our innovations in penology are noted, as in Bixby's paper, but Morris cautions us against a chauvinistic attitude toward the claim of historical firsts. He strongly recommends a "lend-lease" of innovations in corrections.

Yablonsky's contribution is not as interculturally comparative in intent as the two previous articles. His comparisons are with regard to separate segments of American society. The manner in which staff, inmate, and general public attitudes seem to conspire to produce a "doing-time" society is the central theme of this paper. Limited economic support is recognized but is regarded as less crucial than the absence of an active rehabilitative attitude.

Prisons Produce People

A. M. KIRKPATRICK

It is impossible to divorce discussion about the rehabilitation of the offender from examination of the prisons and the process of punishment. From time immemorial there has been a very great reliance on corporal and capital punishments, and these have been deeply imbedded in our social customs. Mosaic law called for restitution and set equivalents—so many oxen, so many sheep for death or moral offenses. The civic glory of the Athenians was such that they believed if a citizen was banished to live among the barbarians this was the supreme punishment. Socrates chose the hemlock rather than banishment. Only as far back as 150 years ago, England and her colonies utilized a great

---

NOTE: Reprinted from *Federal Probation*, 26 (4) :26-33, 1962.

variety of punishment including lashing, branding, mutilation, transportation, death—punishments so cruel and horrible that Boswell had reluctance to describe some of them. In eighteenth-century England there were no less than 200 offenses punishable by death, and most of these were trivial offenses against property.

THE PHILOSOPHY OF PUNITIVE DETERRENCE

Today we look on prisons as a normal type of punishment for criminal activity. But in actual fact, the custodial prison came as a reform against the blood-letting and severity of the punishments of those former days. Prior to the eighteenth century, offenders were held in castles or fortresses awaiting trial or execution of the sentence, or else they were held for debt. The idea of the custodial prison is a relatively recent thing. It came out of the Quaker philosophy about 150 years ago and issued in the Walnut Street Jail in Philadelphia.

The Quakers believed that if they provided work, solitary confinement, and the Bible, the prisoner would become penitent. This was the derivation of the word penitentiary. It was in these eighteenth-century jails—the original jails prior to custodial prisons—that John Howard and Elizabeth Fry began their task of amelioration of the very desperate plight of the inmates of those days. Those must have been places of human despair and desperation.

All previous methods of punishment had been the result of a belief in punitive deterrence. This phrase is very significant in thinking about the treatment of the offender. It reflects the belief that an example should be made of the offender by punishment—often brutal and horrible—which would deter others from committing the offense or ensure that the offender would not again venture to place himself in jeopardy as before.

The beliefs that punishment does deter and that the rougher the treatment the greater the deterrence is deeply rooted in human nature. I suspect it is the natural conclusion of the rational man. But crime and mental illness are not rational matters. Punitive deterrence was based on the assumption that criminal behavior was the result of innate badness and willful wickedness. The field of insanity was believed to be the result of demoniac possession which required even bodily torment to dislodge the demon. During the last hundred years, we have learned a great deal in the social sciences about the nature of human behavior. We know now that it is subject to irrational compulsions with drives motivating action which are little understood by the offender himself or by society.

This custodial prison was based on the philosophy of deterrence—punitive deterrence. The idea prevailed that imprisonment should be a static thing and that it should not only mean a loss of freedom and a degradation of the offender but also a rigorous regime imposing humility and absolute discipline. But what did this type of imprisonment and punishment produce? There is no evidence of anything positive, since crime rates were not reduced. We have developed over the years a hard-core recidivist group of offenders.

MANY PRISONS LACK INDIVIDUALIZATION

Most penitentiaries are as yet large, unclassified institutions with populations overcrowding the facilities and containing persons incarcerated for all types of offenses. There is very little possibility of any internal segregation or differentiation of individual program. It is little wonder that the impact of such institutions on a new inmate is a shattering one. The inmate population has its own systems of social organization and these present a study in social anthropology. There are many cliques and subgroups. Some inmates, because of the nature of their offense, suffer ostracism and have very low status among the inmate population.

The undoubted influence of the "wheels" (the big shots, the controllers, the manipulators) is observable, since leadership always emerges in human associations. We should consider this continuous emergence of leadership when we hear discussion of the building of institutions like Alcatraz designed to drain off the hard-core group. In fact, though there must be maximum security for a residual number of inmates, leadership always emerges when the top group has been removed, and very soon the new leadership assumes much the same role as the previous group. In the maximum-security types of institutions, the inmate leadership is usually opposed to the administration. There is a line drawn between the inmate group and the administration, which establishes a sort of marginal "no man's land" of debatable concerns. This creates an emotional and psychological barrier between the custodian and those who are in custody.

The new inmate has limited choices. He may withdraw psychologically in isolation; he may cooperate with the administration at the risk of losing face, being considered a stool pigeon, and receiving the silent treatment; he may, and usually does, identify with the inmate population, which he feels is the wisest and only practical solution. Experienced institutional personnel believe this structuring of attitudes increases the difficulties of developing effective treatment in the prisons as they are presently organized.

In a prison of this sort (speaking of the maximum- and even medium-security prisons), all activities understandably are weighed by the administration in terms of security. The warden is charged by law to hold in custody those committed to his care. He is not told to treat them. He is told to keep them. Traditionally this produced an ordering-and-forbidding type of discipline imposed from without and with little attempt to find ways by which inmates might internalize these disciplinary controls if there is to be any valid carryover into community living in the free world. There is in these institutions a heightening of routine, monotony, and repetition, with little real individualization. There is a deceleration of living tempo and a sharp reduction in problem-solving due to lack of opportunities for personal initiative and developmental activity. The thinking of inmates is largely done for them, and their essential living needs are supplied.

Regulations and routines become paramount, and privileges assume an importance beyond any reality we on the outside can conceive. By and large there is a constant pressure on the administration to relax regulations and increase privileges, but there are obvious limits to the extent to which this can be done. Hence there is a great deal of criticism among inmates of regulations and a general suspicion of the administration. The inmate group is forced to create its own framework of reality because of isolation from the broader community and the need for self-protection. The mechanisms of self-protection become narrow and self-centered and tend to reject the actuality of social and legal sanction and also administrative policy and practice. The administration has got to be wrong, and as a result, the inmate relationship with officers and even other inmates tends to be impersonal. The common phrase is "do your own time."

Notwithstanding this general impersonality, there is frequently a grouping of two or three inmates containing emotional content and deep feelings of mutual support and understanding. It is obvious that this has to take place among human beings. These relationships often are formed consciously to provide personal support that can be relied on within the general necessity for the presentation of an unbroken inmate front. There is sometimes a deep understanding and sympathy for fellow inmates who may be experiencing real personal troubles.

There is a good deal of tolerance among inmates for one who is really doing "rough time," provided he does not provoke general administrative sanctions. Inmates seem to sense when a man is really under stress or just "blowing his top." Unfortunately it is difficult for the administration to capitalize on these positive feelings, as the only solution in many cases for the inmate under stress would be to provide immediate release to deal with his problem which may be quite external to the prison. This is not within the power of the prison staff.

PRISON SOCIETY HAS ITS OWN CODE OF ETHICS

The prison environment has its own norms and code of ethics largely developed from the criminal backgrounds of the majority of those incarcerated and transposed as the "code" into prison living. Each prison is fundamentally the same in the cultural attributes it exhibits, but each is different in the mode of expression adopted by the inmate group. Their attitudes generally reflect a faulty relationship to authority and often to those who would help. There is hostility to those outside their own group. There is exposure to asocial and antisocial behavior, and with normal sexual outlet denied, there is often aberrant sexual behavior. Most inmates reject the latter, but many accept and perpetuate the heritage of the criminal tradition in this sub-culture.

The reality of cell-confinement with its claustrophobic restriction of mobility grinds deeply into the emotions of many men. Prison neurosis is no empty diagnostic term. Men have frequently said they have come to know every stone, every line, every cranny in their cell. They say they have stood many hours in a sort of hypnosis just counting lines or stones or bricks. Others relate that night after night they have paced their cells in walk patterns, counting the steps. On the other extreme, there may be exposure to dormitory living. This is increasing in our institutions, particularly in those of minimum security. Dormitories call not only for different disciplinary controls by the administration but also for group adjustment among the inmates, which cell living has tended to destroy. There is often real fear on the part of oldtimers about entering such group settings.

The avenues of psychological escape tend to be focused on individual pursuits free from administrative domination. These are obviously study, general reading, writing for the penal press, and cell hobbycraft which is also a means of economic advantage. For want of other incentives, these pursuits may become ends in themselves and often great proficiency is obtained in something of little productive value. Recreational and vocational training are advantages for some but are less of an escape, since they are usually group activities and hence are under the more immediate control of the administration.

In most prisons there is an inadequate work experience, and this is not conducive to good work habits on the outside. There is much overmanning of tasks and much "busy work" which the inmates fully comprehend to be so and regard as personally and socially unconstructive. Men often become soft and flabby in prison. There is great need for understanding to be shown both by management and unions in regard to the problem of prison industries. The development of these, even to their fullest capacity, would be an infinitesimal part of the production of our total industrial complex and no threat to the total economy.

The inmate usually experiences feelings of disgrace resulting from the social degradation surrounding arrest and trial. This seems particularly true of first offenders. On the part of the older hands, there may be irritation at the failure to "get away with it." There has, in any event, been a physical separation from the community and a rejection by society creating emotional reactions and a concept of role with which we have to reckon later on. There is often a weakening of such relationships as may have been previously built up in a family, job, or community, and this makes more difficult the problem of eventual resumption of these relationships. Roots have been torn up and will eventually have to be replanted in a hard and stony soil. There will be increased need for understanding care and nurture.

If we look into the prison culture, we can valuably identify certain factors. First, there has been public degradation connected with the arrest, trial, sentencing, and public exposure. There has been a reduction of social status with the corresponding reduction in the self-concept of role. There has been a physical withdrawal from normal living activities and a thrusting into a strange and threatening environment. When the inmate enters the prison gate, usually he is stripped, searched, and deprived of all his possessions except one or two minor articles such as pen and pencil, lighter, and perhaps some stationery. He is given new clothing and from then on makes no choice of food nor choice of regime. The areas of living in which he can choose have narrowed down to a few personalized things. He finds himself in a unisexual society with sanction against close human relationships or expressions of tenderness, lest these be misunderstood for homosexual approaches. There is a substantial withdrawal of the expression of affection and tenderness so essential to the normal, healthy, wholesome human being.

Obviously this leads to the production of stress and it is interesting to observe the varying kinds of reactions. Regression is noted. Men become "stir happy," "fogged up," and withdrawn in their social expressions and in their relationships with other people. Retreative behavior occurs. There is often some attempt to blur out the reality of time by "brews" (making alcoholic beverages), excessive food consumption, homosexual relationships—anything that will provide sensory satisfaction. Conflict is observed. Inmates doing what we call "rough time" are figuratively beating their head against the wall. Some of my institutional friends do not understand me when I say these men may well be making substantial change, though they are, in fact, causing more trouble for the administration. Manipulation is seen. They are the "wheels" who endeavor to manipulate the administration and turn all situations to their advantage so they can do "easy time" and "make time work for them." Escape is evident. This is illustrated by men who pursue erudite subjects or develop amazing skills in handicraft. Courses in higher education may be escape mechanisms or realistic learning devices, depending on the realism of the motivation. Learning or readjustment takes place. There are positives for some in the constructive use of time for self-examination and positive replanning and retraining for future life in the community.

INMATE CULTURE

But no matter how the inmate reacts individually to stress, there is the sharing of the common status as inmates. He is forced to move into an inmate culture. He may not want to accept the values of this inmate culture, but he has no choice. I can recall, shortly after the last riot at Kingston, talking to one of the inmates whom I had known for many years. He said, "You know I can't say out there what I am saying in here—I just can't say it. I don't go along with all this stuff," waving to the yard. "But I can't say that outside." We were talking about the riot and he was ventilating about it to me, but he did not dare express such feeling in the prison setting outside the interview room.

It is not difficult to discern the no man's land between the inmate and the administration in the custodial prison. We have inherited this legacy and it still persists. This no man's land is a marginal area which isolates staff and inmates from each other, though not in physical terms. They skirmish but they do not really cross. This was initially true in the developing of the relationship of inmates to treatment staff, but the marginal gulf is now broadening and becoming blurry because there is an increased acceptance of treatment staffs. The "bug doctor" is no longer so much of an enemy. He is no longer "stooling" for the administration. When the inmate goes to see the classification department, the other inmates are no longer afraid he is going up there just to pass information to the administration. The inmates are aware that in such institutions there are pipelines of information both into the administration and into the inmate group. This change is also noticeable in relationship to the industrial and vocational training staff who work in a foremanship role more now than they have ever done before.

The inmate culture is compelling and binding, though it is not really unitary. It is, to a considerable extent, a perpetuation of the attitudes of the criminal offender from the outside community into the prison. One characteristic is isolation from staff. The code fosters the idea that you never trust anyone and you certainly do not trust the administration, since administration is authority, authority is capricious, and capriciousness is to be avoided because you do not know what it is going to do to you. If it cannot be avoided, it is to be evaded. If it cannot be evaded, then it is to be manipulated.

Another characteristic is isolation from peers. This is a dreadful thing. One must maintain oneself apart from one's peers as far as the innermost important revelations of personality are concerned. "Do your own time, do it with the least difficulty, get out as soon as possible." "I have got enough weight of time on my shoulders, I don't want the burden of anyone else's." "I don't want to get into any situation that might complicate my chances of parole or might jeopardize my remission."

It is characterized also by a lack of mobility. Certainly there is no upward mobility out of the inmate strata, though there may be regressive mobility. There are barriers to communication with free people. But if there is such communication, it tends to conform to a stereotyped pattern. Movement within the inmate population usually is to regression and reduced status. If it is upwards, it usually results in the creation of the status of "wheels." But it is difficult to move into healthy staff-inmate relationships. Some of the medium- or minimum-security institutions have inmate committees or inmate groups which cooperate in self-government; but these are relatively rare. On the one hand, the uncertainties of staff cause a setting of limitations, and on the other, the concerns of the inmates themselves regarding the danger of revelation also erect barriers to truly spontaneous and mutual relationship.

NEED TO DEVELOP AND REESTABLISH VALUES

The prison, then, should develop a culture which, while containing the criminal offender who has been so identified, somehow produces restorative values. To accomplish this, we must recognize the significance of time, the terrible weight of which we on the outside just cannot understand. Our time is fragmented into minutes for this and minutes for that; but for inmates it is told off by months and years. This time should be utilized in constructive ways for the development of insight and training. This means involvement because there cannot be constructive relationships unless there is participation in a program with some involvement of the fertile capacities of the inmates. We will need to satisfy the basic needs of recognition, response, and new experience. On this level of institutional program, we should involve inmates in the organization and operation of their own environment. While this concept of programming is not yet fully realized, it will come before long.

Then we will have to do something about the concept inmates have of role. We need to find ways to heighten their self-expectancy—their self-understanding of role not as inmates and degraded social beings but as men and not numbers to be locked in and counted. We can do this through programming which provides opportunity for status development and for upward mobility in positive relationships with staff to increase the possibility of their actual role performance. The criterion of role performance should not be, as it usually is today, an adaptation to the custodial setting because such adaptation has no necessary relationship at all to the change of the human being in personality, character or development of insight. In fact, it may be the very opposite and be merely the adaptation to imprisonment.

We need to think of the projection of role performance into the outside community because the real test will determine the capacity for social reestablishment within the free competitive community after the ending of the legal restrictions which have been on the individual. This calls for some prognosis of the inmate's ability to function as a socially and economically productive person. This does not mean that it is our job to remake the basic personality. It is not necessarily an appropriate objective that a man who has lived on "the corner" should be transformed into a pillar of one of our prominent uptown churches. The barriers to this type of chameleon-like transition are very great. Minimally it is necessary to settle for a man who can live within the law and with increasing social and economic capacity to satisfy his needs in the legally accepted fashion in his own cultural setting.

CHANGING INMATE ATTITUDES

It is obvious that we need to find ways of restoring the self-respect of inmates. Attempts have been made at this by provision of amenities and welfare measures which are highly important if inmates are to see themselves as men and not as numbers. But we need to go further as staff and public attitudes permit and make prisons into truly correctional communities which should produce a better product for the protection of the public. Change can be hoped for by differentiation of custodial institutions and also by the reduction of population so that there can be real interaction and interpermeation of the inmate and staff cultures. But we need the recognition by the public that punishment, which will be still there, is not in itself enough; but this treatment and training also bite deeply into a person. If we are really going to help inmates, we must, of necessity, disturb them.

No administration wants a riot or trouble in any kind of institution. We all want things to go smoothly in any organization with which we are concerned. This is a human attitude because we are a punishing and rewarding type of society, and we do not get rewards if we have caused or permitted trouble. But where there is unrest of a healthy kind, arising from treatment measures and situations, effective work may, in fact, be resulting. The present type of adaptation noted, for example, in the compulsive forger does not change the man at all but just enables him to live in a prison. If we are going to help him project different objectives for himself in the outside society, he will need training or treatment. This is undoubtedly going to disturb and perhaps even hurt him emotionally. But this is a necessary choice unless we are going to keep people anesthetized in a regressed or adaptive state. We have to disturb inmates if we are going to change their personality. To change habit formations, we have to get deeply into the individual's emotions, disturb his image of himself in society, and recreate in him a new concept of role and self-awareness of his potential for performance in the outside society.

When we do this, we have to be prepared to "pick up the pieces" because there will be individual upsets and difficulties. When routines and relationships are undergoing change, particularly in a prison which is the most isolated and tightest knit social unit in our community, changes ensue in the relationship between staffs and inmates. We not only will be disturbing inmates but also disturbing staff; therefore they must have the reassurance of effective and accelerated communication throughout the administration with a full understanding of what the new requirements on them are going to be.

In an English prison, I talked to a couple of lads who were out in the garden in this open institution with no walls or fences. I asked them if they would rather do their time here where it was beautiful with gardens, trees, and flowers or whether they would rather do it in a local prison. They both said they would rather do it in a local prison which is like a county jail. I did not pursue it immediately but later came back and said I had been thinking about their comment and wondered why they felt that way. They replied that in the local prison they knew where they stood whereas out here they did not know how far they could go. They admitted that it was a more pleasant place to live with more freedom and opportunity for work and constructive learning; but they still preferred the local security prison where the regulations were stricter but were understood by all and maintained consistently.

They continued that in the present setting, both staff and inmates seemed to be testing each other constantly because the limits were not clear and were undergoing change. This brought discomfort on the part of both staff and inmates since the inmates did not quite know how far to go nor how to interpret this developing individualization instead of the former reliance on the book of regulations and the cleavage in inmate-staff relationships. There was far more margin for skirmishing, since the area of the no man's land was broader.

The same question was asked at another prison and received the same kind of reaction. At another training prison, where I met a very fine administrator, I spoke to him frankly about this and he said, "Yes. We have this, too, in our training prison which is supposed to be one of the show places." He said, "We cannot expect to be immune from it here as we endeavor to move from straight custodial security to correctional processes and programs." The same type of problem will be found, perhaps in less sharp degree, in any social institution where there is an attempt to bring about changes in the methodologies by which staff and inmates have controlled their behavior and relationships. Hence we must be prepared to work very diligently with staff and help them through these problems that they, in turn, may help.

PROBLEMS OF COMMUNITY READJUSTMENT

In Canada, prison aftercare—including the substantial proportion of parole supervision—is conducted by voluntary aftercare societies usually financed for the most part through United Appeals of Community Chests but with some government subsidies. The John Howard Societies are now nationally organized, giving service from coast to coast. The female counterpart is the Elizabeth Fry Society, usually locally organized. In Quebec, there are French-Canadian societies specifically devoted to this type of work, and some church societies also provide help in various centers. The Salvation Army is nationally organized and provides services to ex-inmates.

The first problem, obviously, that men face in the community is that of survival until they can secure work and begin to provide for their own self-maintenance. It is quite an initial shock to leave the security of institutional maintenance and to become immediately a relatively inexperienced and untrained cipher in a competitive economy. How would any one of us like to face the world leaving a strange city, not necessarily a prison, with perhaps 35 dollars in our pocket and a minimal wardrobe involving only one or two changes of shirts, underwear and socks? We would immediately have problems in getting laundry done and getting clothes pressed. But the initial problem would be to secure a place to live and have some assurance of food for a period until remunerative return from employment could be expected to reach the pocketbook.

It is exceedingly difficult to secure employment when the stigma that centers around an ex-inmate is taken into account. He knows he will have difficulty being bonded, although the attitude of the fidelity companies is now more receptive to individual consideration of applications from ex-inmates. He also knows that licensing for ex-inmates of cartage drivers and taxi licenses and for some kinds of food operations is rigorously controlled by police or municipal commissions. He has no unemployment stamps in his book and has to account for the fact that he has no such stamps, has no work record, has no references, and has a gap in his work experience which must be accounted for.

Socialization and even communication with people who have not been in the prison environment present difficulties, since words, symbols, and stereotypes are entirely different. To mix with people and to talk about what happened at the country club, golf club, or service club just has no meaning to ex-inmates who do not think like "Square Johns." They find it very difficult to communicate with any intensity or reality because of the lack of common interests and common past experiences with which there can be conversational and personal identification.

Consequently, their attitude to moving into community

groupings is fearful. This is not only because of the difficulty of meaningful communication but also the fear that some slip will reveal that they have been in prison which, in turn, may create antagonism or rejection which they have experienced before. Their attitude to religion of a formal nature through the churches is often similar and is another of the problems involved in resocialization.

One man to whom I was talking on a Monday morning felt very sorry for himself and hung over. He had been robbed. I recall that he said he had become so lonely that he went down to the "corner." He said, "I knew they weren't good friends down there, but poor friends are better than no friends." This is such a human need that he risked getting robbed, hung over, and "put through the wringer" in order to find human beings with whom he could identify and socialize.

The resumption of family life is not without difficulty. These men return to their families with dishonor. They have been degraded publicly, and their role in the family may have changed entirely. What now are the attitudes of parents, wife, children, or in-laws to their past behavior and to their promises for the future? The resumption of a new role as a breadwinner and as the head of a family may not be as easy as it sounds, since the wife may have been getting along very well on Mother's Allowances or public assistance without his interference. In addition, she has been freed from the pressures of his criminal activities in which he may have brought in stolen goods or various types of equipment needed in his craft for safekeeping. She had had, perhaps for the first time in her married life, some peace from her fears and suspicions or, in fact, from having the police knocking at the door. Is it entirely easy to regain the role of tenderness and the ability to express it and evoke affectional responses? Is it easy to resume the discipline of children who have grown up during one's absence?

Another man developed a discussion concerning his problems in the juvenile court where he had been summoned for beating his son. He admitted freely that he had "licked" him but said, "the trouble with me is that my old man didn't lick me hard enough and I went to prison. I am going to make sure now this guy of mine is going to get licked enough so that he won't go to prison." This seemed to be his serious belief and was based on the concept of behavior as being responsive to external discipline. He had been a juvenile delinquent and felt this had happened because he had not had enough "lickings" when he was young. He took the strap to his very young child because he was going to be very sure he would not follow in his father's footsteps.

SOME PERSONAL PROBLEMS IN READJUSTMENT

There are a number of acute personal problems relating to the time lost in prison, which we call the immediacy complex. There is often a desire to make up for loss of time and to accomplish a great deal much too fast. Coupled with this is the problem of getting a "good front" to impress his fellows that he is "back in the bucks." There is a strong desire to secure and exhibit once again the visible symbols of success.

I had taken one ex-inmate to lunch with me and we were returning on Jarvis Street when a lad approached us, trying to sell a gold watch. Now, it may have been brass; I don't know. But it looked good and my companion simply could not resist it. To him, here was a beautiful gold watch which he could get for perhaps a couple of dollars and so he started dickering. In discussing it with him, I said it was probably not any good and undoubtedly was stolen. His attitude was, "So what, I could get it for two bucks." He had difficulty realizing that even if he had not stolen it, he was, in effect, participating in the theft by the purchasing of stolen property. To him it was a method of getting one of the symbols of success and making clear to his friends that he was back in circulation again and doing well.

A problem often arises as to debts incurred either prior to imprisonment or by families during a man's incarceration. As soon as a number of men come out, they are poised again on the threshold of a finance company. This is a very serious and practical problem and relates often to immaturity of purchasing and financial incompetence.

The problem of bonding is a very real one. I think of a recent discussion with a former safecracker who was now running a business operation and needed to be bonded. He figured he could get the money for the bond, but his problem was that he would have to tell his employers where he had been working during the past few years. He did not believe they would accept the bald statement that he had been working for the Department of Justice. He needed a job reference and thought he would approach one of his pals who had been working for several years and now had a good job at the management level in a construction company. He felt sure his friend would write a letter for him, not only giving him a reference but also saying that he had been working with him for a period of years.

To summarize a fairly lengthy discussion, I simply said to him that he had to decide that he was really going to be a "Square John" or that he was right back where he had been, in the criminal fringe, manipulating his way through society. I suggested that he could not have things both ways and that he really had to make the break one way or another and go over to the "Square Johns" or else operate as part of the criminal group. He found it difficult to believe when I, in fact, suggested that he would get his friend into trouble because undoubtedly his letter of reference would be followed up by the bonding company and this might result in loss of his friend's job. He finally agreed that this was so, but to him it was merely "using the angles" rather than facing up to the true situation in his own problem of bonding. Instead of saying, "Here I am. I have been in prison. I have got the money for the bond. I have got people who recommend me," he felt it was quite in order to get his pal to give him a phony letter.

"WE WEAR INVISIBLE NUMBERS"

We all know how difficult it is to change attitudes, even our own, so in dealing with ex-inmates we must accept a long and tedious development with many setbacks in the readjustment to the community. In expressing some of the attitudes of the ex-inmate, one man wrote the following very expressive paragraph.

> We are the anonymous ones who move among you with wary eyes. We are among you but not of you; constantly on guard, lest by an incautious word or gesture, we may betray ourselves to you, and thereby lose our anonymity—and your respect. You may find us in

your factories, in your garages, on your farms, and sometimes in your offices and places of business. We live next door, work at the next lathe, sit next to you in the movies. In short—we are your neighbors. Yet we are a group of men set apart, divided by our experiences from those around us. We are the parolees from your prisons; still doing time. Although we walk the streets to all outward appearances free men, we wear invisible numbers.

Treating the Prisoner: A Lesson From Europe

F. LOVELL BIXBY

One lasting impression dominated all others in my mind following visits to penal and correctional institutions in five countries of western Europe during the summer of 1959: Retribution—the inflicting of punishment as an end in itself—is not an objective in treating offenders in those countries.

We in the United States are accustomed to hearing theoretical penologists proclaim the futility of expiation, but the basic principle of our criminal laws and penal practices still remains the notion that the transgressor "has it coming to him." In western Europe, an offender is to be controlled and reformed, if possible, but there is no disposition to get angry with him or to seek social revenge for his misdeeds.

Many immediately observable differences in the administration of sanctions follow from this definition of objectives. For one, there is a wider range of extramural dispositions and a greater freedom to use them without incurring public criticism. Suspended sentences, fines, open institutions, parole, short sentences, and recourse to medical procedures are accepted as effective means of social protection and not viewed as dangerous tricks to let criminals off lightly.

There also are differences to be found in the operation and programs of the penal and correctional institutions.

Our notions about the sanctity of custody are incomprehensible to the European penologists. They find it shocking that we prosecute in the courts those who escape because, as one official put it, "It is every prisoner's God-given right to escape if he can."

NOTE: Reprinted from *Federal Probation*, 25 (1) :7-12, 1961.

While we go to great lengths to cut off a prisoner's contact with free society, the European nations do everything possible to minimize isolation from the outside world. Visiting and mail regulations are liberal; furloughs to go home are not unusual; and many prisoners are on a status of semiliberté which allows them to go out daily to private employment and return at night without escort. These practices, together with shorter sentences, extensive use of open institutions, and a genuine effort to give prisoners as much freedom of choice as possible, serve to reduce the danger of turning men into convicts—a danger which Sir Alexander Patterson described well when he said,

> The man who comes in as a criminal is made into a prisoner. All initiative and self-reliance are lost, obeying every order given to him, he comes in time to wait for orders. He develops a desire to please, which makes him furtive and sycophantic. In the external show of order and cleanliness his conduct is model but in inner things that matter he is at heart still a waster, actually more useless and dangerous because he has cloaked his dishonesty with the paint and plaster of a well-behaved inmate of an institution.

English and continental institutions are generally much smaller than ours. A prison for 500 is "too big," and administrators who have visited the United States are appalled by our installations for 1,500 and more, which, they say, can serve no purpose but punishment.

Correctional work as a career has a higher status in Europe than it does with us, and greater care is exercised in the selection and training of personnel, although salaries are not notably better.

Constructive day-by-day contacts between rank-and-file staff and inmates are the major tool of rehabilitation. And the social distance which we require to prevent "fraternization" defeats the very purpose of imprisonment as the Europeans see it. To see guards and prisoners working together is a common sight, but guards standing watch over working prisoners is seldom observed.

The western European attitude toward prison labor differs from ours. Although there is agreement on the principle that all employable prisoners should work, the greatest concern in our country is to avoid competition by prison goods in the open market. Thus we have federal and state laws which restrict prison labor to the production of goods for the state and its political subdivisions, despite the fact that they create a dangerous amount of idleness and featherbedding in prison shops.

There are no such restrictions in the foreign countries visited, where the aim is to provide constructive work whether it be for the state or a private employer, either within or without the prison limits. It seems proper to observe at this point that the European use of the contract system is in full accord with the resolutions adopted by the First United Nations Congress on the Prevention of Crime and the Treatment of Offenders in 1955. The policy statement adopted at that meeting permits recourse to private industry whenever the state cannot provide full employment. It says in part,

> It is the duty of the state to ensure that adequate and suitable employment is provided for prisoners. It is preferable that this be done under the state-use system with compulsory government markets. Recourse may be had to private industry, when sound reasons exist, provided adequate safeguards are established to ensure that there is no exploitation of prison labor and that the interests of private industry and free labor are protected.

In America, particularly in New Jersey, we are inclined to think of classification as our own invention. To find ourselves surpassed in the practical application of classification theory is almost like being suddenly confronted with the fact of Sputnik I. Classification to prevent the contamination of the relatively inexperienced offenders and the differential handling of homogenous groups is the foundation stone of penal operations in Europe. Every country visited had separate facilities for youthful offenders, confirmed recidivists, psychiatric deviates, and "trainable ordinaries," as well as the usual classifications based on sex and close-, medium-, and minimum-custody requirements.

These classifications do not exist just on paper, to be disregarded in the face of administrative pressures such as overcrowding and rising per capita costs. They are, in truth, the bone and sinew of operations and are maintained somehow in the face of every obstacle. This was true even in France, where we found much that seemed harsh and archaic.

THE DANISH PRISON AT KRAGSKOVHEDE

Of all the institutions seen in the countries visited, the Danish Prison at Kragskovhede most completely exemplifies the possibilities of fully applying modern ideas when the climate of opinion of the general public is favorable. It is especially interesting to us in the United States because the authorities frankly admit they got most of their ideas while visiting our country. We must, however, be humble because they have done so much better than we have with our ideas.

The institution is an open facility for adult males who have previously served two or more sentences to imprisonment. The daily census is 420 and the average age is 35 years.

There is a main compound, an adjoining work-shop area, and an honor camp (Raabjerg) a few kilometers away. A narrow-gauge railway connects the three units.

Because the installation, intended originally for collaborators, has a capacity of 1,500, the present population of less than one third that number enjoys ample space and facilities such as are rarely to be found in the United States. The value of this undercrowding is fully appreciated by the central administration and local officials, and there is no thought of filling the institution to capacity to reduce per capita costs.

Within the main compound, inside a woven wire fence, are office buildings, workshops, a school, a reception barracks with 26 single rooms, 4 regular barracks housing 88 men each in 4-man squad rooms, and a hospital ward of 24 beds. A new and unusually beautiful chapel in modern style is the focus of architectural interest.

Three kilometers to the north, a former juvenile camp (Mosbjerg) is now devoted to workshops. One thousand acres of heath have been made fit for cultivation; and the work of reclaiming additional acreage goes on constantly, mostly from the Raabjerg camp.

In its general program, the Kragskovhede prison conforms to the policies, rules, and program of all Danish penal establishments. The restoration of each man to his community as a capable, responsible member is the goal, and the usual facilities for work, school, and recreation are provided.

The really interesting features of Kragskovhede are to be found in a number of unusual practices which have been developed there. These derive to a great extent from the unusual personality and ability of the Governor, Mr. Carsten Raphael, together with the wisdom of the central administration in giving him a free hand to experiment with treatment methods within the rules and regulations of the general system.

The steps by which the program was formulated are significant. All possible instruments of treatment such as classification, education, work training, and recreation were listed, and a staff committee established to study and recommend as to how each should be organized and incorporated in the program. The suggestions of 21 such committees were considered and coordinated at quarterly general staff meetings. After three years, a tentative program was adopted, subjected to trial for two years, and ultimately promulgated as the present basis for Kragskovhede's operations.

Two factors are recognized as having an influence on every inmate. One, which might be called the institutional climate, cannot be tailored to each individual but affects the entire prisoner and staff population. Included herein are such things as the sheer fact of incarceration, the looks of the institution, and the spirit of the whole project. There is evidence that every effort is made to make these factors contribute to rehabilitation. Custody and good discipline are left largely to the insight and understanding of the men themselves; grounds and buildings are well kept and attractive; clothing is of good cut and quality; and food is ample and attractively served. Perhaps most important, staff training is directed toward matter-of-fact firmness, kindness, and diligence.

The other part of the program comprises elements which can be individually tailored, such as work, school, and planning for release. These elements make up the inmate's plan. The institution climate and the inmate's plan seem to be correlated and consistent to an unusual degree.[1]

Classification

The inmate's plan begins to take shape in the reception center. Here, during a period of about three weeks, the necessary information about him is compiled, and he is acquainted with what he may expect from the institution and what it expects from him.

At the end of this period, a program is outlined by a classification committee much as it would be in many United States institutions. At this point, however, appears one of the important innovations in procedure. There is not one but four classification committees involved in program planning and follow-up. Each has four members, including a leader who represents the warden (this may be a deputy warden or a department head); a representative of work training; one from education; and one from the social casework department. A prisoner is assigned to one of the committees, according to his serial number, and no committee has more than 100 to 125 men to oversee. Classification policies and the supervision of classification operations emanate from the governor and his immediate staff.

In connection with classification and treatment, another device known as "home-day" has been introduced. To avoid unexpected interruptions in the working schedule and to assure that necessary interviews and other recurring needs are met, each residence unit has one day a week designated as home-day. The purpose of this plan becomes evident when a home-day schedule is compared with a regular day:

HOME-DAY AND WORKING-DAY SCHEDULE

Time	Home-Day	Working-day
8:00 to 9:00	School	Work
9:00 to 11:00	School	Work
11:00 to 12:00	Changing of books	Work
12:00 to 1:00	Lunch	Lunch
1:00 to 2:00	Paying	Work
	Bathing	Work
2:00 to 3:00	Changing of clothes	Work
	Haircutting	Work
3:00 to 4:00	Interviews	Work
	Disciplinary court	Work
4:00 to 5:00	Shopping	Work

Discipline

The basis of discipline is common sense and fairness. Rules are simple and few, and if the reasons for a particular rule are not immediately obvious, they are carefully explained to the prisoners during their orientation.

Minor infractions are punished by the assessment of a monetary fine to be paid out of an inmate's spending funds, the amount fixed in relation to his income during the previous week.

Many serious offenses which might bring solitary confinement or other severe punishment are dealt with by a disciplinary court on the basis of a written report. Residents of the accused's pavilion may attend the trial, where the reporting officer and the inmate make statements concerning the charges; and the judgement of the court is announced before adjournment.

It was stated that the open-court plan serves to restrain both sides from telling untruths and that some acquittals have occurred. One, which resulted in the discharge of an officer for filing a false report, did much to convince the population that disciplinary trials at Kragskovhede are honest. On the other side of the coin, no dissatisfaction with the plan has been expressed by employees.

Wage Policy

In order to make the situation as real as possible, inmates are paid for their work in institution money in units equivalent to the national currency. According to prison regulations, each inmate must save toward a goal of 150 kroner at release time. This is his capital which may be tapped only for expenditures of vital importance such as keeping health service and trade union payments up to date, renewing pawn tickets to save articles of lasting value, and meeting family emergencies.

Sums over and above 200 kroner may be spent at the inmate's discretion. In fact, practice in spending money wisely is regarded as part of the treatment process. Arrangements for ordering and spending free earnings require no official approval and are conducted on what is referred to locally as a "shop-like" basis. It is the responsibility of the business office to see that an inmate does not spend more than is placed at his disposal.

Group Therapy

Groups of 8 to 10 under a psychologist, meeting four nights a week, have proved successful despite prior fears that Danes would not "open up" and that members of groups might be taunted by other men. This led to the experimental establishment of groups in Copenhagen for men coming out of group therapy at Kragskovhede. These groups, conducted by a psychologist employed by the Danish Welfare Society and given general supervision by the institution psychologist, meet every two weeks.

No evaluation has been attempted, since this work has been going on for only a year. However, in answer to specific questions, it was said that (a) there has been no evidence of using group meetings to plot further crimes and (b) the groups do not seem to prolong dependency because the need to break away is emphasized in group discussions.

Prerelease Program

There has been much talk and a few experiments in America directed toward "bridging the gap" between incarceration and community living on parole. It is a need in correctional treatment that has never been satisfactorily met by preparole units or so-called "halfway houses," possibly because the one attempts to bring the community into the institution, while the other carries the institution over into the community.

A seemingly better practice has been developed at Kragskovhede. All men are released from the institution on a Saturday. On the previous Sunday, each man checks out of the prison, that is, he squares his financial accounts, turns in state property, picks up his own personal clothing and possessions, and completes the signing of any necessary forms and official papers. He then moves to a barracks outside the compound for the remainder of the week before he goes home. This barracks is entirely self-governing, and the rules are limited to the ordinary rules that must govern human beings living in association. The prospective parolees are allowed to visit the nearest town, where they can go to the stores, eat in the restaurants, frequent the bars, and otherwise carry on as free men. They are expected to be back in the quarters by a reasonable hour, generally before midnight, and they are expected to return in a condition of sobriety.

Experience has demonstrated that the first day in the village is a difficult and often very upsetting one. To meet this situation, a group therapist from the institution meets with the prerelease group every Tuesday morning for a discussion of the men's experiences and reactions on their first day in town.

Men who have been through this procedure speak particularly of getting away from the feeling that everyone is staring at them and knows that they are just out of prison. During the week of semifreedom they discover that as they go to the stores, the restaurants, and the movies no one treats them as ex-prisoners; and this helps when it comes time to walk the streets and neighborhoods of the home town or city.

QUERY

How much longer must we in America continue to pay for the luxury of punishing offenders, even though it makes them more antisocial, more inadequate to live in a decent life? Must we go on forever building and supporting huge castles of idleness to "teach a lesson" to the relatively few malefactors we catch and convict?

NOTE

1. This impression, gained from a brief visit, was confirmed in England by a capable English official who had spent some time as a visiting staff member at the institution.

Lessons From the Adult Correctional System of Sweden

NORVAL MORRIS

The Police Court, the local jail, and the penitentiary provide insights into the brotherliness and decency of a country's social system. Visit the art galleries, the cathedrals, the fountains, the squares, try the restaurants, and inspect the shops, and

NOTE: Reprinted from *Federal Probation*, 30 (4) :3-13, 1966.

you will have certain social soundings. Examine how a society handles its poor, its sick, its old, and its antisocial and asocial discordant elements, and you will have quite others. My tastes turn to the latter type of tourism and in particular to criminological and penological wanderings.[1] This preference led to my spending two months in Sweden visiting their correctional institutions and agencies, talking with their staffs and many of their prisoners who are English speaking (and they are numerous), questioning those responsible for probation and parole supervision, and collecting statistical and descriptive materials on their system.[2]

This should be sufficient for a broad overview of a correctional system; it is not, however, anything like adequate for a responsible description of such a system. For this and other reasons, no attempt is made here to offer any rounded description of the Swedish adult correctional system. The purpose is rather to examine certain organizational methods and practical techniques applied in Sweden with a view to assessing their transatlantic exportability, now or in the future. The focus is candidly reformist. The question posed is: What practices in the Swedish adult correctional system merit emulation in this country and adaptation to our different correctional problems? Or, put more succinctly, how can the Swedes help us to escape from our correctional cultural cocoon?[3]

Sanford Bates, of vast experience in American corrections and with wide international perceptions, recently suggested that "America has set the example . . . in several important innovations and developments in our correctional system"[4] and listed, as such, probation, parole, some indeterminacy in sentencing, the juvenile court, the youth court, inmate classification within correctional systems, open institutions, and the prison camp program. It is an impressive list and by and large well justified, though there are dangers of chauvinism in such claims, for in this field, historical firsts are rarely easy to establish.[5]

There is a history of international borrowing of correctional ideas, and it is a process to be encouraged. The problems of crime and the treatment of criminals differ widely between cultures, being set deep into the political, social, and economic structure of the country, frequently precluding any direct emulation of correctional organizations and methods. On the other hand, themes, ideas, and techniques often are entirely capable of adaptation to cultures other than those which produced them, and underlying principles and broad objectives frequently merit consideration for emulation in other and different societies.

Comparative studies are particularly important to us at the present time when the field of corrections in the United States is in such a state of ferment. We are doubtful of our inheritance, skeptical of many of our methods, appalled by the size and diversity of the problems we face, and cognizant of the lack of knowledge with which we work; yet it is also a time of great hope. There is a sense of increasing empathy towards one's fellow man, even the criminal; a desire determinedly to avoid needless suffering, a willingness to experiment, a general striving towards improvement. We have an Attorney General of the United States who presses his far from unimaginative director of the Federal Bureau of Prisons to experimentation and even more rapid development—surely a Gilbertian reversal of traditional roles. And in state after state, the old hard-nosed, tough warden, who knew that nothing could be done, gives way to energetic realists-reformers. At such a time, it is particularly important that we seek to learn the lessons of corrections in other countries.

Sweden is no place for the enthusiastic penal reformer. As William Hazlitt observed, "Those who are fond of setting things to right, have no great objection to seeing them wrong." But the persistent reformer who sees things wrong within his own state may gain from seeing the avoidance of many of these evils in Sweden. Exorcising some of these evils may be facilitated by comparison with one of the most humane correctional systems in the world and one which has achieved close links with the community which supports it.

GENERAL BACKGROUND

Books like Marquis Childs' *Sweden: The Middle Way* and the general interest in the United States in the pattern of life in Sweden have made commonplace some knowledge of the po-

litical, social, and economic structure of Sweden and some understanding of its high standard of living and of its well-developed social welfare system. The national background can, I
believe, be assumed, and we can turn to a general description of
the correctional program in Sweden as a prelude to considering
some of the specific lessons that may be learned from it.

The population of Sweden slightly exceeds 7,700,000. The correctional institutions at present hold, in round numbers, 5,000
prisoners of the age of 18 or above. There are also nearly 3,000
persons of that age range on aftercare supervision. Further,
about 15,500 persons within this age group are on probation.
These figures reflect a crime rate, and certainly an imprisonment rate, appreciably lower than that which obtains in this
country.[8] It is not my present task to speculate on the reasons
for these lower rates, but it is at least worthy of mention that
they are, in part, a function both of shorter sentences and of a
much less moralistic criminal code. It has often troubled me
that the country which proclaims the highest moral standards
in its criminal law, the United States, seems to have the largest
problems not only in attaining those very standards but with
the remainder of its criminal law also. Gambling, sex, narcotics laws of quite amazing virtue, all largely unenforceable, are
to be found in this country but to nothing like the same extent
in Sweden, nor indeed elsewhere in Europe or throughout the
British Commonwealth.

Putting such large speculations aside and returning to correctional problems, the Swedish courts not only try to avoid
committing offenders to penal institutions but when imprisonment is the sentence, the terms of years imposed also are short
in comparison with those obtaining in the United States.[9] The
prison administrators further try to minimize both the actual
terms served and the amount of social isolation and separation
that is involved in a prison sentence. For example, of the 5,000
prisoners, over one third are at any one time held in completely
open conditions.

Finally in this numbers game, it is important to stress that the
5,000 prisoners also include nearly 500 persons detained pending
trial. The fact that less than 500 persons are at any one time de-

tained in jail awaiting trial is a remarkable tribute to the Swedish police and judicial systems. If you doubt it, visit the local jail nearest you and reflect that the Swedish 500 are drawn from a population of 7,700,000. This number does not include people arrested and held in custody by the police; however, police custody is limited to a maximum of four days, after which the offender must be brought before a court and if further detained can only be detained in facilities provided by the correctional system—he then falls within the 500. But the lessons here are not for corrections; they are lessons for a judicial system which the lawyers most urgently should learn in this country.

Pervading the Swedish social and political system is a high level of respect for individual human rights. It is also a very polite society in which citizen treats citizen and the state treats its citizens with punctilious respect. These attitudes lie deep in Swedish social organization and are in no way abandoned when the citizen becomes a criminal or a prisoner. Thus, section 23 of the law on Treatment in Correctional Institutions, 1964, the first general provision on the conditions of imprisonment, provides that "An inmate shall be treated with firmness and determination and with respect . . . injurious effects of the loss of freedom shall be prevented as far as possible."

This humanitarian and egalitarian attitude is indeed the mainspring of the whole correctional system, an explanation of both the low incidence of imprisonment and of many of the conditions and practices within the prison system. This attitude is both its strength and a key to some of its weaknesses. This is what moved Karl Schluyter when, as Minister of Justice in 1932 to 1936, he laid the foundations of the modern Swedish correctional system; and it seems to me to be the main motive of the energetic and imaginative leadership now given to that system by its present, internationally esteemed Director-General, Torsten Eriksson. The predominance of humanitarian and human rights purposes also in part explains some of the weakness of the system—staff training is far from well-developed and that which exists is at a low level of technical sophistication, with reliance being placed very heavily on the personality and decency of the staff member with insufficient attention being given to his training.[10] Research is exiguous and little indeed is known of which treatment methods work better with which categories of offenders; again, the motivation of the system is human respect, not empirical or clinical perceptions.

The prison administrator and the prison officer in Sweden has this advantage over his colleague in many other countries: Swedish citizens generally are intensely proud of their social welfare system. More and more they take their very high standard of living for granted and express pride in their country in relation to its care for the sick, incompetent and discordant elements within it. When they turn to the international field, their national amour-propre is likewise expressed in terms of extensive technical and financial contributions to the developing countries and to the United Nations. The Swedish citizen not connected with prison work will, at the dinner table, express pride in the Swedish correctional system; this is hardly a common experience at the American dinner table. And his satisfaction is not in any clinical skills that the system mobilizes or in its effect on recidivist rates but rather in the fact that the Swedish criminal or prisoner still remains a Swedish citizen meriting respect, continuing properly to enjoy a quite high standard of living, and remaining a part of the community.

Examples of this attitude are frequently to be found in the press, where the prisoners' complaints to the ombudsman[11] often receive considerable press attention. The community appears to be interested in and to take seriously complaints by prisoners which would not in this country merit protracted attention within the walls and certainly would receive no consideration whatsoever outside. This sometimes borders on the extreme. While I was in Sweden, for example, a complaint to the ombudsman by a group of inmates in open institutions that the guards were occasionally at nights shining flashlights into their cells to make sure that they were still there, and that this was a serious interference with their right to a good night's sleep, was taken quite seriously by the press. The prisoners argued that if they were trusted in open institutions they had to be trusted completely. Torsten Eriksson had no great difficulty in satisfying the ombudsman of the need to confirm the continued presence of the prisoners, even in open institutions, and that this was no interference whatsoever with their decent treatment; but the point remains. The complaint was not treated frivolously by the press; it was thought of as a serious issue. The community generally has pride and a sense of responsibility for conditions in their prisons to a much larger degree than in this country and to a larger degree they have given up retributive punitive attitudes. These sentiments are brought to his work by the prison officer who sees a Swedish quality of firm, decent, respectful, and polite treatment between individuals as properly determining his attitude and behavior towards the inmate. It is a great asset, substantially diminishing the alienating and prison subculture-creating processes that are to be found so often in other countries.

SIZE OF INSTITUTIONS AND STAFF-INMATE RATIO

The largest prison in Sweden is Langholmen in Stockholm. This is a traditional cellular prison with a daily average population of 620 in the summer of 1965. Langholmen dates from the early 1850's, is overcrowded (its population occasionally exceeding 700, in an institution designed for 450), and is soon to be abandoned. The Karolinska Institutet maintains a 60-bed psychiatric clinic, built in 1932, in the grounds of Langholmen prison which provides extensive and highly efficient diagnostic services to the courts and the prison authorities. If Langholmen were characteristic of the Swedish prisons, there would be few lessons for us in them; even though by American standards it is a small prison. By Swedish standards it is absurdly large. On the day I went to Langholmen, the next most populous prison in Sweden was that at Malmo, in the south, with a population of 241 inmates.

These statistics tell a story of determinative significance for the system and spell out a lesson that one hopes will ultimately be learned in this country. For the 5,000 prisoners in Sweden there are at present 88 prisons. With a range and diversity of small prisons and with an institutional staff in excess of one member of staff for every two prisoners, with small institutions and small groups of prisoners, it has proved possible to set up a correctional institutional system which avoids the mass anonymity characteristic of the penal system in this country, and which largely avoids the hot-house growth of the evil subculture which has characterized our correctional efforts.

This lesson from Sweden is one that we already know, but it is underlined by the Swedish practice. Our institutions are grossly too large. Sweden has avoided the megainstitution; we should abandon it. There is little point in arguing the merits of this; few will disagree. It is a question of ignorance and tradition masquerading as political and social priorities; readers need no persuasion of the many advantages of smaller institutions. With small institutions, much else that we all seek to achieve in our correctional work is possible; with the megainstitution, little is possible.[12]

WOMEN STAFF

Women are found to be working not only in institutions for younger offenders in Sweden but also throughout their adult correctional system. I do not mean working only in the front offices outside the security perimeter; I mean within the walls and within the cell blocks. And there are women governors of prisons for male prisoners. Only in Langholmen, of the institutions I visited, is there the sense of an exclusively male society. Monasticism is avoided, even in the main long-term institution of Hall which is the central prison for the internment group, who are the persistent and professional criminals; it is likewise avoided for the 18- to 21-year-old group of vigorous males, and indeed when I visited the institution of Mariefred, holding such offenders, the warden was a woman. The advantages of our learning this lesson from Sweden are obvious; women bring a softening influence to the prison society, assisting men by their presence, to strengthen their inner controls, through a variety of deeply extrenched processes of psychosocial growth.

What are the disadvantages or risks involved in emulating this sensible plan, which would be sensible even did we not face chronic staff shortages? I suppose the risks or disadvantages are fourfold: loss of discipline, a barrage of obscenity, sexual assaults, and successful courtship by those we too often see as pariahs. The first I doubt, the second is a matter of staff training, the third is not a serious threat, and the fourth is to be occasionally expected and welcomed. One would not isolate a woman or women members or staff among a large number of recalcitrant hostile male prisoners; the main custodial staff should remain male, as it is in Sweden. The lesson is clear and is that women should be employed within the correctional institution for those skills in psychology, casework, administration, and counseling which they can offer as well as men, and nothing but advantage to the entire correctional system will ensue.

AN INTEGRATED, REGIONALIZED CORRECTIONAL SYSTEM

Under the administrative control of the Ministry of Justice, the correctional administration is responsible for the integrated but regionalized system of corrections throughout Sweden. There are approximately 3,600 employees of the correctional administration, not counting the volunteers who do the actual work of supervision in the community.

Correctional work is regionalized into five geographic groups and into three special problem groups. Each geographic group provides a central prison and a range of classificatory and treatment institutions, prerelease centers and hostels, and extra-institutional facilities. There are, in effect, five operatively distinct correctional systems in Sweden, handling all problems of detention prior to trial, probation, imprisonment, parole, and aftercare in their regions. The three specialist groups—youth, women, internment—are not regionalized in this fashion. The institutions and facilities for the 18- to 21-year-old group are administered as a nationwide system, as are the facilities, institutional and within the community, for women offenders and for offenders sentenced as habitual or professional criminals to indeterminate commitment. Conditional and final release under the indeterminant commitment is under the control of an internment board presided over by a judge or retired judge of the Supreme Court, and with four other members, including a senior lawyer, a member of parliament, usually a psychiatrist, and the director general of the Correctional Administration.

Considerable effort is made to delegate powers to the five regional correctional systems, and substantial authority in relation to the date of conditional and final release of inmates is given to local supervisory boards. There are 47 supervisory boards in Sweden, each serving one or more trial court districts and responsible for recommending the parole of prisoners in its district. Parole is for one year or the unexpired portion of the sentence, whichever is longer.

The total cost of this unified, regionalized correctional system of Sweden, in 1965, was approximately 200 million Swedish kroner; that is, about 40 million dollars. Of this sum, 90 million kroner (18 million dollars) were applied to staff salaries. These costs cover the 15,500 probationers, 5,000 prisoners, and 3,000 parolees.

Such an integrated, regionalized correctional system is, of course, not unknown in this country. The Wisconsin system comes to mind as such an organized structure.

One of the currently contentious issues in the organization of corrections in the federal system in the United States is whether the federal probation and parole services should be joined with the Federal Bureau of Prisons and the Federal Parole Board in a single department administratively responsible to the Department of Justice. Unification and regionalization at the federal level and in a country the size of the United States raise problems of great complexity, with political and jurisprudential penumbrae which at present I would prefer to avoid; let me therefore suggest only some of the advantages of the Swedish unified and regionalized structure for a state as distinct from a federal correctional system.

The advantage of unification of institutional and extrainstitutional processes, of some coherent single administrative structure of probation, prison, and parole, flows essentially from the fact that the link between institutional and noninstitutional correctional processes grows closer and requires overall planning. The prison is now rarely thought to provide an independent, self-contained correctional process; it is seen by all who hope that it will rehabilitate as involving a gradual release procedure and an effective aftercare program all linked into a single rehabilitative plan. And even effective probation is coming to be seen as requiring some institutional supports in an appreciable proportion of cases. The probation hostel may be necessary for some cases; institutional control of leisure in community treatment centers may be needed for others.

And so prison, probation, and parole grow closer together and structurally intertwine. The prison may be required as a base from which the prisoner goes out to work; a halfway house may be used as a release procedure; and aftercare will always be closely linked with the prison program and should provide a continuum of planning and execution of the prisoner's rehabilitative plan. It is hard to provide such continuous institutional and postinstitutional correctional processes and such institutional and contemporaneously noninstitutional processes (halfway house, working out, community treatment center, probation hostel) unless there is the closest of ties between those responsible for these various services.

Continuity of treatment plan and execution is necessary as a release procedure; but it also proves necessary when we apply more effective control mechanisms in our aftercare processes for this reason: at present when a prisoner on parole breaks a condition of his release, the choice facing the correctional authorities is too limited. He can be warned or he can be taken back into custody. Just as we are developing "halfway-out" houses as release procedures, so should we, as does Sweden, develop "halfway-in" houses to provide for those released prisoners who require a period of closer control than can be given when they are relatively free on parole but who do not need to be sent back to prison. This group may not be large, but it is appreciable, and again there is a happy confluence between better rehabilitative processes and less cost.

Another advantage of unification of correctional service should be mentioned. It has long seemed to me that the prison warden, to be entirely effective in his job, should not only be informed concerning probation and parole work but also should have had a period of active involvement in casework in the community. Likewise, it seems to me, the senior probation or parole officer should have had institutional experience if he is to be most effective. This theme is accepted within the Swedish correctional system, and no one reaches a high position in that system without a variety of work experiences both within and outside the walls. Again, the theme of the continuum of treatment services is stressed by the very structure of those services.

So much for the value of unification in a state system. Regionalization needs little justification. It carries forward the theme of avoiding enterprises too large for any single man to have reasonably close and detailed acquaintance with their workings. And there is also in Sweden the advantage, in a community less mobile than that of the United States, of linking the correctional system in each of the five regions close to the needs, opportunities, and social attitudes of the particular social group in which the offender lived and will live; regional differences require appropriate differences in correctional systems. Finally and obviously, regionalization greatly facilitates maintaining closer ties between the prisoner and his family by visits and furloughs than would be possible were correctional administration in Sweden not regionalized in this way.

PRISON INDUSTRY

An aphorism frequently heard in the prison administration of Sweden concerning their work program is: "First build a factory, then add a prison to it." Prisoners work a 45-hour, 5-day week from 7 in the morning to 5 in the evening with 1½ hours for lunch; the able-bodied idle prisoner is rare in Sweden. A few inmates, of course, are employed on maintenance work, but the atmosphere of all the industrial prisons is close to that of a factory. And even many of their very small open institutions are also industrial. One finds institutions of 40 inmates living in lightly built and unlocked and unfenced facilities in which about half the inmates will be engaged in farm work and half will be running a small timber-yard or carpentry workshop. The industries range from small, almost village industries, to substantial mass-production factories. The machine shop industry provides 500 jobs, the wood industry 850, and the garment industry 850. These are the major products, but there are also large laundries and substantial boat-building and prefabricated house building activities (200). Indeed, for the 5,000 prisoners, 2,500 jobs are available within various types of industry, while roughly 1,000 prisoners are employed in farming and forestry activities.

The correctional administration is one of Sweden's largest rural land owners, with 6,500 acres of farm land. The building industry is of importance, with prison labor having recently been used to build several open institutions. There still remain tensions between employers and trade union organizations as to the extent to which prison building should be done by prison inmates for the larger closed and complex institution, but for the smaller open institutions the battle is won and they are largely the product of inmate labor.

The lesson here is one that needs little underlining. Everyone informed on corrections in this country sees idleness as a serious threat to any aspirations we may have. We all know that we face joint opposition from employers and trade union organizations. I would hope that everyone appreciates that this opposition lacks principle and is unjust. It is based on the unacceptable premise that when a person is convicted of a crime and sent to prison he ceases to be a citizen.[13]

The value of the produce of the Swedish correctional system of last year was 60 million kroner (12 million dollars). It seems to me that the stress on production sometimes involves a sacrifice or neglect of vocational training. This may be erroneous judgment and may well fail to take into account the high and universal standard to general education in Sweden together with the value of on-the-job training. It also probably insufficiently allows for the lesser vocational training opportunities when sentences are so very much shorter, both in maximum term imposed and in actual time served, than in the United States.

The average wage of the prisoner in industries, farming and maintenance in Sweden is one dollar per day. The institution of Tillberga, however, within the eastern institutional group, is the first of a series of six institutions of a new character. It is the largest open institution in Sweden, with a population of 120; but unlike most open institutions it is not organized even in part as a farming or forestry camp but rather entirely as a factory. It consists of three "houses" proximate to a large factory for the manufacture of prefabricated houses and also for a certain amount of machine shop work. It has a staff of 44, of which 18 are guards while 13 work in the factory, and 13 are in administration. Most of the 120 inmates are short-term prisoners who come direct to the institution without escort from the courts. Many of them are sentenced for drunken driving and, as is the Swedish practice, have been committed to prison for a short term. Most are under 25 years of age.

When I visited Tillberga, the plan was to pay the prisoners the ordinary ruling wage in the community for the type of work that they do; the inmates would pay for their room and board at Tillberga, with the remainder of the funds being their own as if they were working at large in the community. They would not pay for the guards. This is surely proper; like other people they pay income tax and as citizens they must make a contribution, as we all do, to the costs of prisons. It is improper, simply because they are prisoners, that a larger cost for prisons should fall upon them than on the rest of us. Prisons exist for us quite as much as they do for prisoners.

It will be years, I suspect, before we will be experimenting with the full wages prison in this country; but the logic behind it is compelling and it is only a question of time surely before the advantages to the community and to the prisoners that such a system offers for certain classifications of prisoners bring it into existence. The experiment at Tillberga is an important pathfinder.

ASPTUNA AND RESEARCH

Chapter 28, Section 3, of the Penal Code of Sweden, which became effective on the first of January in 1965, provides that "If the defendant is 18 years of age or older, the court may, if it has been deemed necessary for his correction or for some other reason, order that the probation shall include treatment at an institution. Such treatment shall continue for at least one and at most two months depending on decisions made as it progresses."

The first section of the Code represents Sweden's emulation of some lessons learned from the United States, particularly from institutions that have followed the path blazed by the State of New Jersey in the Highfields experiment. Sweden has built four 40-bed institutions for male offenders; one 15-bed institu-

tion for women is planned. It is intended that selected probationers shall be sentenced under this provision of the Penal
Code to spend between one and two months in such an institution, being involved in group therapy and in a settling-down, motivating, and planning period before they serve their three-year
probation term in the community. Like all other Swedish prisons
which I visited (other than Langholmen), the institution at
Asptuna, which is one of the four built pursuant to Section 3,
Chapter 28 of the Penal Code, is attractive in design and comfortable in its living circumstances. Inmates do not merely sit
about in guided group interaction and in planning their probation experience; there is an active industrial program occupy-
ing their energies for 45 hours per week. These are vigorous
young men who must be kept actively employed.

Overall, it is obviously an excellent plan, and the Swedes are
wise in having learned it from this country and in having so intelligently modified it to their own needs; but I would like also
to draw from Asptuna a negative lesson that we might learn
from the Swedish correctional system—a lesson of what we should
not do.

When I visited Asptuna, the young and intelligent superintendent, having informed me in detail of the background of
the institution, of the organization of its program, and the group
discussions and industrial activities that were daily pursued,
then told me that this was a research demonstration project. I
asked him how he would know if the project had succeeded,
how would he discover if the experiment had demonstrated anything? He replied, conscious that he was being facetious, that if
they had 80 percent success in terms of avoidance of recidivism
he would regard that as a successful experiment. Acting the
graceless guest, I pressed him on this and urged him not to be
so confident of my ignorance. At length he agreed that the
recidivism rate itself would very likely give no guidance whatsoever on whether this had or had not been a successful experiment. He agreed that if by the selection process prisoners so
promising that they were unlikely later to be involved in crime
were chosen, the 80 percent success might indicate an appreciable
failure of the institution; they might well have had 85 percent
success if they had been left alone.

In truth, no matter what the recidivism rate, it will throw little light on the success or failure of the experiment. The offenders were selected for Asptuna at least partly on the ground that the courts regarded them as less likely to relapse into crime than those committed to prison. The failure rate of a group like this under previous treatments was not known. The classification and selection procedures may well influence the rate of recidivism more than the treatment method itself; at least it is impossible to disentangle the relevance of each. A very low recidivism rate may not be desired. What we may prefer is a reduction in recidivism rates among defined categories of offenders with known recidivism rates, and the experiment of Asptuna may be better attuned to the treatment of those who do present a serious threat of future criminality rather than to those who do not.

If every correction experiment is not to be regarded as a success by its innovators in Sweden as elsewhere, we must test it critically by methods capable of guiding future correctional developments; experiments should be capable of failure! The methodology of such research is now well-known to us and there is no excuse in Sweden or elsewhere for our investment of men, money, and materials in projects like Asptuna without any concomitant methodologically sound evaluative research.

In terms of research, we do not have lessons to learn from Sweden; they have lessons to learn from us. Only quite recently have criminological studies commenced at the university level in Sweden and the interest in critical evaluation of correctional methods is still dormant. Sweden would be an ideal country in which to develop criminological and correctional research, since very soon they will be excellently equipped for the coordination of social information about all their citizens. Every citizen now has his own individual nine-digit number made up of the last two digits of his year of birth, two digits expressing the month, two the day of his birth, and three digits completing his number by reference to his position amongst all babies born on that day (odd numbers for males and even numbers for females!)

All social welfare information from Sweden is now being coordinated for every person around his own number, and all such information is being processed for the computers. There is, in other words, a far-reaching movement of high technical competence towards the amassing and effective processing of a great deal of statistical information concerning the population of Sweden in all their contacts with official and quasi-official agencies of the state; but there yet remains insufficient guidance at the technical level, in relation to criminology and penology, for the information which is not accumulating to be structured to produce the maximum gain of knowledge to guide social action in the prevention of crime and treatment of offenders. It is paradoxical how remarkably imaginative and creative the Swedes have been in correctional work in relation to the relative backwardness of their statistical information and research activities, particularly research evaluative of their wide and interesting range of correctional methods.

FURLOUGHS, VISITS, AND SEXUAL RELATIONSHIPS

My first visit to Swedish prisons was in 1955; I well remember my shock at Hall prison on seeing a prisoner's motorbike on which daily he went out from the prison to work on a nearby farm. The Huber law in this country and its gradual expansion from Wisconsin through federal and state correction systems is one of the brighter spots in corrections, and the Swedes have few lessons to teach us on this theme other than that the system works well in their country also. However, in another process which allows prisoners to leave their prisons for defined periods, they do indeed have a lesson we should learn—the furlough system.

Furloughs for prisoners were introduced in Sweden in 1937. At first they were restricted to cases of serious illness or funerals of close relatives or comparable emergencies and to prerelease employment interviews; that is to say, they were restricted in exactly the same way that the current federal legislation[14] is restricted. I hope that it, too, will burgeon, as has the Swedish practice. From open institutions, Swedish prisoners now get home every three months after a fixed proportion of their sentence has been served; from closed institutions they get such home leave every four months. The minimum term they must serve before their first furlough ranges from six months to three years, the latter being the first possible furlough for a prisoner serving a life sentence. The duration of their first furlough is normally 48 hours plus traveling time, while subsequent furloughs are for 72 hours plus traveling time. At present, nearly 8,000 furloughs are granted each year.

Let me not conceal the difficulties that this system is facing. There was an escape rate of approximately 8 percent.[15] How seriously one is going to regard this and whether one will reject such a system because of such an escape rate is a matter of one's judgment of social policy. It should be remembered that all these prisoners are, in any event, going to be released and that furloughs are not given to prisoners who are regarded as actively and currently dangerous, and further that furloughs are better than any other method for maintaining the prisoner's ties with his family and the community in which he will be discharged to live.

Prior to and as a condition of being granted his first home leave, the prisoner will make a leave plan in consultation with a social worker. If he is to visit his family, a social worker will visit them and plan the leave with them also. This is obviously one valuable means of achieving our often-expressed hope for continuity between treatment within the walls and on subsequent parole. Home leave compels both institutional and community planning for each prisoner; further, if he conforms on leave, his own sense of capacity for subsequent conformity is strengthened; if not, the parole board's inclination to avoid his premature release is informed and strengthened.

The advantages of this system are as obvious as are its risks; the question is one of social tolerance. And as I have suggested, the Swedish community is proud of its correctional system and is willing to tolerate an appreciable escape rate as a part of the rehabilitative process they see their prisons as serving.

This should be said, however. One important consequence of the furlough system is the gross reduction of the problem of homosexuality within Swedish prisons. Small institutions and the attitudes and programs I have sketched are important factors in minimizing this problem; so also is the general attitude toward sex in Swedish society. But furloughs obviously diminish libidinal pressures for the inmates and lessen the likelihood of their homosexual expression. Visits also have this effect in many Swedish prisons.

Not in the central prisons in each region, like Langholmen, or Kumla (their most recently constructed, electronic, tunneled, televisioned, space age, industrially sophisticated security prison) but in the other smaller and open institutions which make up the staple of the Swedish prison system, the regularity of, and rules concerning, visits also achieve the twin results of helping to preserve familial ties and of minimizing psychosexual aberrations. Visits are allowed weekly in most institutions. In several institutions, the prisoner keeps the key to his own cell.[16]

In many institutions, wives and girl friends are allowed to visit prisoners in their cells—the conventions of privacy are not officially prescribed, but they are observed. I report a frequent practice, not an official rule. If you contemplate the transatlantic exportability of this practice to the American megainstitution, you will pause indeed; but in the institutional setting of the small Swedish prison, the female visitor, drinking coffee in the small mess halls which form part of each small cell block[17] and visiting her husband or boy friend in his cell does not seem at all surprising.

PROTECTIVE CONSULTANTS

In mid-summer, 1965, there was a daily average of approximately 18,000 adult offenders under noninstitutional correctional supervision in Sweden. Of these, approximately 15,500 are what we would call probation cases, and the remainder are on parole from institutions.

Conditional sentences and parole were introduced in Sweden in 1906, with the work of supervision being undertaken by volunteers in the local community where the offender lived. This voluntary supervision system still obtains, there now being more than 10,000 such supervisors supported by a complex system of 47 supervision boards, each under the chairmanship of a judge or lawyer. The boards have discretion concerning the conditions on probation or parole, variation of those conditions, and termination of supervision orders. They have power, in appropriate cases, not only to terminate probation orders but also to extend them for a period of a further two years, the normal supervision order being for a three-year term. Between the supervision boards and the volunteers stands a professional staff of 150 protective consultants and assistant protective consultants.

This system has the advantage of mobilizing the interest of many thoughtful people throughout Sweden as supervisors. Since the Middle Ages, lay assessors of this type "have constituted a democratic stronghold at the very heart of Swedish public life."[18] The program brings them deeply into the total correctional system, since the system is, as we have seen, unified and regionalized. It tends also to maximize the local community's interest in and support for the probationer and ex-prisoner. Some of the supervisors are professionally trained in the social sciences; many are school teachers; they carry caseloads of two or three (though there seem to be occasional cases of abuse in the system with some lawyers carrying rather larger caseloads of their own clients!). The protective consultants provide the presentence advice and also administer and control the system, introjecting a professional casework element into some cases and advising the volunteers in crisis or different supervisory situations.

This system is not offered as a lesson in itself for our emulation. It seems to me to have certain lessons for us but not to be worthy of copying. It does have the advantage of involving senior members of the local community in the corrections system, of mobilizing those responsible elements in the community for the assistance of the probationer and the ex-prisoner; its main disadvantage is one that permeates corrections in Sweden—it provides little technically skilled social casework assistance to the offender, and there are certainly cases where such is needed.

In this country, the historical progression has been clear and steady: With the development of social work training and the realization of the different demands of skilled casework, the volunteers have been supplanted by full-time paid and (in an increasing number of systems) trained caseworkers. The discourse has taken on the quality of choice—which do we want? What can we afford? This is, in my view, a mistaken choice, and that is why I would seek to draw a lesson from the Swedish practice. The problem is not one of choice, but of the effective deployment of the strengths of each.

Too often in criminological discussions we talk of "the criminal," "the juvenile delinquent," "the prisoner," our stereotypes masking almost the same diversity among offenders as exists among people generally. The correctional needs of one are not those of the other. The voluntary probation officer with a caseload of two or three can do better work with some probationers and some parolees than can the trained professional with his usually heavy caseload. In contrast, the problems which beset some probationers and parolees demand a skill in casework in their treatment which it is unrealistic to expect of the untrained, no matter how dedicated his purposes or how sterling his character.

The problem of classification is thus a serious one but one that we cannot burke. Numbers and finances are forcing us to the difficult task of classification, of building a system in which the professional and the volunteer both have their roles. The professional will clearly carry the burden of the presentence investigation and of advice to the courts; but the work of the volunteer in Sweden and in many other countries should be a stimulus to our developing supervision systems which can maximize the advantages and skills of each in relation to the needs of their clients. Some offenders will require the technical skills of the volunteer supervisor; and a few may require both at different times during the period of his supervision. That both groups are needed is clear; what is unhappily less clear is which types of offenders respond to the supervisory and supportive skills of each, but it is certainly not beyond our methodological competence to find out.

There is this lesson, then, in the Swedish system of supervisory boards, protective consultants, and volunteers which I must underline. It brings the community into the total correctional system.[19] The volunteer, through the protective consultant, establishes contact with the prisoner he will probably be supervising when he is discharged; he visits him and becomes to a degree a part of the institutional correctional system. It is an

important method of lessening the banishment, the social isolation of the institution. And the prisoner will have been tested
in regular furloughs before he is placed under supervision; it
will be known to him, to the protective consultant, and to his
supervisor, that he has a job and somewhere to live and that
determined efforts have been made to preserve such familial and
social ties as he had.

CONCLUSION

Correctional systems reflect social systems; their development
is limited by social and political attitudes. Yet there is an interaction here, too. The creative correctional administrator also can
influence social and political attitudes towards prisons and prisoners. In this dynamic relationship, the Swedish experience has
been most fortunate. Mr. Kling, the Minister of Justice, spoke
at the opening session of the Third United Nations Congress on
the Prevention of Crime and Treatment of Offenders, in Stockholm in 1965, concerning the correctional system in Sweden and
the public's attitude to it. He did not exaggerate when he said
"nowadays there finally exists, rather generally, public support
for the desire continually to improve methods of treatment and
that aggressiveness toward criminals has declined in our country
and has been replaced by a common interest in how to shape
treatment in the best possible manner so that the convicted offender may become a good citizen after serving his punishment."
And the Minister was not expressing a pious hope; rather, he
was describing the most significant factor in the development of
the Swedish system.

These, then, in my view, are some of the main lessons Sweden has to teach the American penal reformer. I have omitted
mention of the many lessons for the lawyer and legislator: their
day-fine system which realistically adjusts the fine to the economic circumstances of the offender; their rational practice in
relation to the defense of insanity to a criminal charge which
avoids with social advantage, the philosophic quagmire in
which we struggle; the expedition of their criminal law processes;
and the simplicity and clarity of their Penal Code of 1965.[20]
The eulogy could continue but is excessive already. Further, the
task facing the Swedish correctional authorities is less burden-

some than ours—they have not known war for 150 years, theirs is a prosperous, homogeneous society lacking subcultural conflict and with a highly developed, community-accepted social welfare system. Even so, in the application of the social sciences, in the mobilization of the skills of the psychiatrist and psychologist to those aspects of classification and treatment in which they should play an important role, in their staff training and correctional research activities, they lag behind many less prosperous correctional systems. The lessons of effective treatment of the psychologically disturbed criminal and the inveterate recidivists are to be learned in Denmark, not Sweden; and there is much that Swedish corrections could gain from this country— particularly from some of our better probation and parole systems, and our developing efforts at research to evaluate our prevention and treatment methods. But why try to turn the discussion into a Correctional Olympics? The point is made—comparative corrections is of importance to penal reform and Sweden is a highly valuable contributor to the pool of shareable knowledge and experience.

NOTES AND REFERENCES

1. This has certain collateral merits. There is an international brotherhood of prison administrators who most generously facilitate travel for those whom they will accept as members; transport is efficient and the food is quite excellent.
2. A declaration of interest is appropriate. The author was for these two months a guest of the Swedish government; his judgment is peculiarly seducible by the charm, kindliness, and generosity of Swedish hospitality and a critical eye may have failed. His conscience is clear; but judge for yourself.
3. John P. Conrad's *Crime and Its Correction,* University of California Press, 1965, is the leading text for those who wish to break their cultural chains and desire comparative understanding of the direction and speed of penal reform in this country.
4. Anglo-American Progress in Penitentiary Affairs. In Lopez-Rey, Manuel and Germain, Charles (Eds.); *Studies in Penology.* Martinus Nijhoff, The Hague, 1964, p. 43.
5. For example, the open institution claim. I am an Australian. My country started as an open institution. And we immediately

began a "working out" plan called the "ticket of leave" system!

6. *Characteristics: In the Manner of Rochefoucault's Maxims*, 1823, p. 148.

7. One praising Swedish social organization frequently meets these replies. Is theirs not a sexually immoral society? Is their suicide rate not indicative of a deep social malaise? In the post-Kinsey age, I doubt the differences between societies in any measurement of sexual high frequency and high fidelity. And concerning suicide rates, it seems to me that the published figures measure differences in honest compilation of figures rather than differences in the incidence of this behavior. We struggle with success at several levels not to classify our suicides as suicides; the Swedes do not. The alleged differences in sexual morality and suicide seem to me more likely to measure the degree of social frankness than the different incidence of the behavior.

8. These figures are also reduced, in comparison with other countries, by the commitment to mental hospitals in Sweden, under civil process, of a group of persons who in our system would be committed to prison.

9. Comparative statistics is an elusive exercise; but the following figures give some support to what is an observable difference. National Prisoner Statistics, published by the Federal Bureau of Prisons, in 1960 reported that the average time a prisoner served before he was released from a state institution in this country was 2 years and 4 months. Compare this with sentences imposed in Sweden in 1964. In that year 10,535 prisoners were received into Swedish prisons on fixed prison sentences. Their division by duration of sentence was:

Sentence Imposed	Total	Percent of Total
All Cases	10,535	100.00
Under 2 months	3,208	31.00
2 months to 6 months	3,973	38.00
6 months to 1 year	2,261	21.00
1 year to 2 years	887	8.00
2 years to 4 years	168	1.00
4 years to 10 years	30	.30
Over 10 years	8	.08

10. On July 1, 1966, the Swedish Legislature provided the legal basis and financial authorization for a much expanded and ambitiously designed staff training program.

11. "Since 1809, an officer of the highest rank and authority, the Ombudsman . . . has been elected by Parliament, invariably from among the most prominent members of the Bench, to exercise surveillance over the way in which public authorities respect the freedoms and rights of the citizens. . . . Every citizen is entitled to address his complaints to (the Ombudsman). . . . No special requirements as to form need be followed, and no complaint is dismissed without investigation." (Schmidt, Folke and Stromholm, Stig: *Legal Values in Modern Sweden.* Stockholm, 1964, p. 5; see also Gellhorn, Walter: "The Swedish Justitie-ombudsman." *Yale Law Journal,* 75:1, 1965.)

12. Wandering around a Swedish prison and talking to a member of the prison staff, at the level of deputy warden, I heard him launch into a bitter criticism of the central correctional administration in Sweden for not appreciating the need for small institutions. I laughed. He was offended. I asked him what he meant by a small institution. He said, "one with a population of approximately 40 inmates." I tried to make my peace with him by assuring him that I had had exactly this conversation with many prison officers in the United States who spoke in exactly the same terms, but who advocated prisons 10 times as large as he was demanding!

13. The contrary argument is "unfair competition." Perhaps the unexpected but just solution is for prisoners to remain or to become union members, their interests vigorously protected by their union!

14. The Prisoner Rehabilitation Act, 1965; Public Law 89-176, 89th Congress, H.R. 6964.

15. Furloughs normally are timed to end at the hour the institution closes for the night. If the furloughee has not returned by then, he is recorded as an "escapee." A majority of escapees are in reality merely late or late and alcoholic returns. The Swedes also register one gallant group as "an abuse of furlough"—those who return on time, drunk.

16. The staff have, of course, master keys, but each prisoner's cell is lockable against other prisoner's keys.

17. The lesson of avoiding central dining halls for the entire prison has of course, been learned throughout Europe and the British Commonwealth; it is an amazing perseveration that they are still being built in this country.

18. Schmidt, Folke and Stromholm, Stig: *Legal Values in Modern Sweden,* Stockholm, 1964, p. 9.
19. For a thoughtful evaluation of the Swedish probation system, see Conrad, John: *Crime and Its Correction.* University of California Press, 1965, pp. 26-29.
20. See Professor Ivar Strahl's introduction to *The Penal Code of Sweden,* translated by Professor Thorsten Sellin and published by the Ministry of Justice, Stockholm, 1965.

Correction and the "Doing-Time" Society

LEWIS YABLONSKY

The following soliloquies attempt to reflect a consensus of attitudes on the part of three different persons about to enter a contemporary correctional institution. They speak from three different points of view: the inmate, the institutional staff, the public.

John Q. Prisoner: Here I go again—back in stir. I thought I could make it this time. I wanted to stay clean but I can't seem to help it. It was an easy mark and I should have made it without getting busted—but that's the breaks.

Well, 5-to-10 won't be too rough this trip. I wonder who's still in. Things were working pretty smoothly with my old bunch when I left last time. I hope they're still here. Let's see— Jim is still in and Joe. . . .

I hear they're still trying that new program. That rehabilitation stuff is still B.S. for my money. What can they do for me? I began talking to the head-shrinker last time and each trip made me feel worse. Who needs it?

I'll do my bit quietly—with no fuss—get out in two and go back into action. I can do two years' time standing on one foot.

John Q. Institution Staff: Here I go again. I remember the first time I walked into this place ten years ago. I really had my mind made up—I was going to save the world. I thought everybody had some good in him—if you just knew how to bring it out and I thought I had what it takes. But I soon wised up.

NOTE: Reprinted from *Federal Probation,* 24 (1) :55-60, 1960.

At first when the older staff smiled at my ambitious ideas for helping the inmates square up, I could shrug it off. And when they called me aside and told me I was "rocking the boat and you can't help these punks anyway" I didn't pay much attention.

But then I began to feel as they did. These guys are rough and you can't really change them. There are a few good ones—who behave themselves in the institution—but they always come back. Most of them are impossible hoods. The only place they'll straighten out is in a coffin.

Just the other day I had to take that new guard aside and wise him up on that score. What an idealist! It's funny to have a new character like that around. He really acts like he can change some of these hoods. He'll learn!

We have to do our time in some ways just like the prisoners. Ha, ha, of course, we get out evenings and weekends. But sometimes I feel we're doing time, just like them.

John Q. Public: I've never visited one of these places before. Frankly, I really didn't want to come. I'm too busy these days at the office to take time off for this nonsense. But with all the other lodge members coming, I just couldn't refuse. Anyway, I always wanted to see whether these places really look like they do in the movies.

I must admit that I'm actually a little frightened. That prison riot they had a few months back was no picnic. You can't really change a criminal—so the least they can do is keep them under control. They should be locked in their cells and kept there. These places are turning into country clubs from what I hear. I sometimes wonder where our tax money goes in these places. The least they can do is have these criminals do their time quietly.

THE "DOING-TIME" SOCIETY

The real problem in correctional institutions today is not only outmoded physical plants, undercut budgets, overcrowding, prison psychopaths, understaffing, riots, and other such sundry and difficult conditions. An essential problem is the absence of active rehabilitative attitudes, objectives, and an attitude of simply "doing time." The offender's attitude of simply "doing time" is not only restricted to inmates but it is too prevalently shared by prison administrators, custodial officers, and the public, even though on occasion there are utterances to the contrary.

The proper response expected of both correctional personnel and prisoners by the public and government is to do your time quietly with a minimum of outcry and disturbance. Although throughout the country today there are some small social service staffs working energetically to "rehabilitate" offenders, by and large the "doing-time" tone of the prison community remains constant. The prevalent notion is that the inmate is to serve out his sentence and the prison administration, at best, is on hand to see that it occurs as humanely and quietly as possible.

As one offender stated: "Rehabilitation in prison is still a dirty word." It is taken lightly, not only by most offenders, but unfortunately, and more significantly, by many prison administrators and custodial officers. Although some lip service is given to rehabilitative effort in general, the prevalent "doing-time" prison philosophy continues to militate against correction.

The central problem of this kind of correctional institution (in name only) is found in the analysis of a prison community. The structure and characteristic of the prison community has been analyzed by many researchers and writers in the field.[1] A central theme in the literature is that the prison social structure militates against correction inherently and, in fact, reinforces negative and illegal behavior patterns which are in conflict with the overall social system. The way in which prison society militates against correction may be illustrated in the following general points, which are each summaries of primary problems of the prison community in particular and correction in general.

INMATE-STAFF DIVISION AND CONFLICT

The prison social structure is divisible into two apparent categories of participants: the inmate population and the institution personnel population. Each strata is clearly and easily identifiable. Each tends to view the other with mingled feelings of distrust and suspicion. There is a reinforcement of mutually hostile attitudes between prison personnel and inmates through stereotyping and autism (distorting perceptions according to needs). There is a tendency toward praise of one's own group and deflation of the other. The prisoner pointing to the prison doctor as a "sawbones" or "croaker," to the warden as a political "hack," and the psychiatrist as a "head shrinker" are cases in point. Institutional personnel, in turn, tend to view prisoners as stupid, shiftless, never-changing, immoral, and recalcitrant hoods.

Some inmates and staff attempt to walk the line between these two divisions; however, this is usually a precarious position. They find at one point or another that it is necessary to take sides, and it is too difficult, if not punishing, to leave one's defined membership group.

The offender when sentenced is, in effect, being rejected by society. He must make some adjustments in terms of his self-concept with reference to his custodial status. He can accept his sentence as being "just what I deserve" or he can begin to rationalize and project the blame for his incarceration on an unfair society.

One characteristic response of the inmate is to rationalize or project and channel his hostility upon the nearest manifestation of society. The nearest objective representation of the outside world, to the inmates, is the institutional staff. They therefore tend to reject the outside social system and its values through stereotyping and responding to the guards and prison administration as negative symbols of a society which has "wronged" them.

THE PRISON "ORGANIZATION MAN"

In prison there are advantages which accrue to the prisoner who becomes an "organization man," sticks to his group, and conforms to inmate values. The prisoner who continues to accept the outside society and its values through not being hostile toward the prison administration (the inside-the-walls symbol of the outside society) may find himself in the difficult situation of being rejected by both worlds—the prison and the outer society. Few inmates have the resources or courage to stand up against the expectations of the prison world which are imposed by fellow inmates with persistent force and clarity. In some instances their norms are more precise than the regulations prescribed by the administration.

The enculturated or conforming inmate does better in prison. He becomes, as Clemmer has termed it, "prisonized." If he accepts "stir" rules, he is accepted not only by his fellow inmates but also by custodial officers who learn to have this kind of negative expectation of inmate behavior. The maintenance of this equilibrium is reinforced by all factions in the "doing-time" society.

STAFF ATTITUDES

There is a similar pressure on guards toward conformity to certain generally accepted negative attitudes and "doing-time" goals of the institution. (Negative, in the sense that they militate against correction.) The new guard is quickly instructed by the old-timer about the "correct" attitudes to have toward "shiftless, recalcitrant, no-good hoods" who will never change. The correctional officer (at whatever level up to warden) who enters the prison social structure with a degree of correctional idealism will soon be cajoled or forced into submitting to the shared "doing-time" norms of both personnel and inmates. He is quickly admonished by both fellow officers and even some old-line inmates with such expressions as: "You'll learn." "You'll see what I mean about these characters." "No cons really change."

To resist these pressures to conform to the "We're all doing time" philosophy takes more courage and strength than most new correctional officers can muster and still do their difficult, demanding, and at times dangerous, job. Moreover, to do their work they require the cooperation of their fellow officers (particularly in dangerous situations) and this may not be forthcoming to "eager-beavers," "rate-busters," or "inmate fraternizers."

CORRUPTED REGULATIONS

Another reinforcement of the negative "doing-time" condition is that understaffed and underfinanced prison administration often falls into the trap of cooperation with the inmate social system to maintain at least an overt image of order and discipline in the institution. They may have to use "squealers," allow prison psychopaths to dole out favors, look the other way when misconduct takes place, and so forth, in order to maintain a degree of order. This practice of "playing ball" with the inmate system may produce short-range benefits of a seemingly quiet orderly institution.

However, at some point, the administration gets the uneasy feeling and begins to recognize that the reins of control and power have slipped quietly into the too-willing hands of the inmate population. In particular, the "prison politician," usually a long-termer and a psychopathic personality, maneuvers himself into a position of central power. When the societal appointed administration moves toward tightening and enforcing administrative rules, resistance tends to develop.

The psychopathic leader, who has the most to lose from a return to institutional administrative order (since he has developed a system of contraband favors and power beneficial to himself) may threaten a shake-up of the quiet "doing-time" situation. His extreme reaction may be exploded in a prison riot.

Riots are only one minor price paid for the maintenance of the "doing-time" society. The main cost is in terms of the salvageable inmate doing his time and coming out with the same, if not a worse, criminal behavior pattern.

THE MUTUAL "DOING-TIME" AGREEMENT

If either the administration or the inmates shift their responses or attitudes about the prison as a doing-time society, it may become a threat to the other faction. For example, an inmate who sincerely defines the prison as being a therapeutic community where he wants to change his illegal behavior may make the custodial officer and the administrators feel uncomfortable. They may have to reshuffle their defined attitudes and stereotyped views of the prisoner never changing and, in fact, attempt to provide therapeutic services. This is a real threat. It may add burdens to an already demanding job and impose demands on the administration impossible to fulfill in terms of budget, staff, and therapeutic staff resources.

In reverse, if the prison administrators take a definite view that the prisoner's behavior pattern can be modified, that he is reachable and can "straighten out," this may produce great anxiety in the offender who will have to modify his rationalized view of society as being unfair, disinterested, and unable to help him. In addition, if he accepts help, he is forced to admit there is something wrong with himself which should be modified. This is something not easily accomplished by an inmate with a calcified set of rationalizations about himself and society. The status quo, although painful and self-defeating in many respects, is less anxiety-producing for him than the drastic changes required in accepting efforts at modifying his personality system.

Given these complex conditions there is a silent agreement on the part of both staff and inmates to maintain the equilibrium of the existing social system.

Unfortunately, the "doing-time" problem analyzed here is not restricted to the prison community. It exists in other areas of correction. A certain apathy and maintenance of a negative status quo between correction officers and their clients can be similarly identified in other correctional divisions, such as probation, parole, detention, and to some extent, in court practices. A certain style of bureaucracy and negative status quo maintenance is the rule rather than the exception. The "doing-time" condition (described in my analysis of prison society) generally pervades the field of correction.

Given this indication of a basic difficulty in our contemporary correctional systems, I will now attempt to describe how this problem might be attacked on at least one important front— the proper utilization of higher education.

CORRECTION AND HIGHER EDUCATION

Correction has become a many-faceted field for dealing with the crime problem. Current policy and practice dictate action on a number of fronts. Validated psychotherapy approaches, restructuring the negative "prison community," improved physical plant, expanded research effort, improved and expanded parole services, halfway houses—all are correctional battlefronts demanding and receiving contemporary attention. Though there are these many points of attack, I would like to emphasize one important front which is continually developing and could play an important role in ameliorating the negative effects of the "doing-time" problem.

The effective education of correctional personnel is crucial to progress in eliminating the "doing-time" problem. In terms of society's control in correctional situations, one of the most influential levers is found in the types of personnel introduced into correctional interaction situations. We do not select our criminals; however, there is certainly an element of selection and definition about who is to be a warden, custodial officer, parole officer, or institutional psychologist. Moreover, we do have some control over the degree and type of education which such personnel need to qualify for certain positions. Although the following comments about higher education and correction refer essentially to the prison community, I should like to suggest that they are relevant to other areas of correctional approach.

Higher Education and the Prison Community

If change is to take place, it must begin somewhere in the structure of the prison society. Either the prison administration or the inmates have to start modifying their definition of the goals and objectives of the correctional institution. It is apparent that the inmate population would find it extremely difficult to modify their position toward defining the institution as a therapeutic community. Therefore, the modification must necessarily come from correctional personnel strongly motivated toward a correctional philosophy, induced by a comprehensive educational process.

The degree and type of education and training which correctional personnel at all levels receive is thus a crucial issue in producing change in the system. In order to crack old-line, strictly punitive pessimistic conditions of many institutions, educational reinforcement of correctional objectives based on social science theory and research should be part of the training of present and future personnel.

This body of knowledge about criminology would necessarily draw heavily from the human behavior sciences. Since the university and college are the only types of educational institution in a position to supply this kind of extensive education, the proper training of correctional personnel should radiate from our institutions of higher learning. Upper administrative correctional personnel should be university trained, with emphasis placed upon as many other levels of correctional personnel being trained along these lines as possible.

This extended education should include some of the following characteristics: (a) concepts and diagnosis of the prison social system, (b) analyses of causation factors and appraisal of the modal or general personality factors of the inmate, (c) clearer definitions of correctional objectives (i.e. is the institution attempting to deal with neurosis, psychosis, reduce anxiety, or modify illegal patterns? These goals are not necessarily mutually related), (d) a definition of the role relationship of the institution to the external society, and (e) selected knowledge of essential contributions of the behavioral sciences to the field of criminology.

This kind of training requires extensive education. As indicated, the only logical educational institution which could provide this totality of educational facilities would be a university or college. The training should not simply give the professional correctional officer a piecemeal understanding of his job but should present correctional theory and the objectives of correction into a "gestalt" which would give prison personnel a point of view to take with them into their correctional work.

The discipline of criminology in terms of its contemporary state of composite knowledge about causation, crime control, the criminal personality, correctional philosophy, and other such areas may be hard put to meet the challenge of educational needs in these areas; however, this demand should have productive interactional consequences. The potential professional correction person may force some remote "ivory-tower" educators specializing in criminology to distill their theoretical and research findings into a form amenable to practical application. At the same time, many old-line prison personnel may find it necessary to modify tightly held but erroneous "common-sense" notions in the light of scientific conclusions.

Part of the issue of making correction truly mean correction through the utilization of education is that it is currently recognized that progress cannot be accomplished simply by expanding the social service staff of an institution. It is increasingly recognized that all members of the institutional staff have some impact on "rehabilitation."[2] Even if it were possible to have one psychiatrist or psychologist per inmate, this is not the answer. It is the day-to-day living and the total prison community which militates against and/or fosters correction. The totality of the social system of the correctional institution must be brought to bear upon modifying the offender's illegal patterns. It is not solely the responsibility of social service or the custodial officer or any other special division in an institution. It is the total social environment of the institution, which must become a therapeutic community. Therefore, the educational impact described must be leveled at all members of the correctional staff.

Contemporary causation theories reveal that it is the "gestalt" of human experiences which produces the criminal offender. In a similar way, it is the total impact of the prison and outside society which may modify the offender's behavior toward a legally conforming direction. Properly trained correctional personnel can direct this therapeutic social impact on the offender. The role of professional personnel in correction must be modified if we are to make any strides forward in correcting offenders. This could develop, as indicated, through modifying the education requirements of correctional personnel, so that they move into action in the institution and community armed with a philosophy of correction based upon and reinforced by an extensive knowledge of relevant criminology.

SUMMARY

The theme of this paper may be summarized in the following points.

1. The real problem in correctional work today is not in such varied and assorted secondary problems as riots, poor food, poor plants, and low budgets. The basic problem lies in the attitude of the members of the correctional social system. In a "doing-time" system, a consensus of attitudes of despair and hopelessness reinforces the offender's negativistic, illegal behavior.

2. As one prime example of this correctional "doing-time"

problem we examined the institution problem. The prison community is a social system with two divisions—correctional personnel and the inmate population. Both tend to share mutually hostile attitudes toward each other which are often reinforced by stereotyping and autism (a distortion of perceptions according to needs).

3. A set of varied attitudes and conditions tends to reinforce the inmate's self-concept of being a nontractable, unmalleable criminal.

4. Any shifts in the frozen perceptions of either correction personnel or inmates cause anxiety and a necessity for changing attitudes on the part of the other. Consequently, the attitude of a prisoner toward the guard and the guard toward the prisoner tend to remain frozen in a status quo.

5. It is apparent that, of the two factions, society has more control over the correction personnel attitude. We obviously have some control in determining the standards and qualifications for the personnel introduced into the correctional situation. Here a primary job can be accomplished in educating personnel with the most effective correctional perspective.

6. In order for institutional personnel to have this proper perspective of their role in correction, they should receive a rigorous educational program which equips them with a philosophy or point of view about their approach and objectives.

7. This kind of education can be accomplished primarily through higher education in a university or college.

8. The education should include a knowledge of such areas of criminology as causation, the prison community, personality factors of the offender, the role of the correctional institution in overall society, and other theories and concepts of social science which apply.

The proper extension and development of higher education correction curricula, in cooperation with ongoing correctional programs, should necessarily stimulate further relevant theorizing and research vital to the total field of crime control. A more extensive and intensified interaction between the field of correction and higher education could have an important impact upon solving one significant aspect of the overall crime problem —the "doing-time" society.

NOTES AND REFERENCES

1. Some notable contributions to understanding the "prison community" relevant to this discussion include:

Clemmer, Donald: *The Prison Community*. New York, Rinehart, 1958.

McCorkle, Lloyd W. and Korn, Richard R.: Resocialization within walls, *The Annals*, May, 1954.

Weinberg, S. Kirson: Aspects of the prison social structure. *American Journal of Sociology*, March, 1942.

2. See *The Progress Report*, Vol. 7, No. 2, April-June 1959, U.S. Bureau of Prisons, Washington, D.C., especially "Group Work in Correctional Treatment," an editorial by Dr. Benjamin Frank, pp. 1-2.

SECTION II

A VIEWPOINT ON TRAINING AND
SELECTION OF CORRECTIONAL OFFICERS

TO anyone not intimately acquainted with the field, Gill's history of the abortive efforts to provide adequate programs of training for corrections may seem unbelievable. It has been a century since the first congress of corrections made their recommendations for training; and yet, even though national institutes of training were established in other countries as early as 1908, no program was initiated in this country until 1928. Such attempts as have been made have rarely been maintained and have achieved only sparse success. The wax and wane of training efforts is documented by Gill in such a manner as to suggest that the nation has a vested interest in maintaining a perspective of the inmate as a "scapegoat." In spite of this paucity of success, Gill seems not to have lost hope for the eventual establishment of an effective national training base. His caustic description of present and past attempts to limit training to custodial functions is particularly instructive. At the present time, there is no evident progress in areas which extend the horizons of officer training beyond the locked grill, the expectant gun tower, and the gray compound wall.

Alexander stresses the necessity of both selection and training. He offers recommendations that have evolved from lengthy experience with the federal correctional program supplemented by academic involvement in penology. A review of the problems inherent to the imprisonment experience, and the manner in which these might be corrected, are central themes of his paper. The difficulties posed by a system which places major emphasis upon custody and defense against inmates have left little room for consideration of new roles for line officers in the major mission. Improved methods of classification and grouping of inmates are urged, as is addition of more highly specialized personnel. Extension of the institution into the community to benefit from the expansion of opportunity which these changes generate is deemed mandatory. The actualization of the major steps made attainable through recent legislation calls for intense scrutiny of recruitment, training, and retraining of present personnel.

The remaining authors in this section, all of whom are psychologists, offer some specific recommendations for training. The papers by both Taylor and Peizer *et al.* plead for attention to the need for positive interpersonal relationships between inmates and line officers. The line officer's essential role in providing these kinds of relationships is seen as the cornerstone of effective programs of correction. Taylor's view of day-to-day contacts between officers and inmates as opportunities for an informal kind of psychotherapy adds a new facet to the role of the correctional officer, for which little training is provided. The paper by Jessor buttresses the above contentions by demonstrating that from a psychological point of view, neither punishment nor simple custody are effective in lessening the likelihood of further antisocial behavior. It is his feeling that custody either does nothing to change antisocial attitudes or actually strengthens them. Corrections is determined as " . . . the provision of an environment and a set of experiences which will facilitate the learning of new values, new orientations, and new expectations which will serve, in turn, to inhibit delinquent acts in the future." Jessor sees the line officer as teacher in the most vital sense and regards his role as central; this broader role offers opportunity for satisfaction as a professional. Both Peizer *et al.* and Jessor stress the requirements of improved selection and recruitment procedures in the hope of attracting uniformly high caliber personnel.

Training Prison Officers

HOWARD B. GILL

In 1870, the American Prison Association adopted the following in its Declaration of Principles: "Special training as well as high qualities of head and heart is required to make a good prison or reformatory officer. Then only will the administration of public punishment become scientific, uniform, and successful,

NOTE: Reprinted from *American Journal of Corrections*, 20 (4) :8-11, 22, 1958.

when it is raised to the dignity of a profession and men are specially trained for it as they are for other pursuits." Yet in America, the first training program of this kind was not organized until 1928. By this time, successful and permanent training courses
for prison officers had been organized in both Japan and England.

METHODS

Training by Exhortation and Rulebook

Within the memory of many prison administrators, the training of newly appointed prison officers consisted of a few well-
chosen exhortations about not fraternizing with the inmates, not
carrying contraband in or out of the prison, not permitting escapes, and not talking about prison affairs outside the institution. There were no "do's." With this, the new recruit was assigned to a post where trial and error prevailed. Lucky was the
new officer who kept his eyes and ears open and his big mouth
shut. At least he learned what was current practice among those
who had survived.

Frequently the new officer was handed a book of rules which
set forth some of the procedures that had evolved over the years
and which admonished him, among other things, to be at all
times "gentlemanly, courteous, prompt, willing, obedient, vigilant,
faithful, industrious, neat, temperate, calm, decisive, receptive,
dignified, firm, tactful, tolerant, frank, patient, discreet and self-
controlled," and even "impressive." He was told to avoid all
"collusions and jealousies and refrain from all discussion of political and religious and other controversial subjects." He must
not use "profane, indecent, or insulting language" within or near
the prison. He must be "circumspect in his way of life in society, careful as to the company he keeps and the places he fre-
quents, and prompt in the discharge of personal obligations,
debts, etc." "Any officer . . . who spends his money for liquor
and gambling will be discharged." (The quotes are all taken
from prison rulebooks for officers.)

Now, there is nothing inherently wrong with expecting a prison officer to be a paragon of all the virtues; it just is not very

realistic. Certainly, it ought not to be considered as "training" for prison work.

Sometimes more modern manuals (which is the new name for prison officers' rulebooks) present a bewildering list of items which a new officer should know. One such manual lists 75 such items which include a mixture of concrete techniques such as "How to maintain records," "How to frisk cells," etc., which can be easily learned by practice, with less tangible, subjective matter such as "How to correct inmates," "How to counsel inmates," etc., which require a great deal of knowledge, training, understanding, wisdom, skill, and insight. Such a list will give any new officer a good case of penological indigestion.

In not too recent times and still in some prisons, "employees and foremen are strictly prohibited from holding conversation with convicts upon any subject disconnected with their duty or labor . . . nor shall they listen to any convict history, or to the history of his crime and case on which he was convicted." On the other hand, many modern prisons now enjoin the correctional officer to be both a security officer and a treatment officer. In fact, it is apparently assumed in many institutions that the prison officer is a jack-of-all-trades with a hodge-podge of duties, mostly security, but with some vague responsibility for treatment. Sometimes the pious sentiments expressed with regard to the latter and then the restrictions put upon it can only leave a new officer so confused as to be meaningless. The prison officer must counsel, but not too much. Nor is any procedure established to give him access to the case records or any authority with regard to putting the recommendations contained therein into effect. Such schizophrenic thinking ought to make a split personality out of any ordinary prison officer; it sure will drive him crazy.

Frequently, the principal use for such rulebooks is to provide the administration with the concrete foundation for placing charges of failure to obey the rules against an undesirable officer. They also give considerable information as to procedure in a particular prison. Thus the strange mixture of pious platitudes, tricky rules, and procedural details provides in many prisons the only basic training given new officers. It is a most unfortunate and inauspicious introduction to penology. The organization of recognized training programs for prison officers is still a prime essential in American penology.

Japanese Prison Association School

As early as 1908, the Japanese Prison Association had established a course of training for prison guards and later followed this with correctional courses for higher officials and for physicians. As reported by Professor John L. Gillin, the subjects in the curricula for these courses for Japanese prison officials and other instructional activities of the Association covered a wide range. They included consideration of European and American prison systems and their histories, criminal law and procedure, jurisprudence, ethics, criminal psychology, sociology, industries, hygiene, architecture, social work, etc. In addition to these formal courses, training in judo and fencing was given. Motion pictures of an educational value were taken from prison to prison. Scholarships were arranged for students of criminal science. Special lectures and publications of interest were also arranged.[1]

British and Canadian Training Schools

In 1925, the British Training School for Prison Officers was established at His Majesty's Prison, Wakefield, England. As originally established, this school operated a training course of eight weeks, four times a year, limited to 30 officers each. Four hours daily were devoted to training. Each officer also performed 96 hours of duty per fortnight and during the eight-week training period performed all the duties of the officers of the prison, being posted for duty to every post in the prison in turn. A series of 37 lectures on as many different subjects from "Security" to "Prisons of the Future" was presented by the Commissioner of Prisons, the Governor of the Prison (warden), and members of the staff.

After satisfactory completion of the course at Wakefield, officers in training are assigned to various prisons. Here they are under practical instruction for another two months' period, supplemented by lectures given by the Governor (warden) or deputy of the prison. This course of instruction covers such subjects as duties of a cell-house officer, reception officer, gate-keeper, shop officer, kitchen, outside working parties, and the care and use of steam boilers and other general duties. In addition to passing a thorough physical examination, each officer must satisfactorily pass an intelligence test and written and oral examinations given by the civil service, the officers in charge of the courses, and the Commissioner of Prisons.[2]

A recent letter (February, 1958) indicates that the program is still in existence under the title of Imperial Training School for Prison and Borstal Officers at Her Majesty's Prison, Wakefield, England.

More recently, in 1946, a Staff Training School was established in Ontario, Canada, complete with living accommodations, lecture room, and gymnasium; and since January, 1953, all new recruits for correctional work must successfully complete a six-week course of training before assignment to an institution. The courses offered at this school include general staff course (5 weeks), physical training and recreation instructors course (8 weeks), cookery course (5 weeks), and primary staff course for new recruits (6 weeks).

American Efforts in Prison Officer Training

On January 23, 1928, Richard C. Patterson, Jr., Commissioner of Corrections for New York City, organized a Keepers' Training School in connection with the Training School for Police Officers of that city. During the winter of 1928-29, Sanford Bates, at that time Commissioner of Correction for Massachusetts, organized a lecture course for prison officers consisting of a series of lectures on criminology and criminal law given weekly at the State House in Boston. The series was given only once. When Mr. Bates later became Superintendent of Federal Prisons (June, 1929), he organized the United States Training School for Prison Officers at the Federal Jail in New York City under the leadership of Jesse O. Stutsman and with the counsel and advice of Hastings H. Hart, Consultant in Delinquency and Penology of the Russell Sage Foundation. In March, 1931, a centralized State Training School for prison officers was established with headquarters at the State Reformatory, Rahway, New Jersey.[3]

New York's Central Guard School

In 1937, one of the most successful training schools for prison officers was established under the direction of Walter M. Wallack in the State of New York. This school, which had its head-quarters at the State Prison at Wallkill, New York, was known as the Central Guard School of the State of New York. It maintained an eight-week training course for new recruits certified by the Civil Service Commission as a result of both written and physical examinations and for experienced officers chosen from the several state penal and correctional institutions. Following the successful completion of the course, new recruits were assigned to an institution for a month of additional probationary service before permanent appointment was granted. The course covered ten principal subjects, as follows:

1. Functions and duties of a prison officer.
2. Inmate characteristics.
3. Influencing inmate behavior.
4. Modern social and economic problems.
5. The crime problem and penal treatment.
6. How New York administers institutional care.
7. Parole.
8. Criminal law and court procedure.
9. Physical fitness and first aid.
10. Firearms and tear gas.[4]

Training with Federal Aid

In 1939-40, the United States Office of Education undertook an experiment in prison officer training as part of its program of Public Service Training. An exploratory project in such training was set up in cooperation with the Board of Control of Wisconsin at the State Prison at Waupun, and as a result of this project an introductory course in Prison Officer Training was prepared by Howard B. Gill for use in establishing similar projects in other states with the help of Federal funds under the George-Dean Act. The introductory course covered 15 principal topics, as follows:

1. General qualifications of a prison officer.
2. Who are prisoners?
3. Why are they prisoners?
4. Special effect of imprisonment on prisoners and others.
5. The prison officer and other officials.
6. The prisoner's point of view.
7. The prison layout and equipment.
8. The prison personnel.
9. The prison program.
10. Escapes.
11. Disturbances.
12. Contraband.
13. Prisoner behavior.
14. Weapons and physical fitness.
15. Laws and professional standards.

Supplementing this introductory course there were outlines for five special courses for watch (security) officers, custodial (correctional) officers, professional and technical officers, staff officers, and probation and parole officers.[5]

None of these training courses or programs has survived. Shortly after the publication of the plan issued by the United States Office of Education, it was held that the provisions of the George-Dean Act did not extend to the training of prison officers, and subsequent attempts to secure an appropriation for such purposes were rejected by the Congress. Both the schools established by the Federal Bureau of Prisons and the State of New York were set up to meet an unusual expansion in the guard force in these two systems, and as soon as the training of these new recruits was accomplished, the schools were allowed to lapse. Otherwise, never has a central training school such as those established in Japan, England, or Canada been set up in the United States.

FEDERAL AND STATE STUDY COURSES

In the place of these earlier attempts to establish prison officer training in the United States, there have appeared a series of new endeavors. As early as 1934, the Federal Bureau of Prisons published a Prison Service Study Course "for the instruction of officers at the time they enter the service and to assist officers and employees already in the service to secure a better knowledge of prison work." This course was used by the Federal Bureau of Prisons for several years until other methods were substituted by a special training officer.

In 1940, the Department of Public Instruction of Pennsylvania issued a study manual for a course in the principles and methods in dealing with offenders, prepared by Helen D. Pigeon. This course covered the police, the courts, probation, penal and correctional institutions, release procedures and parole, the behavior and treatment of the offender, and prevention. The Department of Public Instruction of Pennsylvania reports as late as April, 1958, that this manual

> . . . has been used extensively as reference material in [the] Basic Correctional Training Program throughout the Commonwealth of Pennsylvania . . . [by] people in Probation, Parole, . . . and other phases of the correctional field in addition to the personnel of Penal Institutions.

who have attended in-service training courses conducted in various areas of Pennsylvania. They state, however, that "the publication is now very much out of date."

When the Correction Department of the Army was in charge of the Adjutant General, manuals of instruction called "Lesson Plans" for enlisted men and officers in corrections were issued as early as 1928 and again in 1946. In 1941-42, under the direction of Richard A. McGee, then Deputy Commissioner of Correction, and others, the Bureau of Training of the Civil Service Commission of New York City issued a series of training courses in correctional treatment.

Even these more recent endeavors have waxed and waned as personnel in different correctional departments come and go. The reasons why such comprehensive courses for correctional workers have not seemed adequate for survival are numerous. Two principal reasons impress me. First, such courses have attempted to cover too large a field, including procedures, policies, practices, and principles governing custody and treatment of offenders. And secondly, such procedures, policies, practices, and principles have too often merely reflected the individual experience of the author and the particular system or agency which he represents. In such courses, one is struck with the lack of comparative or critical analysis and with the raw empiricism which passes for general principles. In stressing the operational point of view, such courses are often more useful than academic textbooks in criminology; but they obviously lack the disciplined and critical viewpoint of the professional, objective observer.

The present trend toward breaking up prison officer training into a number of separate units, each serving a special need, should meet these difficulties. This divides such training into four units: (a) pre-service training of students who are interested in corrections as a career; (b) orientation and basic training of new recruits in the policies and procedures of a particular institution or agency; (c) in-service training of permanent personnel in various aspects of correctional work; and (d) professional training of an advanced type for those with experience and ability.

Basic Training

The principal aim of basic training is to orient the new officer in his new job by educating him in the procedures and in the rules and regulations governing the institution or agency for which he is going to work. The intensive part of the training usually consists of a trip or trips to each department of the institution and a talk presenting the program of each department by those in charge. It will include a study of the rules and regulations and the manual of procedures, if any, of the institution. Usually a new recruit is tried out on several posts under the supervision of an experienced officer or he may even be tried out on all posts in rotation. His work in such posts is evaluated by the officer who supervises him, and such evaluation furnishes the basis for grading him as a new recruit. Sometimes question and answer periods are conducted, and written and oral examinations are given. Usually, basic training is coextensive with the probationary period.

Here and there, outstanding examples of good basic training

courses may be found which have been developed by leaders with an intelligent point of view. California has such a course described in Employees Training Manual No. 1, and the State Penitentiary at Canon City, Colorado, offers a good example of such a program. The Federal Bureau of Prisons has two courses for new recruits: the orientation course which acquaints the trainee with the environment in which he is to work through a week of lectures, tours of inspection, and daily group conferences, and the basic course which consists almost entirely of on-the-job training for four weeks, during which the trainee acquires a working knowledge of the functions in every one of the six services responsible for the operation of the institution. For those who have successfully passed performance tests in the basic course, a two-week on-the-job trial completes the training of the new officer. Two volumes entitled "The Way to Prison Work" outline the manner in which instructors should conduct these courses and provide the text for trainees to study.

If training stops here, which it often does, then the type of officer developed is very apt to be the sort who on retirement has been an excellent officer one year—20 or 30 times. His point of view is limited to the single institution where he works. He is usually convinced that there is "one answer in the back of the book"—"the way we do it," and his horizon seldom lifts above the book of rules or the manual of procedure that governs his particular institution. His training consists in hearing from the older officers and supervisors how they have carried on their jobs successfully and in doing the same things in the same way. This is better than no training at all, but it is at best only a start.

Continuous In-service Training

The practice of supplementing basic training with in-service training programs does much to broaden the scope of training prison officers. Sometimes such in-service training merely brings the permanent employees together periodically to exchange ideas and stimulate each other to better work. Frequently this exchange is accomplished through regular staff meetings or conferences, newsletters, publication of reports, and other communications from the central office.

One of the most successful of these staff conference programs is that conducted by the Federal Bureau of Prisons at its Wardens' Conference, Associate Wardens' Conference, and other conferences, usually of several days' duration, held from time to time for different groups of specialists in Federal prisons.

In Pennsylvania, the State Department of Correction has set up a series of staff conferences to be held at each of the institutions for "defining training objectives and pinpointing the goals of the correctional system." The topics recently considered at such conferences include the following:

1. Correctional and administrative objectives.
2. Goals and standards of educational, recreational, medical, dental, and religious programs.
3. How to improve inmate work program.
4. How to strengthen coordination between custody and treatment.
5. How to improve public relations.
6. Purposes, needs, and opportunities for prison staff supervisors.

Again, the state of California has developed a series of manuals for training supervisors, culinary personnel, and business employees. In training administrators, the Department of Corrections follows also a policy of rotation of assignment in the same institution, such as the rotation of lieutenants on various watches and assignment; or of having such employees serve in an acting capacity in the next higher classification, as having the associate warden act for the warden; or by transfer between institutions in the same classification to broaden the base of experience for the individual. These shifts and rotation of personnel are supplemented by a planned series of conferences for wardens and superintendents, associate wardens, medical, business and administrative officers, training officers, and other technical employees.

While all such programs stimulate discussion and build esprit de corps, they may tend toward a process of inbreeding. To avoid this, some in-service training programs are built around a series of lectures by specialists from outside the organization. Wisconsin has conducted such a program in which the history of prisons, causes of crime, the importance of courts, leadership, personality development, and such personal factors as good personal relationships, safety, courtesy, and cooperation have been presented periodically by invited speakers. In cooperation with the University of Maryland, the Department of Correction of that state also has undertaken a series of in-service training lectures at which invited speakers have presented numerous topics of interest. Under a Deputy Commissioner for Training, Massachusetts has recently established a training program conducted in a series of such lectures in a two-week course to which groups of correctional workers are assigned annually. The New York City Department of Correction has recently established a Correction Academy for training prison officers with the help of specialists from outside the Department.

Perhaps the most outstanding program of cooperation in training between a university and state correctional agencies is the Frederick A. Moran Memorial Institute conducted at St. Lawrence University, Canton, New York. Since 1950, an annual full-week Institute for correctional workers has been held at St. Lawrence University, in cooperation with several New York State Departments including Correction, Mental Hygiene, Social Welfare, Civil Service, Youth Commission, and Parole. This Institute announces among its objectives: "To supplement and complement existent in-service training programs with the aid of university specialists and facilities." Approximately 40 courses or workshops, meetings five times a week and led by university professors, correctional administrators, and specialists, are offered to several hundred registrants. No examinations are held (except for those seeking academic credit) and no degrees awarded, but without doubt a significant forum is conducted at which serious and organized effort adequately supported, both professionally and financially, is made to advance the education and training of correction and law enforcement officials.

Another form of in-service training is found in the numerous week-long meetings, including "workshops," held by national, regional, and state associations of correctional workers. The Annual Congress of Correction conducted by the American Correctional Association, the annual meetings of such organizations as the Middle Atlantic States Correctional Association or the Mid-West Correctional Association, the Michigan and the Pennsylvania Probation, Prison, and Parole Associations, the regional Probation and Parole Officers' Conferences sponsored by the Federal Probation Service, and the Institutes of Criminology recently inaugurated by the National Probation and Parole Association in different sections of the country once a year, are typical of this sort of in-service training. There is no question but that much information and a considerable amount of inspiration are generated by such meetings. While characteristic of the American disease called "Conventionitis," these conferences furnish a forum for discussion and serve to create a "climate" favorable to better understanding and an exchange of ideas which is helpful.

As is evident from the variety of in-service programs, there is still some confusion in all this experimentation. All of it is stimulating, but much of it is still provincial and spotty. The lack of continuity and coherence in programs which depend on a series of invited speakers and the difficulty in maintaining such a program over the years are obvious weaknesses. More effective are those programs which are built around operational problems or around the established procedures and policies of a department or institution. In any case, if such programs reflect only the points of view of those in command and reject criticism or ignore comparative analysis, the results may be disappointing. The pamphlet issued by the American Correctional Association entitled "In-Service Training Standards for Prison Officers" offers some valuable suggestions for such programs.

Preserve Training

A third type of training which has rapidly developed over the past ten years is the preservice training offered by numerous colleges and universities. Courses in criminology, law enforcement, correctional administration, and probation and parole are now offered in over 30 colleges and universities. Time was when the number of prison wardens and administrators who had ever read a single textbook in criminology could be counted on the fingers of one hand; some still hold office today. Such examples of prehistoric penology are rapidly disappearing.

Unfortunately, preservice training in the colleges is frequently in the hands of academicians who have had little or no operational experience in dealing with criminals. In their effort to avoid the vocational or technical "how-to-do" courses, they often cling to historical and theoretical considerations of the most general sort. They feel a vague uneasiness in their contacts with practicing prison workers but do not have sufficient experience to question some of the latter's most blatant weaknesses. As a result, these teachers take refuge in stating and restating historical facts without sufficient critical evaluation for modern penology, in threshing over theories of causation without tying them down to the diagnosis of individual cases, and in presenting statistical studies often of only general interest to the operational worker.

More and more, however, the universities are turning to instructors who have had both sound academic and professional training and years of experience in dealing with criminals. Such preservice training.
a combination offers the best promise for future development of

Because of the expense of time and money involved, texts in criminology cover current practices in correctional work in the United States and abroad only partially and spottily. The last survey of this sort made by the Attorney General in 1940 is already completely out of date. Because it lends itself to intellectual precision, a great deal of effort and money has been devoted to so-called prediction studies, with a minimum of time and attention devoted to clinical policies, concepts, or projects. As a result, much research in criminology has proved sterile and unrelated to the operational process. Lack of source material and operational research has limited the development of college training in corrections.

Preservice training in the colleges, however, is having at least two valuable results. It is developing a group of younger workers who can see prison problems with more perspective because they have been exposed to an historical and a comparative point of view. They do not believe the sun rises and sets in a single system or agency. In the second place, a number of state departments of correction are turning to the colleges for assistance in organizing their in-service training programs. California, Michigan, and Maryland have recently turned to their state universities for help in this problem. The cross-fertilization which should result may be very valuable for all parties concerned. Of interest in this connection is the pamphlet published by the American Correctional Association entitled "Suggested College Curricula as Preparation for Correctional Service" which also lists the colleges and universities offering such courses.

Professional Training

Basic training in the procedures and policies of particular agencies is essential for new recruits; in-service training which offers a broader view of correctional work is an excellent supplement to basic training; and injection of historical, theoretical, and critical-comparative points of view offered by the colleges and universities is helping to remove the in-breeding which too often results from homemade attempts at training prison officers. Nevertheless, what one misses from all of these endeavors is a hard core of professional concepts which are universally recognized and accepted by all and which bring together in a synthesis historical, theoretical, and operational viewpoints. Such basic concepts are essential to any profession; they have yet to be developed in the field of corrections.

Such professionalization, however, is not entirely lacking in the training or correctional workers. Ohio State University, the University of Maryland, the University of Wisconsin in cooperation with the State Department of Correction, George Washington University with its Institutes of Correctional Administration (after August 1, 1958, under the auspices of American University), the School of Criminology at the University of California (Berkeley), the Delinquency Control Institute at the University of Southern California (Los Angeles), with graduate courses at San Jose College, California, and the University of Notre Dame which offers an integrated graduate curriculum in correctional administration conducted by Hugh P. O'Brien all are attempting to develop such training on a professional level. Under the inspiration of Dean Roscoe Pound of the Harvard Law School, an early attempt was made to create such a program at Harvard University. Unfortunately, the program failed to establish that synthesis of theory and operations, and few, if any, personnel were trained to undertake leadership in crime control.

At Ohio State University, Professor Walter Reckless has for many years trained graduate students to enter the correctional field as professional workers. Professor Peter P. Lejins is doing similar professional training among both undergraduate and graduate students at the University of Maryland. In Wisconsin, the State Department of Correction has established a program for training probation and parole officers whereby newly appointed officers are paid for half-time work while earning a graduate degree in social work with emphasis on corrections.

At American University, since 1958, a series of Institutes of Correctional Administration have been presented twice a year for the professional training of men and women actually engaged in correctional work. The courses offered may be counted toward undergraduate or graduate degrees with emphasis on corrections or allied areas. The aim of these Institutes is to develop a frame of reference in corrections built around the basic concepts which are professionally acceptable. Through the School of Criminology at the University of California (Berkeley), graduate degrees in police administration, corrections, and allied fields may be earned through the usual university schedules under such professional leaders as Austin MacCormick and O. W. Wilson. At the University of Southern California, the Delinquency Control Institute, under the direction of Dan Pursuit, offers training on a professional level in its field in short, intensive, 12-week institutes.

The distinction between these programs and those conducted as preservice training in other colleges and universities lies in the emphasis given to combining both the theoretical and the operational points of view. This is accomplished first by employing as instructors persons who have had training and experience in the operation of correctional work as well as in the theoretical background and/or secondly by a judicious combination of academic training and practical experience while learning. Also, such courses offer university degrees with special emphasis on correctional administration.

At Maryland, Ohio State, Wisconsin, and California (Berkeley), the programs follow the usual university semester plan, while Notre Dame requires full time for two semesters plus summer school. At American University and Southern California, the institute programs are geared to eight- and twelve-week intensive sessions, respectively, which appeal to the worker who cannot afford either the time or money to undertake a more extensive program. Out of such professional, university training, it is hoped, may be developed that hard core of basic concepts, sound in theory and useful in practice, which will some day be recognized as the foundation of a professional penology.

NOTES AND REFERENCES

1. Gillin, John L.: *Taming the Criminal.* New York, Macmillan, 1931, pp. 30-31.
2. Hart, H. H.: *Training Schools for Prison Officers.* New York, Russel Sage Foundation, 1930, pp. 43-70.
3. Hart, *op. cit.,* pp. 13-27, 31-39.
4. Wallack, W. M.: *The Training of Prison Guards in the State of New York.* New York, Columbia University Press, 1938, pp. 35-144.
5. Gill, H. B.: *Prison Officer Training.* Washington, Federal Security Agency, U.S. Office of Education, Misc. 2309, 1940.

Personnel: The Key to Correctional Change

MYRL E. ALEXANDER

At the Center for the Study of Crime, Delinquency and Correction of Southern Illinois University we are building bridges between the practice of correction and the academic world much as you are doing here at this Center of Criminology.

The world (including the United States and Canada) is deeply concerned with the great unresolved social problems of crime and delinquency. These are vexing problems in every society. With industrialization and urbanization in our modern society,

NOTE: Reprinted from *Canadian Journal of Corrections,* 9:327-33, 1967.

their extent and complexity seem to become more pronounced. Our ability to understand and solve these problems has not kept pace with the growing need for effective action.

Man's knowledge of the physical and natural sciences is far ahead of his knowledge of the behavioral sciences.

Today we know how to put a man in space or how to electronically explore the face of a planet—but we really do not know how to treat the kid next door who steals automobiles, much less how to prevent him from doing it at all. We know how to navigate under the ice of the polar cap—but we do not know what to do with the drug addict.

The world is beginning to ask why we can not solve the problems of crime and delinquency. Millions of people in the United States and Canada are asking why we can not change the behavior of youthful and young adult offenders. What, indeed, is the matter with prisons, correctional institutions, jails, probation, and parole that first offenders cannot more effectively be prevented from continuing criminal careers? As those of us who attended the Stockholm United Nations Congress on the Prevention of Crime and Treatment of Offenders learned, many nations throughout the world, especially the new and developing countries, are looking to us for direction and leadership. They ask tough questions: Can we avoid your high delinquency rates as we move towards industrialization? What have you learned that will help us avoid your experiences with delinquency? What are your more promising techniques? How can you help us? And, after all, do you really know any more about the problem than we do in our simpler societies that are just beginning to emerge?

We in corrections have asked tough questions of ourselves. What beyond containment and control are correctional institutions intended to do? Is this necessary for such large numbers of offenders or are there potentially more effective alternatives? Is there a difference between teaching knowledge and skills to committed offenders and exploring with them the reasons for their difficulties in the first place? Can effective correctional treatment occur in the relative isolation of the correctional institution or must it be geared to community resources? Both in terms of treatment and control, at what point and for what reasons should institutionalization be terminated?

And so, the widespread and growing concern, both within and outside of corrections, has produced a ferment such as we have never seen before. It is a healthy ferment. It is a compelling ferment. It is leading to greater expectations—and to concerted action.

Consider, if you will, that the creation of the prison a little less than 200 years ago was a gigantic stride forward in man's search for more humane ways of controlling crime and delinquency. Earlier methods of punishment had been found ineffective and barbaric: transportation and exile, widespread execution, torture, mutilation, branding, galley slaves, the "hulks"; but Philadelphia Quakers conceived of an institution to which offenders could be committed for a period of time to live in isolation for prayer, Bible reading, introspection—until they became penitent—they called it a penitentiary. The idea swept the world. Later on, the reformatory for youthful offenders was developed principally by the American prison reformer Zebulon Brockway —parole and probation were developed as alternatives to imprisonment. But the prison remained essentially punitive and retributive in practice. The noble concepts and principles of the early founders and the reformers of the nineteenth century were observed more in the breach than in practice. Despite the introduction of behavioral science disciplines to the correctional scene in more recent years, the pay-your-debt-to-society philosophy has persisted both in the criminal law and in popular thought.

In the past 25 to 30 years, many new dimensions have been added to correctional practice. In addition to devising methods of identifying the problems and needs of committed offenders and planning regimens of correctional treatment, much attention has been given the settings in which so-called rehabilitation is expected to occur. Much of the regimentation of traditional prisons has disappeared. The help of public and professional community resources has been sought. It is no longer enough that illiterate inmates be taught to read and write and that prisoners without occupational skills be taught a trade. A

whole new range of educational efforts directed towards interpersonal relationships and the willingness to live up to employers' expectations have assumed new importance. These and
other modifications in correctional practice are reasonable but
it cannot be said that the newer methods are any more effective
than the old. The tragic truth is that we do not know. Crime
and delinquency continue to increase throughout the civilized
world and in the United States this chronic social problem has
now received national attention.

In his message on crime to the United States Congress in
March, 1965, President Johnson said, "We cannot tolerate an
endless, self-defeating cycle of imprisonment, release and re-
imprisonment which fails to alter undesirable attitudes and behavior." The President has appointed a Commission on Law
Enforcement and the Administration of Justice to find the
answer to six basic questions, one of which is: What correctional
programs are most promising in preventing a first offense from
leading to a career in crime? The Congress has responded by
authorizing the expenditure of vast sums for further study and
action in a number of areas of correction and has broadened
enabling legislation which will encourage the development of
new correctional methods. I am sure you have read about the
Law Enforcement Assistance Act and about the Correctional Rehabilitation Study Act which carried an appropriation of more
than two million dollars for a three-year study of manpower and
training needs. The enabling legislation which gives the United
States Bureau of Prisons a wide range of new correctional tools
has particular meaning for us tonight. In brief, this law signed
by the President authorizes:

1. The release of any prisoner to work in the community at
   approved regular employment with return in the institution
   during nonworking hours.
2. The establishment of community residential centers as
   places of confinement for federal prisoners.
3. The use of furloughs of not more than 30 days at any one
   time for purposes of visiting the bedside of a dying relative,
   to attend the funeral of a relative, or for any other purpose

deemed proper by the attorney general (or his designated representative).

These are fairly simple—but revolutionary new—approaches to correctional problems. Each has been used in one way or another elsewhere. But when, for example, the concepts of work release and furloughs are considered, it becomes obvious that the rusty doors, the gates of the correctional institutions have been unlocked. Offenders who have been responsive to education, vocational training, and group therapy, and have reached a stable degree of maturity and competency need no longer wait for an artificial and magical date of parole or release—they can be moved into a normal community setting for professional placement and work under competent guidance. Upon return to the institution during nonworking hours, continued education, advanced vocational training, and individual and group guidance can be provided. When roots begin to develop, life in a community residential center will be available for modified protective help to those who need it. Then parole can be considered with a complete range of demonstrated facts and selection criteria never heretofore available to paroling authorities. New motivations for offenders to achieve attainable goals will have been assured.

These are but two of a number of the newer, tradition-breaking correctional concepts which destroy the ancient customs, prejudices, and shibboleths which have bound and confined the cramped correctional practices with which we have learned to live. Now, much more is being demanded.

The implications of this kind of accelerated correctional evolution—or revolution, if you choose—almost stagger the imagination. Consider a few:

1. The correctional institution must be oriented externally to the community, rather than internally to an artificial community behind walls, fences, and grills.
2. Emphasis in program must be directed toward the more promising, the less confirmed in delinquent and criminal behavior, especially the youthful and young adult offenders.

3. Since the typical offender is of normal intelligence but substantially retarded educationally and with minimal employable skills, those deficiencies must be corrected through vastly changed and innovative educational and training techniques.
4. Training must be directed toward the realistic world to which the offender will return—not to the stereotyped training which happens to be available within the institution.
5. Since human behavior is so little understood, a wide range of behavioral disciplines must be introduced and coordinated in a truly interdisciplinary search for improved techniques and knowledge.
6. A system of sentences, parole, and release based on time intervals—often serving to defeat initiative and preclude the recognition of attainable goals by the inmate—must be replaced by a flexible system based on more immediate and attainable goals within the comprehension and realization of the offender.
7. The total impact of the institutional experience on the offender is dependent on the climate, purposefulness, realism, and skills in human relations of every facet of institutional experience.

I submit that we cannot afford to wait another 200 years for corrections to come of age. Confronted as we are with clear demands for revolutionizing the entire system of corrections, the basic question becomes: How can we generate incisive changes? It is my conviction that this can be achieved only through people—through staff—through personnel management that is skilled and dedicated to producing change.

BASIS FOR CHANGES

But however clear and simple the concept of change through personnel management may be, the development of new and innovative personnel processes is difficult and complex. I submit that any constructive change in personnel practices must be based on:

1. Broad-scale retraining of all personnel in the existing organization.
2. Creating a vastly broadened base of recruitment.
3. A boldly conceived policy of personnel development.
4. Selection for promotion based on excellence, achievement, and potential for growth.
5. Explicit training and evaluation of staff assigned to supervisory and management responsibilities.

I realize that there are many other principles of personnel administration which are applicable to virtually any organization. These five will suffice to illustrate my thesis if you will permit me repeated references to our own experience in the Federal Prison Service.

Retraining of Existing Personnel

The Bureau of Prisons is undergoing far-reaching change as a result of recent legislation, and it is not an easy task to reorient over 5,000 people to new correctional concepts. The essential steps involved in attempting to do this consist of anticipating the changes to be made, devising methods of acquainting employees with change, and identifying the new tasks and responsibilities that will be required of all employees.

With optimism that the new legislation would be passed in the 1965 session of Congress, we began preparations for it a year before when a conference of all institutional wardens and principal Bureau staff members was held. With a preliminary appreciation of the operational changes that would be effected, study groups comprised of wardens and Bureau staff members were appointed to reexamine and prepare proposals for change in the areas of education, vocational training, industries, personnel administration, utilization of institutions, research, and evaluation. These groups worked throughout last winter, and in May a wardens' seminar was held.

The findings and recommendations of the study groups were reported and discussed. Each of the study groups utilized the services of large numbers of institutional and Bureau staff persons. Through this kind of involvement of large numbers of people, there was broad understanding throughout the Prison Service that dramatic changes were imminent. With passage of the enabling Rehabilitation Act of 1965, we adopted the following technique of helping all personnel become acquainted with the specific changes that were in the offing. A list of questions about work release, home furloughs, and community residential centers was prepared using typical questions solicited from staff persons of all levels. A number of these questions indicated that many employees felt concerned, or were threatened by, some of the changes in long-established methods. A Bureau staff meeting was held in which typical questions were asked by a moderator. A tape recording was made of this meeting and copies were made. Bureau staff persons experienced in personnel training took these tapes to the various institutions where they were used as the focal point of local staff discussions. In addition, written materials were prepared and sent to the Personnel Development Officers in each institution. Together with regular Bureau publications, every employee in the Federal Prison Service is thus beginning to become acquainted with the changes and the reasons for them.

The anticipated changes which the law now authorizes will have far-reaching effects in new program requirements and the functional responsibilities of personnel. Caseworkers who have been oriented to strictly institutional diagnosis and classification must now concern themselves with broader goal-setting and become involved in programs which are oriented to rapid training and intensive treatment related to work release in the community. Educational staff members can no longer rely on traditional course materials and teaching methods. Educational achievement must be attained more rapidly than before. The content of educational courses, teaching methods, and techniques of motivation must be revised to meet the new demands. This is equally true of vocational training in which the trades to be taught and the role of guidance and placement personnel face new challenges.

Unquestionably, the greatest problem is that of identifying new roles for line personnel—call him correctional officer, guard, or any other name—and identifying effective ways of retraining him. For many years, we have recognized that it is the line officer who has the most direct and continuous contact with inmates. We have trained him well in making counts, judo techniques, firearms proficiency, and the day-to-day mechanics of institutional activities, but we have given him virtually no help in acquiring the basic skills of influencing and changing human behavior.

In 1964, the Ford Foundation awarded a grant to the Center for the Study of Crime and Delinquency of Southern Illinois University to conduct a broad-scale study curriculum which might best be included in a two-year Associate Arts degree program for correctional officers. Such a curriculum was devised, and although it needs to be validated, we expect to use it in training a group of our own correctional officers during the coming year. Subject matter includes general psychology, adolescent psychology, and other content relating to human development. Skills in English, writing, and verbal communication are included. Some of the elements of a liberal arts education are planned. Finally, basic principles of guidance and counselling are to be incorporated. Part of the course also will be devoted to the practice of corrections during an intensive two months and a junior-college–level thesis will be required.

It is the goal of this kind of curriculum to create subprofessional practitioners for functional roles as members of correctional teams. This anticipates a level of performance comparable to the nursing and medical technical specialists who support the practice of medicine.

Broadening the Recruitment Base

The problem of recruiting professionally trained personnel has been essentially twofold: the practice of corrections has not been viewed by professional people as offering rewarding careers, and correctional administrators have not communicated to colleges and universities their professional requirements. In consequence, recruitment has been limited to people available from civil service registers. For example, in 1964, we discovered that although there were a number of vacancies for trained librarians in our institutions, only one or two of the incumbents in these positions had been professionally trained for the jobs they held. We had become accustomed to appointing to these positions persons with any kind of college degree. They were not skilled in the techniques of library management, reader guidance, and other specific abilities which trained librarians can bring to correctional practice. We immediately began contacting universities in sending out a general dragnet for trained librarians. A few have been recruited and eventually all of our librarian positions will be filled by persons trained in this specialty.

As correctional practice becomes more sophisticated, there will be continued need for a greater variety of specialized personnel. We will need persons trained in academic and vocational guidance and experts in employment placement. In the area of social work, we will need specialists in group work and in community organization. We have anticipated the need for anthropologists as we inaugurate intensive training programs.

If we are to find such people, we must raise recruitment standards and develop new ties to the academic world. In the Federal Prison Service and in a number of the more progressive state correctional systems, direct working relationships with universities and colleges are being explored. Several mutually beneficial undertakings are becoming apparent. A few institutions now offer educational courses at the junior college level which are taught by college or university faculty members. In other instances, university departments of sociology, psychology, and education have found our institutions to be laboratories of research and meccas of practical experience for advanced students. Several of our institutions are certified for the supervised field work of social work students. At a half dozen institutions, university students are making substantial contributions to personnel development. In some instances, institution staff members are conducting seminars and teaching credit courses on university campuses. From a recruitment standpoint, relationships such as these are highly important.

Personnel Development

An ongoing program of personnel development is essential both to the training of staff and growth of the organization. We have found two methods to be particularly effective—rotation for the purpose of broadening the experience of personnel and providing opportunities for specific professional training. In too many traditional correctional systems, the average employee might spend his entire career in one institution or indeed on a single job within the institution. I firmly believe in a policy of rotating work assignments in the Federal Prison Service. For example, all correctional officers must be rotated through a variety of jobs at intervals of three to nine months, depending upon their skills, performance, and experience. Consistent with this policy, it is virtually impossible for an employee to be promoted to a supervisory level at the institution where he is assigned at the time of promotion. The average federal prison warden today has acquired experience in at least five or six institutions during his career and the majority of them have been assigned to central office staff positions at some stage in their development. Planned rotation not only gives the employee a variety of work experience, it provides management with greater opportunities for assessing ability and potentials for further growth.

Other techniques which we have found to be effective are frequent training conferences and seminars for personnel at all levels as well as frequent participation at national conferences and institutes. Special training courses are held for supervisors and persons who are thought to be candidates for promotion to supervisory positions. With increasing frequency, selected personnel are detached for specialized training. For example, one of our top staff people is now engaged in a six-week training course for career federal executives in program budgeting. An assistant director has just completed a two-week course in government for top career federal officials conducted by Brookings Institute. Another of our mid-career fellows was selected for a full-year's residence at Princeton University's Woodrow Wilson School of Government.

Selection for Promotion

In any organization, the methods of selecting persons for promotion is the acid test for training and development programs. In a career service, these must be based on performance and continuing assessments of potentials for further growth. The most effective techniques available to us are performance ratings and the use of promotion selection boards. The performance of all of our personnel is evaluated at regular intervals. Not only is this good personnel accounting, but it provides a structure for documenting actual accomplishment with which to identify future promotional potentials. In the Federal Prison Service, we are much more fortunate than correctional administrators in some jurisdictions in that we are authorized to use promotion boards made up from our own executive staff. This insures the exercise of group judgment on the part of key personnel who share the overall administrative responsibility. In my judgment, this method is far superior to the more common procedure wherein an employee's chances for promotion depend too heavily upon his ability to pass a written test and survive an oral examination by a panel whose members are not in the least accountable for the management of the agency.

Development of Supervisory and Management Staff

No organization and no unit of an organization can rise above the level of its management and direction. In these days more than ever before, correctional supervisors and administrators must be highly trained and skilled in the principles and techniques of effective administration. They must know and understand the importance and processes of decision making as well as how and when to delegate responsibility and authority; and they must have an appreciation for the intricacies of communication. These are elements of good management which can be transmitted and learned, and their practice is as critical to correctional management as to the management of any other enterprise. Indeed, I think that if time permitted, I could convince you that correctional administration is one of the world's most intricate management jobs. Think for a moment about the responsibilities of a warden of a modern, rapidly developing correctional institution. He is held accountable for the entire institutional community involving the control, care, and training of inmates, the effective use of staff, and the expenditure of vast sums of public money. He is expected to develop a close-knit staff team which can function harmoniously and with mutually understood purpose. These team members come from a wide variety of separate disciplines and specialty backgrounds, yet the warden must weld together a dynamic organization designed to train, treat, and produce marked changes in the behavior of the institution's clientele.

With the foregoing in mind, at least two conclusions are evident. First, correctional administration and practice must build strong bridges to higher education. Recognition of this fact accounts for the location of recently built or planned institutions near universities and other community resources. Second, personnel administration is seen as one of the primary tools for correctional planning. Unlike bygone days when the staff of the personnel office busied itself with clerical routines, effective personnel management requires the technical skill and direction of personnel administrators who are particularly trained and qualified in this area of management.

The concepts and methods of corrections are changing rapidly. It is my view that the purpose of correctional administration is not only to keep pace with these changes through effective recruitment, training and use of staff but to employ imaginative personnel management as a means of stimulating and inducing those changes.

While I have limited my remarks to the practice of corrections in the institutions, I am convinced that parallels can be found in the practices of probation officers, parole officers, the judges of criminal courts, and parole authorities. Correctional institutions deal with a relatively small percentage of the total number of convicted offenders. For them, institutions are but one step in the continuous process of corrections. As the concepts of change through personnel management become more widely spread throughout the entire correctional spectrum, we can look forward to the day when the question of whether methods can be designed to drastically reduce the rate of recidivism will be answered firmly and positively. I am optimistic that that day is not far off.

Treatment in Prison: Problems in Training

A. J. W. TAYLOR

Imprisonment sometimes creates more problems than it sets out to solve. Man cannot be trained to acquit himself well in a free society while he is himself in captivity. Nor can he be taught to select his friends with care if society places him among well-chosen and qualified criminals. The one-sex community, the limitations of freedom, the restricted opportunities for choice and expression, unavoidably impose restrictions that may hamper or completely prevent the growth or adjustment of personality. For these reasons, most communities in the Western world have adopted the policy that prison should only be used as a last resort. Lesser penal measures, together with skilled supervision, are frequently used as an alternative to imprisonment, certainly for the younger offenders and where possible for older offenders. Despite this, however, cases have arisen to suggest that imprisonment can be beneficial. Positive treatment within a prison, however, faces two main difficulties in addition to the problems outlined above. First, a prison is still thought of as punishment rather than as a place for rehabilitation. Second, the prison staff usually has no feeling of worth.

Men Sent to Prison as Punishment—Not for Punishment

The staff of a prison works against the historical background of prison as a place of punishment. The current trend is to refer to imprisonment as punishment, but this change of preposition implies a change of attitude that has not yet completely been made. Society at large has not yet lost its feeling for deterrence and retribution in punishment, and to some extent the staff of a prison feels compelled to function in line with society's attitude. Principles of reformation and rehabilitation, and the individualization of treatment, are not easily augmented in a punitive setting. Even if the principle of treatment is accepted, it is frequently neglected in order that staff accommodation and routines may be directed towards the urgent daily problems of

NOTE: Reprinted from *Federal Probation*, 27 (1) :11-13, 1963.

supervising a paranoid community. Immediate problems seem to be more important and real than those of distant rehabilitation in free society once sentences have been served.

Feeling of a Job Well Done Often Denied the Prison Staff

The second difficulty arises from the accumulated inertia that forms part of the stagnant world of the prison. Everyone needs to feel that his job brings worthwhile results, but in the face of the stream of failures who may return to prison, this feeling of worth is frequently denied prison staff. Inmates who succeed or reform merge back into society and draw no attention to themselves, but the repeated offenders stand out clearly as examples of failure. In the face of constant criticism from the wider community, as well as disappointment from seeing failures return to prison, staff has to look elsewhere for measures of self-regard. One measure may ultimately be in the adoption of a philosophy that, "in the light of our present knowledge we cannot guarantee success in this very difficult field of reforming criminals, but, given the backing and respect of society at large, we could move forward confidently, making the most of the knowledge that we do possess."

Even the professional worker within prison will experience feelings of failure, but he may derive comfort from the observations of his professional colleagues, as noted by Glover[1] and Wolff,[2] concerning the difficulties of working with "neurotic characters." He may also be fortified by the knowledge that apparently formidable areas have yielded to the constant march of the scientific approach. Mental deficiency, insanity, tuberculosis, and alcoholism have gradually become areas of hope rather than despair. Hope, self-respect, and personal worth among the staff of institutions, no less than among inmates, depends on a vigorous research and penal policy translated to action.

In prison, we are concerned mainly with individuals and not the broader issues such as economic conditions, industrialization, and complexities of society that may be involved in the causes of crime. At times, the "main offender" in the family may well be a wife, who, because of her own neurotic disorder, precipitated criminal conduct in her husband; a social caseworker can be of value in helping to restore harmony in a "discordant" home. Within prison, however, it is necessary to decide at what point to attack crime. The first offender may merit much consideration, but it is never possible to say with any degree of certainty that any recidivist is a "no hoper." Statistics also indicate that crime is a young man's game and that many repeated offenders fade out around 40—the "climacteric" of a criminal career. However, there are sufficient examples of the young active criminal changing his outlook and behavior to suggest that we are not justified in allowing them to run their full course up until they are 40. Even the persistent offender can provide a rich field for research because we know little of the recruitment and training of professional offenders. The ultimate goal in any treatment program is that of prevention, but since prison staff deals with those who have already committed their first offense, it is the function of other agencies to reach back beyond the point at which the offense was committed in order to stabilize the individual, his home community, and society.

INFLUENCE OF STAFF THROUGH PERSONAL EXAMPLE

If a prison is sufficiently small, the staff can bring their influence to bear through personal example and contact with inmates. This is the point that was emphasized by Maconachie[3] a century ago but has regrettably been avoided by many penologists since then. We cannot get to know men if they are merely numbers. The prevailing trend is towards encouraging formal group counselling in prison, but in our determination to bring hope and enthusiasm to overcome inertia in prison, we are in danger of destroying much of the valuable work that goes on at an informal level. We must not assume that groups are non-existent because there is no fixed group meeting nor observable framework for selection, discussion of topics, and leadership control of groups. In fact, prison officers do much valuable work as wing officers, gangers, and instructors. Frequently the men allotted to them assume a unit and look to them for guidance and help in a variety of matters that are quite unrelated to their immediate work. In this way, the relationships that are built up are so frequently of the highest order. In one case, an inmate referred to his officer as his "Dad," and this remark was made with such feeling as to indicate a true respect in which the officer was held.

Any change of personality and outlook only comes through healthy relationships with other people. In stressing that training officers bring their influences to bear upon the inmates, we must be careful not to underrate the healthy relationships that inmates may have with authority. The disciplinary staff deals with difficult, unstable, and frequently truculent people, and in their dealings with them sometimes can give inmates their very first experience of being within a firm but fair community. So many inmates have not experienced qualities of personal justice from close members of their family, or indeed others with whom they have associated on the personal level, that a healthy experience of discipline can be as much a positive factor contributing to a changed outlook as any other beneficial experience. In this sense, "discipline" is a measure of maturity, not the mark of a big voice, big chest, and big boots.

AIM OF THERAPY

The aim in any kind of therapy is to induce positive relationships, and the method of achieving the end is of less importance —within an ethical framework. It is essential that the need be met and not that it be met in a particular way. Were an attempt made to put all officer-inmate relationships on a formal plan, the artificiality of the situation would destroy the spontaneous growth of understanding that sometimes exists between the two sides. Moreover, the officer would frequently feel ill-equipped to act as a group leader in a discussion for a set time, and the inmate would revert to his natural suspicious antiauthoritarian frame of mind and would be less likely to disclose his confidences. On the side of formal groups, we are lucky in New Zealand in that we have a good ratio between reformative personnel and inmates. It is therefore possible for these highly trained nonuniformed members of the staff to run "formal" discussion groups. In Wellington Prison, with an average daily muster of 150 inmates, there are no less than six groups of different kinds run by the welfare officer, parole officer, chaplain, priest, Alcoholics Anonymous, and psychologist. The interrelationship between the groups and the leaders is such that there is little overlapping but occasional cross-reference in order to meet the needs of the particular inmate. The important thing is that the uniformed staff does not have its own custodial role dislocated by being expected to run formal groups. At the same time, the relationship between officers and the formal group leaders is such that they frequently join for discussions on the progress of inmates, and they seek ways in which they can help the members of the reformative team. This mutual understanding between the uniformed and nonuniformed staff is a valuable aid towards bringing about a hopeful and harmonious atmosphere in places that are traditionally sterile monuments to human depreciation and misery.

GOOD WILL ATTRACTS TROUBLED PEOPLE

Prisoners are people, albeit difficult people. In our optimism, we should not forget that it was the rebels who defied the highly organized group methods of the North Korean brainwashing machine. Resistance has to be overcome, and while there is no simple remedy, good will is a vital basis for therapy. Good will is a philosophical and emotional orientation to mankind in general and to the needy in particular. Good will attracts troubled people and inspires confidence. It may be measured by the number of inmates who approach the psychologist of their own accord rather than through official routine, where neither party has ulterior motives. If good will is spread through formal and informal groups in prison, the way is open to provide a wide range of differing therapeutic skills from persuasion to counseling and psychotherapy, as the case requires. Informal groups, no less than formal groups, have a valuable part to play in rehabilitating offenders.

NOTES AND REFERENCES

1. Glover, Edward: *The Roots of Crime*. London, Imago, 1960.
2. Wolff, Werener: *Contemporary Psychotherapists Examine Themselves*. Springfield, Thomas, 1956.
3. Barry, John Vincent: *Alexander Maconochie of Norfolk Island*. London, Oxford University Press, 1958.

Correctional Rehabilitation as a Function of Interpersonal Relations

SHELDON B. PEIZER, EDWARD B. LEWIS, and ROBERT W. SCOLLON

INTRODUCTION

Our purpose here is not to describe or promote a program for rehabilitation but to pass on some observations that we have made, as psychologists, regarding the rehabilitative process in correctional endeavors. Our observations of the functioning of rehabilitative programs, of groups of inmates, and of the behavior of individual inmates have led us to the belief that the concept of "interpersonal relations" is one of the most useful keys for understanding and promoting the rehabilitative process. Aside from our personal observations and experiences, a backlog of psychological theory gives support to this concept. Newer contributions to the study of psychotherapeutic processes and the psychological study of social learning have demonstrated its usefulness.

We regard the rehabilitation of inmates of correctional institutions as a learning task. When most people think of learning, they think of books, classrooms, and the practice of physical and verbal skills. Most of our learning, however, occurs outside of the classroom situation and before and after formal education intervenes in our lifetime. Rehabilitation of the felon or misdemeanant may include vocational training, learning of the three R's, and formal indoctrination in the rules and regulations of society; but we are primarily interested in social learning. We hope to change the inmates' attitudes toward the institutions of society and towards individuals. We hope to make inmates more respectful of the rights of others, more highly motivated to seek social acceptance, and more realistic in their views of the relationship between themselves and society.

Except, perhaps, for a few extremely retarded inmates of institutions for the feeble-minded, every human being has learned some of these social orientations. The majority of us have not

NOTE: Reprinted from *Journal of Criminal Law, Criminology, and Police Science,* 47:632-639, 1956.

learned these things through books and lectures but through our relationships with other people, particularly our parents and friends. We have learned them by imitating the behavior of these prestige figures, motivated by a desire to gain acceptance from them.

As psychologists, we are necessarily interested in the factors involved in learning and training; as correctional clinicians, we are interested in changing the individual to meet society's criteria for citizenship. We therefore offer our particular point of view in regard to the rehabilitative process.

THE REHABILITATIVE PROGRAM

Though many aspects of prison routine are rehabilitative in intent, it is in three major areas that rehabilitative design is most clearly apparent—the disciplinary, vocational, and moral training programs. These divisions are somewhat arbitrary, since the total program is educational in a broad sense. The program reflects the values of our society as well as the common perception of the felon as a person deficient in those areas of development which the program aims to stimulate.

The prison disciplinary program should be recognized as a means to the end of inculcating self-discipline. External controls, physical or symbolic, may have the temporary effect of minimizing undesirable conduct. Whether such controls will lead to the modification of behavior under circumstances of greater freedom (i.e. parole) depends on the learning which takes place. It appears that large numbers of inmates resist the learning of an abiding fear of punitive consequences. Thus, the punishing features of the disciplinary program are probably rather insignificant for long-range learning.

Prison rules and punishments are neither more nor less arbitrary than rules and punishments on the outside. The same may be said of their palatability. The crucial question regarding rules is whether they serve practical purposes; the crucial question regarding discipline is whether it induces acceptance or only conformity. Footdragging compliance and halfhearted verbal expressions of agreement are commonly encountered symptoms of conformity without acceptance. Good behavior in the face of certain punishment for misconduct is not surprising and is insignificant in the development of self-discipline. The disciplinarian is responsible for communicating the purposes which underlie the rules he enforces. It would, of course, be naive to assume that all inmates will accept the social rationale for institutional rules. On the other hand, it becomes quite easy for an inmate to justify hostility to rules which appear senseless to him. Whatever the disposition of the inmate—to accept or reject discipline—he is hard pressed to justify rejection of rules which are reasonable and punishments which are fair. In making it difficult for the inmate to cling to distorted views, we increase the chances of his adopting new ones. It is a long stride from the acceptance of good intent and acknowledgment of judiciousness in the disciplinarian to the expression, in daily conduct, of mature self-discipline. However, such acceptance appears to be a prime requisite. It can be induced but not demanded.

It is difficult to see how rehabilitation could be accomplished in a prison setting without a work program. If what is learned "inside" is to be generalized to the "outside," relative normality of living must be maintained within prison walls. Certainly, then, emphasis on productive activity and the development of employable skills is not misplaced. Faith in the rehabilitative value of vocational training is not always justified, however. Unskilled status is no longer indicative of marginal employability. Though at first glance a prison population may appear to be distinguished by its plethora of "men without trades," it is questionable that this attribute truly sets the prison population apart from groups of similar social and economic standing on the outside. In this day of mass production, a worker may have long tenure and relatively little technical skill. The most important goals of the work program may not be achieved because they are less easily defined and communicated and less readily measured than are skills. Unless one accepts work realistically, can adopt himself gracefully to a place in the hierarchy of power which exists in the employer-foreman-worker relationship and appreciates the values of stability and reliability, vocational skill has little adjustment value. The prison work-supervisor or vocational instructor can influence these work-attitudes only insofar as he is capable of establishing rapport with the inmates who work under his guidance. It is necessary that the work supervisor take pride in his vocation. A cynical instructor can scarcely communicate positive work attitudes or ideals, since his own conduct will unfailingly reveal his negativism. When rapport is cited as a requisite for attitude development, it may be mistaken by some to mean the sort of overly casual dealings which wise prison administrators discourage. This is not the intended meaning. The requisites for true rapport appear to be a genuine idealism regarding rehabilitation and a genuine respect for the inmate as a human being. The vocational instructor is in a highly strategic position. Just as in his role of skill-teacher he can observe and correct skill-errors, so as a teacher of work-attitudes he can observe and correct expressions of attitude. Unless, however, he is accepted by the inmate as someone who matters, his rebuke or word of praise or admonition will have little constructive value.

Just as the goal of discipline is self-discipline, so the goal of moral training is moral choice. Ideally, penal institutions might strive to nurture life philosophies or value-systems which would sustain socially approved and morally upright behavior. It is probably true, however, that well-developed, integrative philosophies of life are the exception rather than the rule, even among persons on the outside of prison walls. In any case, such human attributes are complex and appear to develop slowly out of experience rather than to appear full blown as a consequence of limited teaching, example, or exhortation.

The aspects of prison life most obviously aimed at moral training are the religious program and the disciplinary program. It is doubtful that enforced attendance at church has the hoped-for effect of stimulating moral growth. The fact of force is sufficient to induce negative attitudes in many inmates toward chaplains, sermons, and the entire ritual of the church service. Church attendance can and should be made attractive without the introduction of either rewards or punishments. The relationship of religious study and religious experience to moral growth is difficult to assess. The immediate value of such study and experience is sufficient to justify the program, whatever the long-range consequences. However, since long-range effects in moral growth are desired, every effort should be bent to make moral choice an issue in evaluating conduct.

Moral values are communicated in various ways. From the avidity with which inmates seize on incidents demonstrative of lack of morality in officers, it is apparent that example is an effective communication method in this area. While the bad example may be seized upon to bolster the inmate's rationalization of his own amoral or immoral conduct, the good example cannot be indefinitely ignored. However, reliance on example alone is unwise. Many opportunities for direct instruction or counseling arise in the course of routine activities within the prison. Moralizing probably has little value as a stimulus to inmate self-examination and critical evaluation. On the other hand, a clear statement of moral principle without condemnation of the inmate as a person would appear to be a vital aspect in the effective handling of disciplinary incidents in or out of the institution court room. It is not enough to jail a man and strive to arouse feelings of guilt and self-dissatisfaction. Opportunities for bolstering self-esteem through approved and significant accomplishments must exist. The calculated risk of a "trust" program appears to be well-justified by the gains in self-regard occasioned by the experience of being trusted and the accomplishment of proven trustworthiness. Institutionalized "trust," however, is probably less effective than the personalized trust which is implicit in the humane and judicious dealings of a good correctional officer. Identification with a figure who represents an adequate character model precedes the development of conscious ideals. This identification is fostered on the level of interpersonal dealings. The beginnings of moral life-philosophies can and should grow out of these interactions of inmates with officers.

SOME INTERPERSONALIZED REHABILITATIVE TECHNIQUES

Where the motivation for an individual's delinquency lies within himself and results in a pattern of behavior unacceptable to society, it is plain that "cure" or rehabilitation will have two phases: (a) the process of unlearning old behavior patterns and (b) the process of relearning new ones. While most penal institutions provide satisfactory examples of "new" and "acceptable" behavior patterns, the attempt to motivate their acceptance by inmates is largely exhortative, and threat of repression remains the principal sanction for their acceptance. There is no love lost or given in the average prison, nor are there any particular incentives offered for the abandonment of old patterns of behavior. In short, the basic rehabilitative necessities are ignored in present penal practice in that the "unlearning" half of the prescription is omitted altogether, and "relearning" is made unlikely since motivation is externally mobilized by the threat of repression rather than rewarded by the introduction of incentives.

The "cure" of the delinquent demands a change in behavior patterns in the direction of social conformity. Such change is a very basic thing, involving, as it does, a reorganization and reintegration of the individual's entire relationship with the world in which he lives and the people with whom he comes in contact. His attitudes, social techniques, and emotional expectations must all undergo considerable alteration. This necessitates the development and communication, within prison walls, of a stable, supportive, rewarding identification matrix, as well as a system of sanctions which would operate to deter from the old and induce acceptance of new social perceptions. Without providing both of these requirements, any correctional program must fail. People do not easily abandon long-term behavioral adaptations which have served an emotional purpose. Imprisonment itself does not necessarily convince the offender of the inadequacy of his delinquent behavior.

In the attempt to foster the development of such an "adjustment matrix," correctional administration must consider two major factors, the first, orientational, and the second, interpersonal. The orientation of the correctional institution should be one which places emphasis upon positive rather than negative sanctions whenever possible. It is always preferable, in the training of animals, children, and felons, to provide something to look forward to rather than something to look backward on. In order to foster new behavior, it is advisable that such behavior be made to appear worthwhile in the inmate's eyes. Rewards for acceptable behavior should be instituted and emphasized wherever possible instead of punishment for unacceptable behavior. This is not to imply that punishment has no place in correctional custody, but merely that its exclusive or even primary use is to be avoided. Rewards which have been used successfully include the awarding of "good time," the development of incentive training programs and pay scales, and the attempt to introduce "progressive" custodial functioning.

Incentive programs accomplish several ends. On the job, for example, incentive pay and differential housing will foster the development of healthy competitiveness. The area of competition is one in which most delinquents prove inadequate and may indeed be a key to one of the most important goals in their retraining. Delinquent individuals are notorious for their rejection of the very goals for which the rest of society competes. If the inmate's comfort and personal sense of worth within the institution were to depend upon taking advantage of the incentives which are offered him, then this training would seem quite useful in the rehabilitation process. In addition to fostering such concern with socially approved goals and motivations, the incentive program would provide an additional inducement to the inmate to learn habits of vocational industriousness and stability so essential to satisfactory extramural adjustment. In brief, the prison should become a representative example of the social reality inherent in striving for individual reward.

In speaking of "progressive" custody, we refer to a security system which is facilitative rather than regulative. It is quite natural for the psychologist to observe the correctional setting from a primarily rehabilitative point of view. It is also to be expected that he will consider the primary purpose of incarceration to be the rehabilitation, rather than the custodial care, of inmates. This being the case, he tends to view problems of custody in their relationship to rehabilitation, and acceptable custody becomes that process by which rehabilitative aims are best facilitated. Too often we encounter the anomalous situation in which rehabilitation is limited, or even entirely regulated, by the demands of custodial personnel for a more "secure" institution. The requirement of prison security for the protection of society is not to be denied, but the will of society for the reclamation of its felons is better served by a well-controlled rehabilitative program than by the single-minded purpose of running a "quiet" institution.

Another extremely important aspect of rehabilitative technique lies in the effort to maintain consistency of routine and of rehabilitative function. Once the basic orientation of the institution has been set forth in terms of positive sanctions, reward for acceptable behavior, incentive for social productivity and progressive custody, the problem becomes to impress upon each inmate the inevitability of the consequences of all his behavior, whether compliant or otherwise. Thus the reward for acceptable behavior should be no less certain or speedy than the absence of reward or even punishment for unacceptable behavior. More than this, resort to negative sanctions should be limited to situations in which the security of the institution or potential harm to another individual are clearly involved. Too often, punishment deteriorates to the level of "routine discipline," and custodial officers no longer require the justification of serious offense to warrant serious punishment. For example, to bring an inmate before the institution court and free him from detention upon finding that he was innocent of his offense is an injustice, since the detention constituted a priori punishment. Again, the use of a correction cell in the case of an inmate who speaks out of turn is an unjust punishment in consideration of the magnitude of the offense. The "tone" of an entire institution most usually depends upon the manner in which routine infractions are handled, the justice of the handling, and the emotional interactions of the people involved.

If the interpersonal requirements for correctional rehabilitation are to be met, the caliber of custodial and professional staff becomes a matter of primary importance. These people must all possess the personal and social attributes which would make them acceptable as character models. Staff members for whom asocial, acultural, or even antisocial behavior holds any fascination whatever, or who are personally conflicted or prejudiced in this area, are likely to become disruptive elements in the attempt to maintain institutional discipline and morale. For example, the officer who looks upon heavy drinking as the measure of a man or who sees in promiscuous sexual contacts the primary means of asserting his masculinity is a poor person to be given authority over inmates with similar problems. Certainly, the moral and ethical requirements for staff members, at least in the performance of their specific duties, should be set and maintained at a high level. Example is an important educational principle.

In general, it may be said that too much has been left to chance insofar as the personality attributes and attitudes of institutional administrators and custodial officers are concerned. We should expect maturity, responsibility, and self-sufficiency in our officers. We should choose people capable of responding to the "needs" of the inmates rather than their "wants" or impulsive desires. True rapport does not imply personal involvement with the inmate or with his asocial characteristics but the ability to understand and the capacity to accept and respect him as an individual on the basis of those values and attributes which even the worst felon shares in common with the rest of humanity. The custodial officer must possess the stamina, drive, intelligence and interest to discover and support the positive attributes on which social acceptance is predicated.

In connection with this subject, it is worthy of note that psychologists and other professional personnel are frequently accused of "mollycoddling" inmates. One "mollycoddles" when one responds to peripheral, immediately satisfying requests which the inmate may make. Conversely, one builds character and self-respect when one responds to the inmate's long-range, realistic needs. We are not concerned with making life, either in or out of prison, comfortable or immediately rewarding but rather with creating in the inmate the ability to postpone immediate satisfactions in favor of more solid, long-term, socially approved goals. In order to accomplish this, we must provide satisfactions for such behavior when it is noted within the walls. Habit, after all, is built upon experience.

When we have staffed our institution with mature, responsible officers, who can function not only as disciplinarians but also as character models, and who have the ability to form rapport and to become objects of identification for the inmate body, then we can begin to rehabilitate by responding to the socialized, realistic needs which the inmates express and by treating each inmate as an individual worthy of recognition for his social advances and capable of accepting responsibility for his personal deficiencies. Any institutional administration whose object is to rehabilitate must take into consideration the necessity for individualization of program and discipline. Too often, when inmates appear before institutional disciplinarians, offenses are punished rather than people. External circumstances and individual responsibility as well as the nature of the infraction itself should enter into consideration in an individualized disciplinary approach. There is no substitute for humane judgment. Institutional officers and officials are prepared to render such judgment only when their own anxieties and asocial personality tendencies or prejudices have been recognized and integrated into mature personality patterns.

It should also be remembered that the rules of consistency, fairness, individualization, positive outlook, and provision of incentives are as vital to the maintenance of officer morale as they are to the fostering of inmate adjustment. Just as the "tone" of an entire institution depends upon the manner in which routine matters are handled, the justice of the handling, and the emotional interactions of the people involved, so the morale of the staff depends upon an adequate and progressive personnel policy.

SELECTION AND TRAINING OF CORRECTIONAL OFFICERS

We have noted above what some of the characteristic demands should be in regard to personnel who must handle interpersonal relationships in prison situations. It should be evident that we must select institution personnel with regard to their ability to relate to inmates without hostility, without emotional dependence and untoward involvement, and with a perceptiveness as to inmates' motivations and needs. We also wish to select men who can serve as models for imitative behavior and who generally possess emotional maturity and stability. In the past, lack of consideration of such qualifications and the inability to attract large numbers of good personnel would have made it difficult to apply such criteria. At the present time, we should be more cognizant of the necessity for such qualifications. In general, most correctional institutions are now better able than formerly to compete for personnel on the job market. Because of generally increased salary scales, we should be able to apply more rigid selection criteria.

Normal intelligence, suitable literacy, and good physical condition and stature have been the main criteria for selection in many institutions. While educational requirements are many times taken into account, it would seem that personal effectiveness might be more a function of the ability to learn quickly than of past accomplishments in education. We certainly would wish to select fairly intelligent men with aptitude for education and training. These things are easy to ascertain through the use of standard intelligence and educational tests. Finding men with the requisite personality qualifications is a somewhat more difficult task. But personality descriptions and predictions of behavior are made in regard to inmates of most correctional institutions, and a similar job could be done quite readily in the selection of correctional workers by existing trained personnel. The psychologists, psychiatrists, social workers or counselors who routinely make such descriptions or predictions of inmate behavior could make similar predictions regarding job applicants. It would not be the place of such staff members to recommend the hiring or turning down of applicants but to lay before the hiring body the information on which they might make their judgments.

Various interview techniques are available to these trained personnel, as well as recognized psychological tests, particularly those of a projective nature. These projective tests present unstructured stimuli such as ink blots, pictures of people, unfinished sentences, etc., and force the applicant by means of his personal perceptions and emotional reactions into structuring the material. We can gain considerable insight into the applicant's emotional maturity, his ways of dealing with problem situations, and his usual modes of interacting with other people.

Taking the applicant on a short, informal orientation tour of the institution may serve several purposes. With an eye to selection, we may make observations about him and the way he views the job and his future co-workers. This would also provide some initial job training and a basis for establishing emotional security on the job by letting him see the institution as a whole and enabling him to make his first contacts with his future co-workers. Another by-product of this orientation tour is that it will afford opportunity for the applicant, prior to his final commitment, to assess any misgivings he may have about the job.

As long as we have criteria upon which we can agree, selection would seem to be a soluble problem in view of the fact that we already have trained personnel for the job. Training in interpersonal relationships should prove more of a problem, since little attention has been paid to it in the past and since training of personnel in correctional institutions usually deals strictly with matters of custody. Most hiring officers in such institutions want applicants who can "get along with people" but seldom consider the problem of training them for the task.

How can we train officers in interpersonal contacts? The device which most quickly comes to mind is that of the "critical incident technique." Using this method, we may bring before the trainees frequently found problem situations and their possible answers, in order to prepare them for such situations as they may meet in the future. These situations may be presented orally, they may be acted out by other officers, or they may be presented by sound motion pictures that can be prepared by the training department. Acting out the situation in the style of "psychodrama" or "role playing" might be a very effective way of helping the trainee to identify with inmates and other officers. Since the trainee is going to have to deal with such situations on the spot, we also provide him with problem-solving techniques by withholding the answers until he himself has rehearsed possible solutions in a give-and-take group discussion.

At the same time, it should be the job of the training leader to make clear to the officers that they are handling concrete situations in which their own emotional responses are important.

He should help individual trainees to understand their personal responses and help them clarify their own attitudes and feelings. It should be emphasized that feelings of hostility or sympathy are not necessarily bad or a handicap in doing the job, if they recognize and make allowances for such feelings in dealing with inmates and with other staff personnel. At the same time, the instructor trained in psychotherapy or counseling can help the individual correct irrational emotional responses.

After the trainee has completed his orientation and is actually working with inmates, there should be a continuing program of "brush-up classes" and group discussion regarding specific problems which he faces on the job. Again, interpersonal relationships, feelings, and attitudes of new personnel should be clarified and corrected by training supervisors. In addition, psychiatrists, psychologists, counselors, etc., should make themselves known to the trainees and be available for counseling on problem situations of an interpersonal nature which may arise on the job.

Along with the training program, the institution staff should make every effort to integrate new officers into the institution— to make them feel emotionally secure, necessary, and part of a team. Such emotional security is important if the officer is to be effective in his dealings with other people. This attempt can be helped by a consistent personnel policy and by making the officer feel that his work is understood and appreciated.

We have noted above the desirability of stringent selection and training of correctional personnel in regard, particularly, to interpersonal relationships. It would seem that to further rehabilitative programs for inmates, we must put as much effort into educating and selecting officers as we do into the diagnosis and treatment of the inmates whom they are to help rehabilitate.

SUMMARY

It is common opinion among authors that correctional rehabilitation is achieved as a function of interpersonal relationships. From the point of view of psychologists who have had opportunity to observe the correctional situation in all its ramifications, the authors have attempted to set down the procedural assumptions which underlie the general philosophy of rehabilitation, including, within a general educational frame of reference, the vocational, moral, and disciplinary training aspects. These are discussed with a view toward distinguishing between exhortative, repressive, and truly identified means of achieving such education. Techniques designed to foster rehabilitation are then discussed, with a view toward the orientation of the institution and the interpersonal requirements which must be met. Emphasis is placed upon the use of positive rather than negative sanctions, reward in place of punishment wherever possible, progressive custodial functioning, and consistency of program. A third topic deals with the need for custodial officers who are capable of serving as character models, competent to respond to the true needs of the inmate, capable of achieving adequate rapport and of dealing with inmates as individuals. Finally, recommendations are made for the training and orientation of such personnel.

A Behavioral Science View of the Correctional Officer

RICHARD JESSOR

It is clear that there is pervasive ferment in the correctional field, ranging from simple suggestions for change in procedures to fundamental challenges at the very structure of contemporary correctional institutions. Strong stresses are apparent against the twin legacies of retribution and restraint, but these stresses do not tell us which course is best for the future. In recent decades, however, a point of view has developed, based both on theory and empirical findings, which has definite implications for correctional work and for the role of the correctional officer in that work. I am referring to the viewpoint of behavioral science—including the traditional disciplines of psychology, sociology, and anthropology, and the newer developments in community and social psychiatry. Fully aware that there are no easy answers even to the simplest problems, I want nevertheless to push as far as possible some implications which I see as emerging from developments in behavioral science. These im-

NOTE: Reprinted from *Federal Probation,* 27 (1) :6-10, 1963.

plications suggest to me the need for a fundamental and far-reaching reorientation in correctional work.

THREE SOURCES OF FERMENT IN CORRECTIONAL WORK

The ferment which is widely perceived has a number of sources. Changes or pressure for change in correctional practices have come from simple humanitarian considerations and concern for human dignity. This has led, in turn, to revulsion at the more extreme measures of punishment. More recently, and perhaps more important, this has led also to dissatisfaction with the so-called benign procedures of custody. Concern has been expressed about the routinization and the meaninglessness of life in prison, the mortification of individuals subjected to institutional regimentation, and the processes of depersonalization which occur when large groups of inmates are herded about. Such concerns abound in the recent sociological literature, and they are more or less applicable to any particular institution. Some of the most penetrating descriptions of these aspects of institutional life have been made in a recent book *Asylums,* by Erving Goffman.

A second source of ferment, beyond humanitarian considerations, is the sheer lack of demonstrable success in reducing crime through incarceration. This is a fundamental fact that raises doubt about the adequacy of correctional work. Besides the acknowledged high rate of recidivism, there is considerable concern that incarceration itself may contribute to resumption rather than termination of criminal activity. If this is the case, then the entire correctional system is, of course, working to its own disadvantage.

The third source of ferment is the one that I want to elaborate —ferment generated by the development of research and theory in the behavioral sciences. Ideas about crime and delinquency have changed in recent decades, not this time for sentimental reasons but because of the convergence of implications from work in the social and behavioral sciences. These implications are relevant to an understanding of criminal or delinquent behavior. Such understanding, in turn, has implications for efforts at correction. When we have considered some of these issues, we will be in a better position to say something about the correctional officer and his job. Our concern with the correctional officer will be limited to those who function within a correctional institution.

CRIME AND DELINQUENCY AS LEARNED BEHAVIOR

We have learned over the past decades that crime and delinquency cannot, in general, be referred to as innate and inherited factors. This may sound like an obvious statement to many, but it has very powerful implications, not all of which, unfortunately, have funneled down to those persons who are in intimate daily contact with inmates in our institutions. The point of view of behavioral science is rather to consider crime and delinquency as learned behavior. Like any other behavior patterns, delinquent behavior is considered to be an outcome or a consequence not of little-known processes of inheritance or even of illness but rather of fairly well understood processes of learning. Such learning processes are those by which values, expectations, attitudes, and orientations are transmitted to members of the society through socialization and experience, both indirectly and directly. If this viewpoint is valid, we have to consider all learned behavior. We have to ask these questions: What are the interpersonal and socioenvironmental conditions which have fostered its learning and which maintain its occurrence? What are the conditions under which change can be effected? How does or can the correctional experience fit into this process of change?

With respect to the first question, demographic studies have consistently shown that most inmates of correctional institutions come from the lower strata of our society. We have gone beyond the early simplistic interpretation of this fact, the notion that poverty or crowding per se causes crime. But what does seem clear at this point is that growing up or living in the lower strata of our society may have two general kinds of consequences, both of which are relevant for the incidence and prevalence of antisocial behavior. The first of these has to do with the direct learning about what life is like. The lower-class occupant cannot help but learn that life is a series of chronic frustrations with respect to those very things that society seems to hold dear and in its mass media and in its educational systems stresses—success, status, wealth, prestige. These values, of which the member of the lower stratum is aware, are unlikely to be attained by him, a fact of which he also becomes aware. These rewards—rewards he has been socialized to seek—being unattainable, their withdrawal or their loss cannot be a deterrent for him. The loss of status, the loss of success, and the loss of social approval no longer serve as deterrents to illegitimate behavior as they do for many other people. In short, to summarize this first consequence of growing up in the lower socioeconomic strata, the delinquent learns that he has no real stake in the larger society and hence really has nothing to lose by violating its norms. The essential idea is that chronic frustration of aspirations toward society's values (the plight of the lower-class member) leads to alienation from that society, hostility and resentment toward representatives of the general society, and repudiation of the norms of the larger society.

While this generalization about one consequence of learning in the lower strata obviously has limitations, it does summarize certain emphases in behavioral science research on crime and delinquency, especially the emphasis upon anomie—the breakdown in normative consensus—and upon the formation of delinquent gangs as a way of repudiating middle-class norms.

The second major consequence of lower-class membership which emerges from behavioral science research is the learning of certain personal attitudes, subjective orientations, or personality attributes which indirectly may facilitate or generate antisocial behavior. Let us develop the implications for crime of two of these subjective orientations often cited as characteristic of the lower strata, or as aspects of what Oscar Lewis has called "the culture of poverty." The two I refer to are short time perspective and feelings of external control.

Time perspective refers to the span of time that is encompassed in day-to-day choices, actions, and decisions. If time perspective is short, only the immediate or fairly immediate consequences of an action or choice are considered in behaving. If time perspective is long, the remote or distant consequences tend to be considered at the time of action. The relation of time perspective to delinquent or nondelinquent behavior may be seen if one considers that much of delinquency and crime involve actions with immediate consequences that are positive or gratifying and long-range consequences that are negative or punishing. Thus rape or drunkenness may be considered to be immediately gratifying to an actor but negative only in the future—that is, if apprehended, if fired from a job, etc. Conversely, much of conforming behavior in our society—for example, going to school and studying long hours—are immediately negative and positive only in a long-range sense, for example, ultimately getting a good job. It can be seen, then, that insofar as a person considers only short-range consequences of his actions, much of delinquent or criminal behavior has positive outcomes and much of conforming behavior has negative outcomes. A short time perspective, then, may be seen as conducive to impulse-gratifying behavior, often criminal or delinquent. To the extent that short time perspectives are characteristically learned as subjective orientations in the lower strata, to that extent does lower-class membership lead to indirect socialization for crime.

The other illustration of subjective orientations which have been mentioned in the behavioral science literature as characteristic of the lower or deprived strata is termed feelings of external rather than internal control. By external control is meant the feeling that one has little control over the consequences of one's actions; instead, one feels that what happens to one is controlled by outside forces—by fate, luck, chance, or other persons. This orientation means essentially that what happens to one is not a consequence of what one does. Such a subjective orientation becomes important to our consideration of crime in the following way. If it does not matter what one does, if whatever is going to happen to one is going to happen, then obviously there is no sense in planning, there is no sense in depriving oneself of immediate gratification as a pathway to later rewards, there is little sense in learning from one's own experience. If it is a matter of chance or fate, one may as well do what one feels like doing at the moment and let things take care of themselves. Clearly, a subjective orientation of this sort also would seem to conduce to immediate impulse-gratifying behaviors and, to that extent, to increase normative violations.

To summarize, our interpretation of contemporary behavioral science has led to consider crime and delinquency as learned behavior. It has led us also to inquire about the conditions of such learning and, as a partial answer, it has suggested that at least some portion of crime may be an outcome of the lower-class learning situation. The latter seems to generate two consequences: the development of hostile and resentful attitudes toward the larger society as a consequence of chronic frustration of legitimate aspirations; and the learning of certain subjective orientations or personal attitudes such as short time perspective and feelings of external control. The former consequence would seem directly, and the latter consequence indirectly, relevant to the incidence and prevalence of crime.

CORRECTIONAL WORK IS EDUCATION

With this picture of at least some criminals and delinquents in mind, we have a further question to ask from a learning point of view—namely, what are the conditions under which a criminal or delinquent can be changed (can learn alternative ways of behaving), and how does or can the correctional experience fit into this process of change? One thing seems clear. Neither punishment nor simple custody should be effective in lessening the likelihood of further antisocial behavior if our picture has any validity. Punishment can easily be construed as simply a continuation of the chronic frustrations which have led to prison in the first place. It simply becomes a reinforcement for animosity toward authority. Custody, per se, should have very little rehabilitative effect, since it either does nothing to change these kinds of attitudes or actually strengthens them. If one looks at the situation of custody, the inmate's world is almost entirely and often capriciously controlled by outside forces. He is rarely told why something is being done, why regulations have been changed, why dispositions are being made. Or if he is told these things, he is not a part of the process of making those decisions about himself and his future. Since explanations about regulations and information about policy and program changes are not often provided for the inmate, the effect of custody is simply to strengthen the already established idea that the world is controlled outside himself, that there is no sense in planning, that things happen capriciously, and so on.

What emerges positively from these considerations, in my opinion, is that correctional work must be construed within the general area of education. I prefer the term "education" because it carries with it none of the analogies to medicine which the term "treatment" implies, and because it emphasizes the learning viewpoint more than the term "rehabilitation" does. Therefore, I am going to use the language of education. The conclusion which I wish to draw is that correctional work neatly fits the model of education. It is the provision of an environment and a set of experiences which will facilitate the learning of new values, new orientations, and new expectations which will serve, in turn, to inhibit delinquent acts in the future.

If we follow this view out, the correctional institution must be seen as a school—to be sure, a special school—for special efforts to teach special problem students. And the correctional officer must be seen as a teacher. The basic question, then, is what kind of school and what kind of teacher can best accomplish the objectives which we have set for correctional work, the teaching of new values, new expectations, and new orientations about self and about society?

IMPLICATIONS FROM "THERAPEUTIC COMMUNITY" WORK

I believe we have to move to a wholly reorganized type of institution, one which represents a minimization of custody and a maximization of education in the broad sense in which I am using that term. Again, there is an area of work in the behavioral sciences which is germane to our problem and which suggests where certain guidelines may be found for reorganizing correctional institutions. I am referring to the work which has been done with severely disturbed mental patients, in changing the hospital milieu, in "opening" the hospital as an institution, in linking the functions of the hospital more closely with the outside world. This work goes under the label of "therapeutic community" and has implications for both the structure of the correctional institution and the role of the correctional officer.

The main considerations in the therapeutic community literature are these, and I would like to mention them because they bear on the kind of "school" I am talking about.

First, the settings of the institutions represent, to as large an extent as possible, the normal aspects of family and community life. They are richer in stimulation and attractiveness; there is less segregation between the units in the institution; they consist of smaller units rather than units involving large masses of people.

The second major characteristic of these institutions is that the roles of attendant and nurse become minimally custodial and are primarily defined in terms of social interaction with the patients. In traditional mental hospitals, the attendants were the lowest strata of the hospital social structure and were usually poorly educated. The parallel with correctional officers in many penal institutions is clear. In a therapeutic community, however, attendants and nurses become one of the main instrumentalities for therapeutic work.

The third thing that seems to be extremely important in the therapeutic community idea is that the total social organization of the hospital (in our case the prison) is, in itself, a vital force for treatment, not simply the background for treatment. The entire structure of the institution, its formal organization and administrative arrangements, has to be convergent upon the idea of treatment (in our case, education).

Fourth, provision is made for inmates to take an active part in the affairs of the institution. There is a shift in the hospital situation from restraint or custody to self-regulation. Instead of the hospital patient being viewed as a passive recipient of therapy or treatment, he is directly involved in the process of his own rehabilitation.

Fifth, the entire ideology of the institution is necessarily shifted. For correctional institutions, this means a shift in ideology from "pulling time," by both inmates and staff, to a climate of change, of development, of education.

Finally, the therapeutic community involves close linkage and interdependence with the outside community rather than the current general practice of isolation and segregation from the larger community.

All of these characteristics of mental hospital change which have emerged from the therapeutic community studies have clear-cut relevance for our conception of the correctional institution as an educational institution. It may seem at first glance that there would be too many obstacles in the way of such radical reorganization in the correctional institution. Equally severe obstacles had been foreseen in the mental hospitals, also, incidentally, charged by society with custodial responsibilities. It is heartening to learn that many of these problems disappeared when the institutional atmosphere changed and rehabilitation became the primary and the avowed aim.

THE NEW ROLE OF THE CORRECTIONAL OFFICER

From all this, the role of the correctional officer becomes somewhat clearer. Of all the personnel in the institution, he is the one closest to and in daily interaction with the inmates. As with the transformation of the attendant's role in the mental hospital, the role of the correctional officer must now come to be seen as central and critical, if not indispensable, to the reeducation of the inmate. Neither guard nor keeper, the correctional officer has now to be seen as teacher and mediator of the process of education.

The teaching by the correctional officer is both direct and indirect, and the success of each of these approaches is entirely dependent upon the closeness and meaningfulness of the officer-inmate interaction and relationship.

By direct teaching, I mean semididactic discussions with the inmate about society, about the relation between behavior and its consequences, about the importance of planning one's future, about the relation between skills and opportunities—the whole gamut of social experience which had either never been learned or had been learned in distorted fashion.

By indirect teaching, I mean the teaching that goes on when one person is a model for another. The correctional officer as model is not so much a perfect or ideal as he is a human being, fallible but well-intentioned, authoritative but not authoritarian. From a relationship with such an officer, the inmate stands to learn new and more benign attitudes about authority figures and about the larger society.

Thus, by both direct and indirect teaching, the correctional officer in his new role would seem most likely to influence and reshape precisely those factors we described earlier as mediating crime, the personal values and orientations conditioned by exposure to the learning environment of the lower socioeconomic strata, the culture of poverty.

Obviously, new standards of selection for correctional officers will have to be adopted to implement the kind of role I have sketched. If the correctional officer is to be the prime vehicle for correctional work, it is clear that we need intelligent, flexible, nonauthoritarian, educated, "people-liking" kinds of individuals. We need, also, better in-service training, not simply, as at present, on how to maintain custody but on such things as how to break the routine, how to get individuals to assume initiative, etc. We will need to train correctional officers, too, in the understanding of the sociology and psychology of delinquency. The adoption of such standards of selection and training may actually make it easier to recruit personnel, since the correctional officer's job will be seen as an active, critical, responsible, professional one rather than a routine custodial job.

One final thought seems to emerge from what we have been talking about. That is that the correctional officer functions not only within the correctional institution but also between the correctional institution and the larger community. The way of thinking about correctional work that I have outlined poses new obligations upon him. One of these is to educate the public to accept greater openness in the institution. No longer can we afford to evaluate the adequacy of an institution in terms of whether it is well-painted, clean, and has few escapes. The public, as it did with the mental hospital, must learn that the best correctional institution has to be evaluated in terms other than these obvious but superficial standards. The correctional officer has also to educate the public to provide a stake in the community for the inmate and to work toward eliminating the culture of poverty which we see as a major breeding ground of crime.

CONCLUSION

Perhaps these remarks represent sheer idealism. I should like to think they do not. I have tried to elaborate my own view of some contemporary developments in behavioral science and to draw out their implications for the correctional field. Much more research needs to be done, of course. Nevertheless, I believe that hard consideration of why we do what we do today and of how it could be done differently will lead us to creative ideas about making the correctional institution more of a school and the officer's job more that of a teacher. In this way, I believe society can begin to acquit itself in that most telling of all its responsibilities —how it treats or responds to its own deviants.

SECTION III

THE INMATE AND HIS SITUATION

THIS section presents an unusual vista. The viewpoints expressed represent a broad cross section of background and experience, ranging from the academic to that most intimate position of one whose freedom is already forfeit as one of corrections' failures. A lifetime of contact with the field of corrections as the son of one of this country's outstanding penologists makes Cozart's contribution, written around the experience of volunteer teacher in a correctional facility, particularly relevant. His remarks are knowledgeable and cogent. The need for a broadened perspective of what it means to suffer confinement, of the psychological impact of imprisonment, and of the image distortion resulting therefrom are lucidly described.

Stressed by numerous social psychologists is the tendency to dehumanize the legal offender, i.e. to view him as something so different from us that we cannot picture ourselves in his special, deplorable circumstance. Porterfield deprecates this "we-they fallacy," illustrating the concept with relevant choices from a variety of literature. Misconceptions which maintain this fallacy lead institutional staff to behold the inmate as a breed apart. Eradicating this fallacy is a major task for society and institution.

The recent experience of Merklin demonstrates that Porterfield's assertion is not empty rhetoric. The extent to which the "inmate code" contributes to the destruction of a personal life style and thus militates against the maintenance of the inmate's own highest values is shown. Merklin's tenure as psychiatrist in one of the nation's major penal facilities led him to view confinement as degenerative. The extremity of his position leaves him with meager hope that incarceration, under present terms, can be of real value.

Johnson notes inmate participation in activities which seem calculated to enhance self-esteem. That this has meaning is evidenced by the type of participation—independent—and sum-

125

mation of activities—various and praiseworthy. From Johnson's viewpoint, effectiveness in rehabilitation will be a function of the use of character strengthening opportunities. He points out that avoidance of the destruction of self-esteem which follows as a consequence of incarceration is the primary value of probation.

Lipschitz observed that in the past 35 years, improvement of the care of inmates beyond improvement of facilities has been negligible. His concern is with the legal rights of offenders. The subtle manner in which these rights may be denied him by institutional coercion and judicial footdragging leaves the inmate little room for relief.

The theme of teaching by example emphasized in the preceding section is echoed by Chaplain Leffler. The need to train in such a manner as allows the enhancement of the officer's self-esteem without damage to the self-esteem of the inmate is again stated. Leffler views the demeaning of others as equally demeaning to the self; this should be regarded as a weakness in a correctional program.

The final article if offered by a man with the most professional perspective—a recidivist. Hodge (a pseudonym) was serving a life sentence as a habitual criminal at the time of the original publication of his article. With particular forcefulness, he directs attention to the fact that the eye-for-an-eye philosophy increases resentment and antagonism. Without asking for sympathy for the inmate, he reviews many issues which must be faced and dealt with through broader training.

The Man Who Waits in Between

WILLIAM R. COZART

What do you say to a man in prison? Do you tell him that his life need not come to a standstill? It has. That time need not hang heavy on his hands? It does. That the prison need not become his whole world? It is.

What do you finally tell a man in prison? . . . This man whose cell is a reminder that he is required to answer what he has made

NOTE: Reprinted from *Federal Probation*, 25 (2) :27-30, 1961.

of himself. This man whose shoulders ache under the weight of an unalterable past. This man whose glance may not quite look you in the eye because he cannot yet look himself in the face.

What word to you finally bring to this man—now that you have classified him on your IBM, analyzed his psychological sicknesses, dissected his behavioral patterns, and determined the shaping forces of his environment? Does his life still matter? Agreed— it does. But what do you tell him about himself that will make the world his home again, his future fresh and new?

These are painful and perplexing questions and give the lie to cheap, easy answers. Answers, though, apparently are possible, for every single prison and correctional institution now in existence embodies, at least implicitly, some kind of reply. But, recently, a number of students at Harvard University have been forced to grapple with these questions in a new and exciting way. And the story of the students' struggle is the story of an opportunity which lies open to any prison which seeks to utilize the fullest possible methods of rehabilitation.

UNIVERSITY STUDENTS SERVE AS INSTRUCTORS

In the Cambridge-Boston area, as in most large cities, the local hospitals, schools, mental institutions, and settlement houses are seriously understaffed. As early as 1900, steps were taken to meet this problem with the establishment of the Phillips Brooks House as an instrument for mobilizing student social work at Harvard. In the years that followed, numerous committees were created through which Harvard students could volunteer to help these understaffed agencies undertake new programs or improve existing ones. One of the most extraordinary recent developments in the work of Phillips Brooks House has been its Prison Instructors Committee. This Committee actually sends college students behind the walls of neighboring state correctional institutions to teach a variety of courses to the inmate population. The results have been overwhelmingly favorable, both among prison authorities and inmates, and among the student teachers themselves.

The creation of this Committee has triggered a lively discussion in both the academic world and society in general concerning the philosophy of prison work itself. The points of view of Mr. Citizen run to extremes and might be labeled "liberal" and "conservative":

The Liberal:

Let's begin by agreeing that capital punishment is an irresponsible denial of life. It denies a man the possibility of becoming anything other than what he is. Killing him does not help him. It just snuffs out a future that could make him into a new man; it just satisfies the public's thirst for vengeance. Moreover, one cannot demonstrate that capital punishment has measurably reduced the number of offenders. Not severity, but certainty of punishment is the best deterrent to crime.

Just as a sudden execution is indefensible, so a prison sentence must not become a prolonged execution, a kind of living death. A man is sent to prison as punishment, not for punishment. While he is there, the prison's program of rehabilitation must offer him the chance to become a better man. The prisoner's opportunity for a liberal education, as offered by the Harvard student teachers, is a great step in this direction.

The Conservative:

Well! So we now have prisoners taking courses in psychology and music appreciation! What are they going to have next—air conditioned cells and swimming pools? A fine way for a man to pay his debt to society: making society go in debt with all this pampering!

Besides, what do these wet-behind-the-ears Harvard men, with their high-sounding theories, know about the real world, the world of crime and murder? Do they really expect their prisoner-students to take them seriously? Anyone knows that the only reason an inmate takes a course is just to get out of his cell!

So the conflict rages and will continue. Meanwhile, one might ask the student teachers themselves for their reactions to teaching in prison.

INMATES WERE FRIENDLY AND RECEPTIVE

Paul R., graduate student in economics, said, "It is true that an inmate can sign up for a course just to escape the boredom of his room, but his usual motivation is primarily academic. Most inmates have an amazing respect for education. Many feel that if once they had taken advantage of their own schooling, their lives might have turned out differently." Paul, who also teaches an undergraduate section at Harvard, often comments that inmates are more genuinely interested in their subjects than ordinary college students.

Frank L., a senior in English at Harvard, said, "Again and again these men show their surprise that someone is willing to take an interest in them. They have a general feeling of lonely hopelessness, and coming to class helps fill their need for companionship and meaning."

My own experience was with a class in psychology at the Norfolk, Massachusetts, Correctional Institution. For 9 months, eight other Harvard University students and I taught there one evening a week, offering courses in psychology, philosophy, science, music appreciation, art, higher mathematics, creative writing, Spanish, and Russian. Having had no experience in prison work, we arrived for our first night of classes with some misgiving. In fact, *The Colony,* the inmate publication at Norfolk, described us in this way: "The college student teachers entered their prison classrooms as warily as if entering the cages of wild animals, their opinions of inmates pre-formed by screaming headlines and overly-lurid gangbuster-type radio and TV melodramas. They were unanimously astonished to discover that most convicts just did not fit these descriptions."

This was true. We found the inmates, on the whole, friendly and receptive. Classes were kept small and informal. Mine, for example, was limited to eight students and thus could be conducted on a seminar basis with a minimum of lecture. The ages ran from 18 to 65. Two were college graduates; three had never completed the eighth grade. Nevertheless, all were equal to (and insisted upon) a course in psychology which was as rigorous as college level.

Reading assignments were kept flexible. Those who were able (about half of the class) read deeply into the works of the most creative minds in depth psychology—Freud, Adler, Jung, Fromm, and Binswanger. For the others, a series of selected passages was assigned as a minimum reading requirement. All, however, read far beyond the minimum assignment and seemed hungry for more and more books. Many books were accessible, thanks to the generosity of the Boston Public Library, which lent several copies of each text for an almost unlimited period of use.

CARRYING ON A DIALOGUE WITH THE PRINTED PAGE

The weekly discussions ran an hour and a half in length and were always lively—and often heated. Most difficult, though, was the problem of training each student to read a book on his own, to carry on his own dialogue with the printed page. Inmates, as most college students, tend to feel that if something is in print it must be sacred, and one disagrees with the text at his own risk. To encourage an inmate's own individual reflection, we used the technique of "reading reports." After each reading assignment, each student turned in a reading report which included two sections: (a) a summary paragraph of what the writer had said, which indicated whether or not the student had grasped the structure of his thought and (b) an original paragraph by the student, which took issue with the writer's point of view and stimulated the student's forming his own opinions. In this second section, a student would frequently appropriate what the reading meant to his own life situation. For example, here is one inmate's response to an assigned article on the problem of anxiety and fear:

> In the anxiety about any special situation, a man also confronts his anxiety over the general human situation. My problem is not merely to understand what it means to be man in prison, but what it means to be man in the world. And the world for me, even my prison world, is a place of precariousness, uncertainty, uneasiness—a place where there seems to be no bottom to things. Because the world is this way, and because I am an anxious man, I strive to establish objects for my fear: this particular guard, the parole board, a distressing letter from my wife. At least these are worries you can put your finger on, and are not the vague, shapeless dread that you sense lies behind the mirror when you shave in the morning—the dread that makes you feel, "here it is, another day of nothing."

It is doubtful whether many college students, after a first reading of the problem of anxiety, could have written such a perceptive paragraph.

The class, of course, had its problems. There were personality conflicts between prisoners; there was some racial discrimination on the part of the older men. But, throughout the year, it was amazing to watch the way the men began to listen to each other's opinions and take each other seriously; to watch an old man's face light up as he read Browning for the first time and discovered that old age need not be a curse; to hear a teenager who was about to be paroled tell of his decision not to rejoin the gang but to make a fresh start on his own.

Perhaps the most any teacher can ever do is to open doors through which a person may come to discover the meaning of his own life. In any case, the Harvard student teachers came to feel that, in the course of the year, doors were opened—some slowly, some painfully—but far wider than before. And this raised questions for us about the relationship between a liberal education and any prison's program of rehabilitation.

RESTORING MAN TO HIS FULL HUMANITY

Surely the fundamental mission of a prison is rehabilitation; but what does this word "rehabilitation" really mean? Could it not be defined as "the restoring of a man to his full humanness, to his capacity to be a whole person"? If so, then it is the courts' role to ask, is this man right or wrong? But the prison's primary question is, Why is this man not whole? A man's wholeness must be the concern of the program of rehabilitation; for this reason, the prison must provide a structure whereby a man may be given insight into himself—not merely clinical data but a new perspective on what it means to live as an authentic human personality. This means that the prison must go beyond merely supplying an inmate with purposeful work, with recreation for his leisure hours, with craft and hobby shops in which he can develop his creative skills. These functions of a prison are, of course, important; but, taken by themselves, they neglect the most crucial dimension in any human being: his inner world, the world of his hopes and fears, the world of his attitudes toward himself, the world of the images by which he lives.

After all, what exactly are correctional institutions correcting? Are they not correcting a man's false image of himself—the image by which he pictures himself as a man who controls life on his own terms, who takes whatever he wants without concern for the rights of others, who brings terror to his fellow man while achieving his own security? Is this not what we mean by a "criminal": one who, out of his distorted image of himself, violates the orders of society, because he pictures other men as things which must serve him, instead of picturing himself as the servant of other men. It is upon man's inner world of images, therefore, that the prison's program must focus; for it is the false images, the flaws in a man's character, which a correctional institution must correct. This is not naive logic, but a realistic appraisal of the nature of man. A man's ethical actions flow out of his interpretation of himself; if his self-interpretation is distorted, his actions inevitably are—as a man thinks in his heart, so he is.

It is at the point of man's interpretation of himself that the goals of the prison administrator and the goals of a liberal education coincide. For education's mission is to enable a man to discover his true self-image and to reject his false one. And this is precisely the goal of the prison. Both are seeking to restore a man to his full humanity, to what Emerson called "an original relation to the universe." If a prison provides a man with the opportunity for a liberal education, it can help him to sense the vastness of his own life, to picture himself not merely as Number 8411 in cell block A, but as a unique, unrepeatable individual in the cosmic drama of human story. It was out of this sense of his own individuality that the teenager in my class spoke of his refusal to live in terms of the image of the street gang but to live genuinely as himself.

This, in part at least, is what we must say to the man in prison: that it is possible for him to recover his lost wholeness. He knows that it is lost, as he brings to our hands the pieces of a life that once held promise. He asks to be made whole again; though he may gripe and swear against the prison system and its staff and daily routine, he is all the time asking to be made whole. It is for this he waits. Behind him lies the man he no longer is; before him lies the potential man he has not yet become. He remains the man in between—the man who waits in between—the "No Longer" of his past and the "Not Yet" of his future, who waits for the prison to restore him to wholeness, to rehabilitate him. And, as we have seen, if the prison's method of rehabilitation includes frequent courses in the humanities taught by concerned college students, the man in prison has an even greater opportunity to seek and to obtain the fullest meaning he can for his own life. It is essential that he have this opportunity not only in order to become a better citizen but because it is his human privilege.

The "We-They" Fallacy in Thinking About Delinquents and Criminals

AUSTIN L. PORTERFIELD

No subject receives more attention than crime and punishment. Perhaps none is less understood or more in need of elucidation. There are many sources of misunderstanding in the field. One of them is the we-they fallacy in thinking about delinquents and criminals. Because of its significance, it seems important to consider (a) the nature of this fallacy, (b) its sources, (c) its consequences, and (d) ways of overcoming it.

THE NATURE OF THE "WE-THEY" FALLACY

When "one of the judges of the city" asked Kahlil Gibran's "prophet" to "speak . . . of crime and punishment," the "prophet" said:

> Oftentimes have I heard you speak of one who commits a wrong as though he were not one of you, but a stranger and an intruder upon your world. . . . But . . . even as the holy . . . cannot rise beyond the highest . . . in each of you . . . so the weak cannot fall lower than the lowest which is also in you. . . . The robbed is not blameless in being robbed. . . . Yea, the guilty is oftentimes the victims of the injured. . . . The Prophet.

Our unawareness of our kinship to the criminal of which Gibran speaks is here termed the "we-they fallacy." Blinded by it, we treat delinquents and criminals as strangers in our society, as though they belonged to a different order of beings from ourselves, with subhuman motivations. They are people who are "lower than the lowest" which is in us. We are capable only of what Gibran calls the "god-self": "Like the ocean is your god-

NOTE: Reprinted from *Federal Probation,* 21 (4) :44-47, 1957.

self; It remains for ever undefiled. . . . But your god-self dwells not alone in your being. Much in you is still man . . . much . . . not yet man . . . but shapeless pigmy. . . ."

We are not aware of the "shapeless pigmy" in ourselves; but we see in criminals—the they-group—something which is "not yet man," for which they ought to be punished. Necessity requires that we overcome this we-they fallacy before we can learn what the offender is like, do much to prevent crime, or properly treat it. We cannot overcome it, however, until we become more fully aware of the forces that produce the fallacy. What are some of them?

SOURCES OF THE "WE-THEY" FALLACY

The spirit of revenge is often confused with the idea of justice in American society. Since this spirit, often sadistic, grows out of contrasting the behavior of the delinquent or the criminal with the self-I-should-like-to-be rather than comparing him with the self-like-his-own that I might have become in his situation, it becomes the center of our emphasis; for it contributes to our widespread inability to say with John Wesley, as he observed a desolate derelict, "There but for the grace of God go I."

Some of the factors in this attitude are: (a) our lack of knowledge of the forces that have produced ourselves as contrasted with the forces that made the offender what he is, (b) the erroneous thinking of some influential schools of criminology, (c) the psychology of the ingroup and the outgroup, and (d) our tendency to blame others for our own mistakes, to satisfy our repressed impulses vicariously, and to prefer vicarious punishment for these impulses instead of atoning for them directly.

Lack of Knowledge of Different Situations

Most serious students of human nature are aware of the influence of social situations in the development of personality; but the general public is largely without this awareness. Since it is not enough for teachers, clinicians, and probation officers to understand this principle and to be able to "take the role of the criminal," the idea will have to be communicated to the great body of our citizens, who alone can make an effective program possible, in order that they can develop the same capacity.

The Influence of Erroneous Theories

Lombroso is often called the "father" of scientific criminology. He did perform the service of calling the attention of students to the criminal as a person with a significant past; but too much of this past was linked with the biological rather than the social process. The Lombrosian theory of atavism—of the criminal as a throwback to an earlier stage of the evolutionary process, who contains the "shapeless pigmy" and "much . . . that is not yet man"; of the criminal whose "not-yet-man" nature is observable in bodily "stigmata of degeneracy"—is a source of the we-they fallacy in the popular mind, whether the general public ever heard of Lombroso directly or not. Earnest Hooton at Harvard and William H. Sheldon at Columbia University have each in their own way constituted themselves a kindred source of this difficulty. The Dick Tracy "comic" strip is an ally of this learned society which constantly paints the criminal as having a different shape from ourselves.

This we-they type of thinking is hard to divest of its hydra-heads, as we shall see further in discussing its consequences.

Ingroup and Outgroup Psychology

William Graham Sumner outlined the psychology of the ingroup and the outgroup in the *Folkways*. Whether we are a given family, church, class, nation, race, or party, we form such an ingroup; and like those given to self-laudation in Sandburg's *Four Preludes on Playthings of the Wind,* we are inclined to chant,

> We are the greatest city,
>   the greatest nation:
> nothing like us ever was.

Thank God we are not like the others-groups: "pig-eaters," "cow-eaters," "uncircumcised," "jabberers," "barbarians," "dagos," "wops," "Huns," "greasers," "Chinks," "ickies," and "Gooks." While it is common practice for people to chant their own praise in words such as the daughters of Sandburg's decadent city, it is equally common practice to pour contumely upon the people whose cultural patterns differ from their own. *It is almost criminal not to be us.*

It is not surprising, then, that we are tempted to take the same attitude toward anyone whom we can associate with delinquency or antisocial behavior which is disapproved by our social class. We should lower the age for the death penalty below 15 years and abolish the jurisdiction of the juvenile court except for misdemeanors, one state legislator believes; but officials act leniently toward a former state land commissioner who steals the state blind! At least, their bark is worse than their bite. The ingroup must hold together. The outgroup, made up of little people, "must behave itself" or take the full consequences, often as "the victim of the injured."

The Tendency to Blame Others

Also important in the persistence of the we-they fallacy is the psychology of the not-me as contrasted with the "god-self" in the language of Gibran. In his *Interpersonal Theory of Psychiatry,* Harry Stack Sullivan speaks of the three selves developed by the child: (a) the good-me, (b) the bad-me, and (c) the not-me.

The child recognizes the good-me as the self approved by the mother. He acknowledges the bad-me as the self disapproved but not hidden so far away that he can deny its existence. But he develops uncanny emotions, as Sullivan calls them, of awe, dread, loathing, and horror associated with parental disapproval of his behavior. The self that does these things is surely not me, not the real me. The "god-self," the good self, could not stoop to uncanny impulses.

As a consequence, a child who plays alone may invent a bad associate whom he represents as telling him to do all these disapproved things. This imaginary mischievous playmate is a not-me. You should punish him. He needs it. The bad-me needs it also; but there would be no bad-me if it were not for this other self. I am mad at him for making me bad. He made me do it.

The child who does not play alone does not need to invent a playmate of whom he can say, "He made me do it." If he does not do wrong but sees some other child doing wrong things he would like to indulge in himself, he tells adults who deal out punishment to the offending child—punishment that makes the tattler feel self-righteous; better than the offender. The tattler's good-me has been vindicated, his bad-me atoned for vicariously, and his not-me properly punished.

Parents may react with antagonism to the youthful tendencies which they see coming to life again in the new generation. One's youth may be almost completely hidden from his present self, as the writer discovered recently while reading the letters he wrote as a teenager and as a young man. I had pushed this brash young other-me far out of the kin of the present me! If there was in my youth a not-at-present-me because I have repressed him, it is not easy for me to deny kinship with offenders and to resent it when I see my own antisocial longings expressed in the behavior of the criminal?

We are hard on members of our own family who have unfortunately yielded to temptations that have been strong in us. We are still harder on the members of the next man's family. Our anger grows against lawbreaking persons of our own class. It is hotter against members of other classes who offend members of his own class; but it hardly knows any bounds when it is directed toward a disreputable minority member who offends a member of our own group. The other-selves of outgroups are surely not-me. Thus the we-they fallacy supports the good-me-not-me fallacy and vice versa. The less kinship we recognize with others, the more we are willing to punish them, and the more likely we are to get pleasure out of that punishment and to confuse sadistic satisfaction with a sense of justice. Many thoughtful people have suspected that lynchings involving burning and emasculating the victim are associated with sexual frenzy of the kind for which the victim is being tortured, whether he is guilty or not.

CONSEQUENCES OF THE FALLACY

Some of the unfavorable consequences of the we-they fallacy have been deeply implicated in the discussion of its sources. More specifically, however, we go on punishing the offender without developing the capacity to imagine ourselves in his place and to see that he is made like us and that he responds as we might in similar situations. We therefore do not promote programs that are directed toward developing situations in which criminal behavior is less likely to develop or in which the criminal or delinquent may change from behavior that is destructive to responses that are constructive in nature. We cannot see that it is unjust to any man or child to forget that he is a man instead of a wild animal; that his humanity needs to be increased by discipline and reeducation, rather than reduced to the status of a caged wolf. Instead of working to this end, we may let positive programs languish for lack of funds. We may condone grotesque situations in jails. We may either scorn probation and parole or do little to establish satisfactory programs because "they cost too much." Then we condemn the outcome of what we have provided as though its failure represented the failure of the best that could be supplied.

It may be repeated that this we-they fallacy is hard to escape. It has survived many deaths. It is not willing to yield to the implications of the data (as given in studies like my *Youth in Trouble*[1]) which show that college students who belong to us— to the we-group—do the same things with surprising frequency as children who get into court; but when the court children do these we-things, the behavior seems to us more seriously significant. They ought to be punished for these we-acts. We ought to save our children from becoming like one of them, so the we-youth can pursue the image of the "god-self" undisturbed by the image of the "shapeless pigmy."

To save the we-children from the they-children, people in one city would not let a guidance home for predelinquent children be established on an acreage already owned by the county on the Eastside, though it had been approved by the seven district judges and the county judge acting as the "Juvenile Board," and private citizens were willing to build the home without any cost to the taxpayers.

The largest delegation of citizens ever to show up at the courthouse for any hearing protested against it. "No . . . no . . . no!" the crowd shouted when one of the commissioners said, "Let's try to sit down and work this thing out." "This would not be a home for incorrigible boys," explained the presiding judge. "It would be for boys who are emotionally disturbed . . . boys who need help . . . boys you would take into your home." The Eastsiders laughed. "You can laugh if you want to," the judge responds, "but I wouldn't mind if they put the guidance home on land backing up to my house." "Well, put it there then," he was told.

A minister, speaking for the Eastsiders, said that "we should build a boy's ranch out in the country . . . not on the Eastside." He believed children in the area with whom these boys went to school might be corrupted by them. He said our children might "put a hero crown on a boy who has been in trouble." Another man wondered whether the presence of Negro children in the home might not complicate the school situation.

Eastsiders remembered that Westsiders, who favored the location of the guidance home on the Eastside, had recently forced the city and county to relocate a health center already under construction on grounds that were close to a "cultural area" on the Westside because there would be a VD clinic in one wing of the building. *We* object to *them* on either side of the city. Thus the consequences of the fallacy become painfully clear.

OVERCOMING THE FALLACY

In outlining the first source of the we-they fallacy, it was pointed out that it is not enough for teachers, clinicians, and probation officers to understand its nature and its outcomes. Objective thinking will have to be communicated to the great body of citizens who alone can make an effective program possible. Objective thinking does not belong to a large enough body of those who ought to be in a position to communicate it, however. The minister mentioned above is without insight into the problem; and most college people, even faculty, react almost instantaneously with the opinion warmly expressed that "we must not coddle the criminal. Justice demands that he be punished. Therefore—" and the conversation often comes to an abrupt end.

These respondents do not understand that the sentimentality which Dostoevski attributed to Russian juries in a given period (see his Diary) has no place in the theory we advance. This sentimentality made the jurymen's sense of participation in the crime so keen and their capacity to rationalize the criminal act so great that it was hard to convict a criminal who had a smart lawyer. This sentimentality operates with the same results where crimes in the name of "honor" are involved in some areas of the United States.

An opposite tendency, described by Dostoevski in *Crime and Punishment,* is not included either. Under its sway, the people justified the status quo, called for the death of the criminal it produced, baptized him before he died, and cried with joy over the repentant sinner's fitness to live in heaven, while putting him to death because justice demanded it! *What is included is the ease with which we rationalize a self-interested sense of justice.*

In order to overcome the fallacy, then, the leaders in the field who already have the requisite insight need to demonstrate the difference between a constructive program of reorientation and the "coddling" process of an undisciplined experience in prison. Then, difficult as it may be to train a sufficiently large cadre of understanding leaders and communicators capable of teaching the principles involved in overcoming the fallacy, it seems that there can be no other way of doing it. Public school teachers, ministers, lawyers, judges, legislators, literary artists, newspapermen, members of the police, and many others beyond the bounds of the clinic and the university campus—many besides the readers of *Federal Probation*—need to become aware of the problem. Perhaps those who already have the insight, by employing every avenue of communication now available, can be the little leaven that leavens the whole lump.

NOTES AND REFERENCES

1. See also Porterfield, Austin L.: *Meanor for Adjustment.* Fort Worth, The Leo Potishman Foundation, 1967, Chap. 7.

Prison and the Concrete Mind

LEWIS MERKLIN

The institution with which I have had to live for the past two years is on a mesa near the Pacific, bordered on one side by extensive fields of flowers and on the other by the western head-

NOTE: Reprinted from *The Center Magazine,* 2:90-91, 1969.

quarters of the Strategic Air Command. It is the only federal youth institution west of the Rockies; it houses 1,200 men under 25. The population turns over almost annually and the average stay is two years. Inmates are from all over the Far West, mostly California, and many of them are recent transients from other parts of the nation. A third are there for interstate auto theft; another third are there for smuggling or interstate transport of marijuana. The rest are serving time for bank robbery, fraud, refusing military induction, hard narcotic offenses, interstate transport of other goods, and various offenses committed on federal property. Ten percent are returned to prison for parole violation; of the parole violators, 70 percent have repeated their initial offense of interstate car theft. Roughly 30 percent of the population is Negro; ten percent is Mexican or Indian.

Over the past two years, this profile has reflected a significant "shift to the left" with a major increase in marijuana and selective-service offenses. It is clear that the change in the prison population reflects the major social concerns of the young: drugs and the draft.

The location of a prison between missile sites and marigold fields is paradox enough, but these simple facts of geography also represent the current social issues affecting its population. No longer the preserve of the classically delinquent "low rider," the prison is becoming an intense experience for young men of all social classes and from various ethnic origins. The possibility of imprisonment has become much more real to a larger community of the young, and in the most concrete sense, a much larger community of the young is being brought to prison. This broadened contact with prisons may arouse greater interest and quicker action in prison reform and, more important, careful thought regarding problems within and without prison walls.

One easily noticed result of the change in the prison population has been a steady increase in physical violence. Bruises, fractured jaws, and stab wounds are the major results which come to medical attention; over the past two years, the prison hospital has been flooded with such cases. Hefty changes in the social equilibrium are being resolved by hefty means. The standard solution for homosexual pressure is "fight it out," and I have heard prison officials advise inmates to settle conflict with their fists, preferably near a guard who will then "break it up quickly."

It is the sincere belief of prison employees that they are actively involved in "correction," "rehabilitation," or "the program." I have never met an inmate who, with a guarantee of professional confidence, has felt that. Nor have I met a psychiatrist who has viewed imprisonment as therapeutic beyond the fact of restraining the most assaultive or vicious of men. There are programs which provide some men with a high-school diploma; others provide "vocational training" that is useless in the marketplace. Some men have been able to use prison as a means of staying away from drugs, but the easy access to all sorts of contraband does not facilitate abstention. If a man is not rehabilitated, treated, or cured in prison, what, then, does he experience?

Whether it is anxiety, depression, panic, psychosis, or depersonalization, the man in prison experiences psychological mutilation. Sometimes this mutilation is supplemented by murder, physical assault, or sexual aggression; it is expressed as well by suicide, self-mutilation, or impulsive dashes for freedom before the eyes of guards who "shoot to wound." The unwitting but relentless function of the prison is one of deprivation: it deprives the inmate of physical mobility, of a sense of community, of the usual heterosexual experience, of ordinary goods and services, of privacy, and even of his name. The extent of these individual deprivations is great, but it is as a system of total social deprivation that the prison facilitates individual psychological deterioration.

While it is the official belief, unshakable in public, that the "mission" of the prison is rehabilitation, the conduct of affairs within the walls is oriented more toward the maintenance of uneventful custody. Former Attorney General Ramsey Clark is only the most recent to decry the fact that 90 percent of prison budgets goes toward custodial expenses. Such organization as there is operates to process men through the place with an efficiency as good as, or better than, that necessary to handle their files. Short of riot control, procedural matters are primary—to insure efficient flowthrough. As with most institutions, the prison is concerned with sustaining itself and its employees; there is an inertia and stolidity which is maddening even to the icy systems analysts who are the latest breed of prison reformers. The few functioning programs in education are designed to meet the need of the institution rather than the individual needs of its inmates. The demands of the prison managers are met and exercised by the guards, who are not notably flexible men.

Rules are enforced without explanation and often by caprice. Any questioning inmate is disciplined for "disrespect for authority." Few men who enter prison with residual respect for informed opinion are able to maintain it in the face of successive waves of resentment of despotism. The rage provoked by thoughtless quotation from the rule book generates the radicalizing effects of incarceration and further polarizes antagonistic groups, foreclosing any possible growth. Subject to the eternal but selective vigilance of guards who regulate every waking and sleeping moment, prisoners are held in passivity or isolation which soon flattens out to hostile, sullen dependency. Faced with harassment and hassling, inmates must learn to live with the guards whose "shot," or disciplinary report, can postpone parole and thereby destroy hope and thought of future time, and with other inmates whose fists, knives, or penises can make present time intolerable.

Men I have known in prison have found themselves caught between three forces: the demands of the prison authorities, the implicit inmate code, and their own personal sense of life. It is a rare man with the integrity, will and perversity who can maintain anything approximating a personal life-style in prison. Some remnant of this sense of life may be salvaged at the price of an extended sentence, a long tour in the isolation unit, or a fantasy life which, if discussed, brings quick demands by the guards for psychiatric consultation. This is not to say that every life-style is socially viable; many men lead self-destructive lives. The loss of dignity and self-respect throughout the prison population, however, is quite different. A sense of personal life is systematically eroded by demands of the prison rules and the code of its inmates. The longer a man spends in prison, the less access he has to his own internal promptings of emotions, feelings, memories, dreams, and reflections. The social organization and the physical barriers of the prison induce a mental state less permeable to shades of meaning, metaphorical thinking, abstraction, time perception, and sensory awareness. This is often expressed as "spacing out," "impaired concentration," "unreal feelings," "turning to stone." It is as though the mind, formerly free to roam at least in fantasy, is also brought within the limits of the prison. For some men, there is a growing sense of personal alliance with the rigidity of the institution and its staff, expressed through the development of increasingly authoritarian and rigid attitudes. This process may well be that of negative identification, as described by Erik Erikson and others. Whatever its form or content, the process is dehumanization.

The prisoners' own code is an effective instrument in dehumanization. The code emphasizes isolation from feelings and responsive exchange with others. It marks a clear border between inmates and guards. While this has obvious protective value, it forecloses any human encounters between inmate and guard, and establishes an unbreakable polar relationship.

The cardinal rule of the code is "Never snitch." Any contact with guards is assumed to have snitch potential. The second rule of the code is "Never notice anything." This relates specifically to direct and open responses to other inmates. It may best be expressed by the following illustration. A man was walking down the main corridor of the prison when he saw another inmate lying on the floor, bleeding from the head. His initial impulse was to help him, but his action was to go immediately to his cell and stay there. The group of prisoners who talked with me about this agreed with his action and his reasons for it. He said that he feared calling a guard to help because the guard would think him the culprit, or would at least subject him to extensive interrogation. Inmates who saw him call the guard would consider him a snitch. To aid the victim himself would invite a similar beating by the initial culprit. Finally, his solicitude would suggest that there was a homosexual tie between him and the victim. This acceptance of the inmate code is representative and doubly impressive in that the narrator and the concurring group were conscientious objectors, imprisoned largely because of issues of personal responsibility.

At times, feelings of anger and unfocused rage can frequently be aroused with sufficient provocation. The third precept of the code, "Do your own time," functions to prevent eruption. No matter how extreme the stress, from family chaos to parole disappointment, it is to be taken with no show of emotion and no inner feelings are to be shared with anyone. This is the most difficult task, but one that is learned with time and institutionalization. While the code is adaptive to prison life, it is otherwise a psychological dead end.

The code develops largely out of fear. The fear of the "unseen fist," pervades the institution. It is the metaphorical fist of the prison authorities who retaliate by giving the prisoner a hard time, and the bare-knuckled fist of the inmates, who retaliate more directly. In an absolutist atmosphere, the code establishes the illusion of dignity through endurance. Its evolution, quick acceptance, and universality demonstrate its value in maintaining psychological distance; but it is a distance maintained by a carapace of isolation. The code meets the needs of the institution for stability, but it separates the individual from any potential personal growth arising from his experience. Instead, his time is denied and constricted, or he becomes as rigid as his captors. In either case, what is perpetuated is the alienation from self and from the society which maintains such institutions.

The Prisoner and Self-Respect

O. G. JOHNSON

In an article entitled "Value to Prisoners of Participation in Public Service Projects," published in the December, 1956, issue of *Federal Probation,* Gordon Fuller describes the excellent response of State Prison of Southern Michigan inmates to these projects and gives an explanation for this response. There is much to be gained, as Mr. Fuller suggests, by thinking through the reasons for this behavior on the part of prison inmates. Why,

NOTE: Reprinted from *Federal Probation,* 21 (3) :56-58, 1967.

indeed, do prisoners participate so well and so constructively in times of emergency and in times of need?

The December, 1956, *Federal Probation* also notes that a group of inmates at Southern Michigan Prison distinguished themselves by hard work in cold weather to attempt to rescue several construction workers who were caught in the collapse of a partially constructed building in Jackson, a short distance from the prison. It is important to know why the inmates behave in this manner under certain conditions because, presumably, if conditions are right they could show this kind of behavior in their everyday living. If prisons are to be truly rehabilitative, they must find the answers to problems like this.

WE LEARN FROM BEHAVIOR IN UNUSUAL SITUATIONS

We can learn much about the behavior of people in normal situations by observing their behavior in abnormal situations. This is particularly true in psychology where it has been axiomatic for a long time that one can learn much about normal behavior or the behavior of normal people by studying psychopathological behavior—the behavior of abnormal people. The same kind of reasoning applies to the behavior of the prison inmate when he donates to the March of Dimes Fund, gives of his limited funds to help an orphan he will never see, or works long hours under uncomfortable or hazardous conditions to help other people. If we understand their behavior under these abnormal or unusual conditions, this understanding should be helpful in working with them in normal or routine situations.

Mr. Fuller explains this behavior primarily in terms of a wish on the part of the inmate to identify himself more closely with free society. This identification, says Mr. Fuller, is reinforced when the inmate participates in any kind of public service project. He then finds that he can satisfy his needs in socially acceptable ways and this constitutes a learning experience for him, the "discovery of the inmates that positive attitudes and socially acceptable behavior are recognized and rewarded."

Quoting Mr. Fuller, "Psychologically basic needs of the individual inmate are fulfilled and sociologically his identification with the free society group is reinforced." He describes one of these basic needs of the individual when he says "he (the inmate) gradually achieves a sense of self-worth and feels that he is playing a significant role in an important and worthy cause." It is just these "basic needs" and the "sense of self-worth" which need to be examined further because it is here where the explanation of some of this unusual prisoner behavior lies.

RELATING CONCEPT OF ONESELF TO THE OFFENSE

Let us think for a minute of the individual as he is about to commit an antisocial offense. Even though the crime has not been planned, even though it is an impulsive, spur-of-the-moment offense, the individual undoubtedly contemplates himself in relation to the act. He wonders, although not so specifically and directly, "is this the kind of thing that I can do or would do?" Everyone does this except in the case of extremely routinized and habitual behavior such as eating with one's fork or shaving or running a punch press. For example, old ladies do not turn cartwheels because they do not look at themselves as persons who are capable, either physically or from the standpoint of their own feelings of personal dignity, of performing this act. A student does not cheat on an examination even when the opportunity is present because he does not look upon himself as a cheater, even though he may feel that he is likely to fail the exam. Anyone who reads the newspaper knows that it is newsworthy when someone steals from a church or from a blind man, takes an old man's life savings, or runs off with the March of Dimes collection can. These items are newsworthy because it is difficult for people to believe that anyone would do these things. Said in another way, it is hard for people to understand how anybody could "lower himself" to the point of stealing from such a worthwhile or helpless source.

The young man who drives off with somebody else's car must, at some time previous to the commission of the act, and also while he is committing the act, accept the concept of himself as a person who is morally capable of doing so. The offender may come to look at himself as a person capable of committing antisocial acts in two somewhat different, although related, ways. One may be a direct lowering of the self-concept, generally as a result of many ego shattering experiences in his relationship with other people. This is often a repeated failure when the individual attempts constructive activities. One may speculate here on the effect on an individual's self-concept of repeated failures to keep a job, particularly when one observes the record of vocational instability of so many inmates. The other way in which an individual may come to perceive himself as a person capable of unlawful behavior is through the process of rationalization of his act or intended act. When looked at in terms of the self-concept, it becomes apparent that rationalization is an attempt to make the act of committing the crime compatible with the individual's view of himself. If one can build a satisfactory set of rationalizations for his acts, he is more likely to be able to retain a greater degree of self-respect. That is, he is less likely to suffer a marked lowering of his self-concept. The Hungarian rebels of October, 1956, furnish us a good example of a group of people who were able to act in direct and violent opposition to the laws of their country and yet come through this "unlawful" behavior with enhanced self-concepts. The political and economic facts of life in Hungary gave them more than ample rationalizations for their unlawful behavior.

INMATE'S DESIRE TO BOLSTER SELF-RESPECT

The immense social value of probation comes from the fact that it protects the offender from the ego-shattering experience of incarceration. The person on probation is not stigmatized by the term "jailbird," "ex-con," "inmate," or any of the other terms which are so damaging to his sense of self-respect. He does not need to look at himself as a person who has done time. He is protected from being identified with the prison population. If probation did only this, it would still be well worth its cost.

The inmate coming into the penal institution very often presents his rationalization pattern when first interviewed by a counselor, social worker, psychologist, or psychiatrist. "I didn't know what I was doing." "I blacked out and don't remember anything that happened." "I got in with a bad bunch of guys." "A colored man can't get a decent job." "I was drunk and didn't know what I was doing." All of these are crude, though genuine, attempts to make his antisocial behavior more compatible with his self-concept. Some inmates spend much time and energy in perfecting and refining their systems of rationalizations. The inmate will often find a buddy or a group of buddies who will support his rationalization system or even suggest new ones. The experienced counselor knows that before the inmate can give up his unrealistic rationalizations, he must be helped toward greater self-respect by direct ego support and by development of his assets along constructive channels, through a rehabilitative prison program.

Most inmates spend some time in prison attempting to repair and bolster their own self-concepts. There are many ways in which they attempt to do this. Some of them participate in athletics, some work steadily and hard in prison industries, some attend the academic school or take college extension courses, some learn a trade, some work as trusties, some read what they consider better literature, some work at handicraft, some work on the prison paper, some write stories, some give blood or volunteer as subjects for medical research.

The important point here is that the many worthwhile activities in which prison inmates engage are directed primarily at the improvement of the inmate's self-concept. Everyone has a need to be needed, primarily because it is flattering to the ego to feel that others are dependent upon one. A highly successful salesman whom the author once knew had put this principle into practical operation in his work. He made it a point, when first talking with a prospect, to ask the person for something—a glass of water, a match, a chair, anything to get the prospect to do something for him. This gave the prospect a feeling of having some vested interest in the salesman, and tended to smooth the way for a sale. Penal institutions can apply the same practical psychology in their rehabilitative programs, giving inmates greater feelings of self-worth and also giving them some greater feeling of responsibility for, and interest in, the society of which they are part.

Seen in the light of what has been said above, it is not at all surprising that prison inmates adopt war orphans, courageously and selflessly fight forest fires and floods, give their blood, and volunteer as subjects for medical research. The need to respect oneself is a powerful one. The penal institution which is most effective in rehabilitating its inmates will be the one which supplies the greatest number of ego-building opportunities for the greatest number of its population.

A Lawyer's View

LOUIS LIPSCHITZ

Thirty-six years have passed since I first represented a man charged with crime. If our statistics of the duration of life sentences are accurate, then I have served the equivalent of at least two life sentences at the Bar and perhaps three. Looking back, it seems much shorter. Looking ahead, a life sentence is still a long time.

So it is with a man who is charged with crime. His future holds but little promise in store for him. Jails and prisons are awful places. No one who holds hope for himself or his future can ever become adjusted to the loss of his liberty, even if his misconduct warrants such punishment.

The views I here express are not based on any studies of criminology, nor am I attempting to explain the causes of criminal behavior. I am primarily concerned about the man who is about to go to prison and what scars he will bear when released.

There are many intelligent persons at all levels of learning who will think or say, "Why be so concerned about criminals? Society is entitled to be protected from violators. Why not show some concern for the man who has observed all the rules." It appears that the man who has followed the rules has had the willpower to do so. He does not, and did not, need help as does the man who failed to resist his weaknesses. It is the malefactors who need aid, whether in or out of prison, and very little is being done for them. Our prison buildings are improving but care is only slightly better than it was 35 years ago. Our hospitals and mental institutions, which could give therapy and care to those charged with or convicted of crime, are just as lacking in sufficient numbers of trained personnel as they were years ago.

Note: Reprinted from *The Prison Journal,* 43 (2) :25-27, 1963.

What have we accomplished by our scientific approach to the solution of crime, its causes and responsibilities? Has the knowledge we acquired in any way contributed to the solution or reduction of the causes of crime? Do we have less crime today than we had years ago? Are there fewer criminals? Are there fewer crimes? Are the crimes less serious? Have we reduced the hardships suffered by society because of the crimes committed: Has the released prisoner a more receptive world to live in? Is he better received? Have we done anything to effectively prepare him for his release? These questions must all be answered negatively.

My first concern has been about the plight of the man who is in prison and will be released. He has had certain rights and obligations while confined. He did not forfeit his constitutional rights by being confined. He still has the right to confer with counsel, to be free from mistreatment and physical abuse, to keep in touch with members of his family and close friends. He has access to the courts to vindicate these rights. He has the obligation of proper behavior and compliance with prison rules.

There are many sensitive areas in a prison other than those dealing with security. Violation of these areas may have a direct effect on the inmate. He may be loath to criticize a keeper for fear that the issues of fact raised by his complaint may be decided adversely to him. This will reflect in the attitude of the prison officials on a parole application. The inmate may be reluctant to show any physical weakness for fear that other inmates will take advantage of him. The inmate may not want to reveal his mental suffering because of the effect it will have on his family when they visit him.

The prisoner is conscious generally that he has rights but is reluctant to enforce them. He may be considered a "troublemaker." If he insists on asserting his legal right, he is given very little assistance or encouragement within the prison. He may want to challenge the validity of his conviction and not have available legal assistance. As I look back, I recall instances where prison officials have refused to mail requests to lawyers. Prison regulations imposed restrictions on mailing privileges. These, I am happy to state, have been somewhat relaxed. Even though the inmate now has access to the courts, the law reports contain cases where the courts have been reluctant to review the facts to make certain that the rights of the prisoner have not been denied.

The United States Supreme Court has recently given greater recognition to the rights of a defendant to be represented by counsel. Our own appellate courts, however, have shown great reluctance to recognize such rights when the prisoner appeals from the refusal of his petition for habeas corpus. The prisoner is thus left to his own devices in pursuing his appeal. In some cases, his failure to enclose an adequate number of copies of his petition for release has caused a denial of his application. In other cases, his criticism of his keepers has limited his access to the courts. He may have failed to allege all of the facts necessary for relief because of ignorance and his plea is rejected. Our courts claim that there is a flood of applications for relief whenever a new decision gives greater recognition to the rights of an imprisoned man. As the number of such applications increases, we hear complaints that many frivolous applications are filed which add to the burdens of an overworked judiciary. This may be true, but many of these problems could be solved by assigning counsel to inmates who seek legal aid. The lawyers so assigned would properly advise the prisoner as to the feasibility of his application for relief and discourage many of the repeated petitions which seem to add to the tasks of the overworked judiciary.

There have been many cases in which the petitions for relief were meritorious. The prisoner who does not receive guidance may then have difficulty in properly preparing and presenting his facts and his legal position in court. The assistance of legal counsel is crucial at this point. The inmate rarely has such legal aid available to him if he or his family are destitute. How can he have respect for our legal processes if they are only available to the affluent prisoner? The prison libraries do not contain the necessary law books to guide the prisoner in his new endeavor. He should have available the legal material to properly enable him to seek his release if counsel is not available to him. Access to courts is meaningless unless effective.

My search has disclosed the existence of rules which restricted the time and place for such research, even where legal material was available. This restriction has been approved by some courts who feel that "jail house lawyers" would cause frivolous petitions to be filed.

There have also been instances in which the rights of prisoners to privately confer with their counsel have been refused. In these instances a guard was present supposedly to protect the prisoner from his lawyer or vice versa.

Censorship has created problems. The right of privacy is not recognized. Mail is censored, irrespective of the person to whom it is addressed. The courts in which questions of censorship are raised dispose of these issues by stating that prisoners do not have an absolute right to use the mails. The courts have generally refused to pay any attention to the complaints of prisoners dealing with their rights to communicate. The number of letters that may be sent out of prison are limited. The identity of the recipient must be established and approved. This is usually done by some guard, who may not in every case have the capacity to understand the communication needs of the prisoner. The usual answer to the courts when such matters are raised is, "We think it is well settled that it is not the function of the courts to supersede the treatment and discipline of prisoners." To obtain relief, he must show that the keepers arbitrarily, maliciously, or intentionally violated his rights—a superhuman burden!

Society has improved its living standards. Very little has been done in our state prisons to improve surroundings for inmates or those who visit inmates. Screens or partitions and bars are found in many visiting rooms. Toilet facilities are at a minimum. Children who visit a parent prisoner are shocked at what they see. The prisoners look to their children like animals in a zoo. Even these cautionary and security measures do not deter a search of the visitor. The Federal Penitentiary at Lewisburg presents an entirely different picture. The inmates are permitted to speak with their visitors in surroundings which are equivalent to a comfortable living room. The Federal prison authorities have not been concerned about the fact that a wife is permitted to kiss her husband when she greets him or that the father may caress his children when he sees them. Why this closer contact should instill fear in other prison authorities is difficult to understand.

There probably are many other ways in which prison officials can improve the lot of those who have wronged society. I leave it to their ingenuity.

On Being Human in the Prison Community

RABBI WILLIAM J. LEFFLER

It is generally assumed that the major function of a prison staff is to run the prison and to see to it that the prisoners behave themselves. I do not accept this idea.

I believe the primary function of a prison staff is to teach—to instruct each prisoner in what it means to be a human being. He should teach not just in a formal sense, but by his day-to-day behavior, by his actions and his attitudes, as he confronts the prisoner in every situation—in the corridor, on the job, in his quarters, in recreation, at meals.

Even before he accepts his official table of organization designation, each staff member, from warden to turnkey, should regard teaching as the first responsibility of his job. The term "teacher" ought to be prefixed to every job title. Admittedly, as a teacher, the staff member will not be completely successful with all his pupils. No teacher ever is. But if he does not consider teaching as the most important aspect of his employment in the prison, he really is not participating in the rehabilitation program of his institution.

TEACHING ROLE OF THE ENTIRE PRISON STAFF

If we are to achieve a deeper understanding of the role of the prison staff, we need to develop a greater understanding of what this role of teacher should be. We need to understand that the staff person is employed to minister to the problems, needs, and concerns of the prisoner during his efforts in this direction. Every possible opportunity should be afforded him during his period of incarceration to develop as a human being. This means that regular in-service training programs will have to be established for the staff, so that they will have a fuller appreciation of what it

NOTE: Reprinted from *Federal Probation*, 32 (2) :30-32, 1968.

means to be a human being ministering to the needs of other human beings and not just prison staff overseeing a lot of prisoners. This means, also, that the staff will have to start thinking of prisoners as their brothers in the Biblical sense of the word—as created in the image of God—even though they have erred and are being punished, and that they remain human beings. If the attitude of the staff can be altered to regard themselves as teachers, the prisoners will gain an insight and understanding of what healthy human relationships can be and begin their rehabilitation by establishing these relationships with members of the staff as well as with one another.

ON BEING HUMAN

The characteristics of "human beingness" are numerous and varied. No one list could possibly exhaust them all. To name but a few, they include compassion, a sense of justice, courtesy, mercy, patience, thoughtfulness, humility, reverence for life. The person who is incarcerated often lacks many of these traits in his personality makeup. If his incarceration is to be at all meaningful to him, it has to be viewed by the prison authorities as a learning experience for the prisoner—not just a period of commitment to prison, separated from society by walls and bars.

Certainly not every prisoner can be expected to comprehend the error of his ways, but if the time spent in prison is going to serve a constructive purpose, then the prison must become a school—a school in which the residents through their daily associations with the staff at every level, can come to understand what it means to be a human being. Only in this way will the prisoner comprehend some of the lessons which his incarceration is supposed to teach him and be able to return to society better equipped to live as a more useful, productive citizen. Only in this way can the prison really assume its role to reclaim offenders and fulfill its teaching function.

This change in function and goal certainly will not be easy for the staff to comprehend or implement. There will be repeaters—many will fail the course over and over again. But if we do not make the effort, then the prison serves no constructive role so far as the prisoner is concerned. Punishment without learning is futile and serves no purpose. Every parent knows this. The same principle should apply to our institutions.

There are many people on the staff of our prisons who have never considered that teaching should be their primary function. The recent reports from the Cummins Prison Farm in Arkansas indicate, indeed, that those responsible for administering that facility did not understand that a prison is a place for teaching and experiencing human relationships. The sheriff of one of our large county jails, who confiscated all prisoners' radios and books, certainly does not think of himself as an instructor in a school on how to be a human being. This teaching concept is not found in most county and city jails today.

More heartening is the report in the *New York Times,* of February 14, 1968, describing the Parchman State Penitentiary in Mississippi, in which Superintendent C. E. Breazeale is quoted as saying: "We're trying to think of the man when he's getting out." One might suspect that the interest in the Parchman Prison occurs because it is unusual and not because it is the usual method of treating prisoners.

Before the member of a prison staff can fulfill his teaching function, he first has to know what it means to be a human being. We cannot define this term specifically, but we can, through everyday relationships, help the prisoner experience what it means to be a human being.

DO NOT UNTO OTHERS . . .

Hillel, a Jewish sage who lived some 2,000 years ago, stated Jesus' Golden Rule in negative terms that are most relevant to our consideration. He taught: "That which is hateful unto you, do not do unto others." A staff member knows the kind of behavior that irritates him, angers him, and raises his hackles. This is where he should start teaching what it means to be a human being—by not treating prisoners in a way he would not want them to treat him, for they are as human as he, even though their humanity may not always be apparent.

Ashley Montagu, in his book, *On Being Human,* states: "One cannot love and respect anyone unless he has a genuine love and respect for himself."[1] Erich Fromm also points out the interrelatedness between regard for oneself and respect for others. He writes: "It is true that selfish persons are incapable of loving others, but they are not capable of loving themselves either."[2] To love another person, or in the language of the Bible, to "love thy neighbor as thyself," one must first ask: What do I think of me? Do I love myself? If he can answer these questions in the affirmative and believes he is a worthwhile human being, then he will achieve self-esteem and will act independently of what others think of him. This self-respect will show in his treatment of prisoners.

Rabbi Menachem Mendel of Klotzk, a nineteenth-century Hasidic rabbi, taught: "If I am I because I am I, and you are you because you are you, then I am I and you are you. But if I am I because you are you, and you are you because I am I, then I am not I and you are not you."[3] This statement is also germane to our discussion of self-respect. One's regard for himself should not depend upon the attitude of others toward him, nor of him toward them. The prison employee who has to bolster his own ego by demeaning a prisoner cannot possibly teach the prisoner what it means to be a human being. He does not know himself, and so it is impossible for him to transmit it to another person. Only if he loves himself first, only if he respects himself first, will the staff member show it in his behavior toward others and treat every prisoner as a human being, as important in his own right and not in comparison with someone else.

We may ask what sort of training might be required of all prison personnel in order to instill in them the necessary respect for themselves as well as for the prisoners. As one possibility, I believe that sociodramas, with staff members playing the roles of prisoners and staff, might do wonders to begin to get the idea across. The staff member who has to play a prisoner in such impromptu dramas would have to feel the inhumanity of much of the present attitudes in order to respond properly. And the staff member who plays the role of staff would have to think through his personal actions and attitudes also. He would have to be more self-conscious of what he says because of the nature of a sociodrama. Discussion growing out of the reactions to these dramas would also help to bring to the surface some of the in-humanity of much of prison life today.

Play readings of different kinds dealing with prison situations, followed by discussions, might be tried. Peter Weiss' *The Investigation* might bring about some worthwhile insight. Lectures by former inmates who have successfully returned to society are another way of communicating to the personnel the importance of respect.

A teacher cannot teach that which he does not know or understand. A prison staff member who does not respect himself cannot teach self-respect to prisoners, nor expect to receive respect from them.

PENITENCE AND FORGIVENESS

"To err is human." How frequently we forget that no human being is perfect. Religion acknowledges the human failings of all of us. The Roman Catholic Church has the Sacrament of Penance for the erring communicant. Judaism has Yom Kippur, the Day of Atonement, a holy day of prayer and fasting, devoted to contemplating one's sins and emphasizing the necessity to respect and to forgive others. Protestants have their Sacrament of the Altar and their services of public confession.

Before one can forgive others, however, he must first know how to forgive himself. Each of us is reticent to admit his own faults, though we often are quick to criticize the faults of others. If correction is to be a major concern of our prison system, then those who are on its staff have to start with themselves. They need to be able to admit their own errors and accept their own shortcomings—not to be limited by them, but to learn from them and thus try not to commit them again. Only in this way can the staff rise above their own behavior and establish the relationships which are necessary to fulfill their role as teachers of "human be-ingness."

This will not be easy to do. All too often the prison staff concentrates on the sin aspect of the prisoner's past behavior and overlooks repentance and forgiveness. They condemn him for his crime and for his waywardness, and forget that Scripture teaches us that God wants the sinner to turn from his evil ways, to repent, and to learn how to live in conformity with His will. Here, too, is an important lesson which needs to be taught in every possible way to the prison staff concerning their daily relations with the prison population.

We call our prisons penitentiaries. They are institutions established to teach the meaning of penitence. Traditionally the prisoner is supposed to be a penitent. He is confined in order to learn what it means to repent, to change his ways, to start life afresh. But he cannot learn unless there are teachers—persons who can teach him how to alter his values, who can show him what forgiveness means, who can encourage him to be a human being because they are worthwhile human beings themselves, who can help him admit his past errors because they can admit their errors, who can urge him to transcend his past mistakes because they know how to transcend their past mistakes in life and can function despite their prior difficulties. This is a vital task for the prison staff. There are no other people with whom the prisoner has daily contact and who can teach him repentance and forgiveness.

The day-to-day association between the prisoner and the staff ought to be a constant learning experience for the prisoner, with the staff member teaching the prisoner that human beings do make mistakes (that even prison personnel are subject to error), that one can rise above his short-comings, and that he can pardon the other person and reestablish an honest relationship with the person who has erred in life. This aspect of the teaching role is indispensable for the prison staff if they are going to teach "human beingness."

WE ARE ALL HUMAN BEINGS

The comment and discussion now going on about our prison systems would indicate that the methods we have used in the past have not been as successful as might be hoped for and that perhaps other methods might be tried. My suggestions may seem somewhat idealistic, but unless we have ideals which we can translate into concrete programs, we are left directionless. I believe our prison personnel should stop thinking in terms of staff-prisoner relations and begin thinking in terms of human relationships—of one humanity, and that they begin to see as one of their major functions the teaching of human beings who have erred and who lack self-respect—what it means to be a human being in the very best sense of the word. Such a change in approach, I firmly believe, would accelerate the rehabilitation process within our prison system, a goal for which we all strive.

NOTES AND REFERENCES

1. Montagu, Ashley: *On Being Human.* New York, Hawthorn Books, 1966, p. 113.
2. Fromm, Erich: *Man for Himself.* New York, Rinehart, 1947, p. 131.
3. Quoted in Buber, Martin: *Tales of the Hasidim—The Later Masters.* New York, Farrar, Straus and Young, 1948, p. 283.

The Rehabilitation Process: A Prisoner's Point of View

RAYMOND C. HODGE[1]

At the outset it must be recognized that rehabilitation cannot be forced on a person; the desire must originate within the individual. Careful and conscientious guidance may lead to recognition of the benefits in rehabilitation, and the rehabilitative tools (guidance in education, vocational and avocational skills, development of pride in desirable personal traits and personality factors, etc.) made available, but he must be led, never forced, to use them for his personal benefit. When an offender reaches the full realization that his rebellion against extant social mores (motivated perhaps by a desire to hurt) is more injurious to himself than to any other person; that in so rebelling he wounds those loved ones whom he has no desire to hurt as much or even more than the ones whom he wishes to hurt and that repeated rebellion and retaliation will eventually alienate even those whom he holds most dear; that he, himself, is the one suffering most; that others have, or will, perhaps, eventually cease to suffer on his account, or to even care, then, if he can be prevented from wallowing in a morass of self-pity, he is ready to utilize the tools of rehabilitation, for the desire will originate within himself.

No hard-and-fast rules can be strictly applied to lead an in-

NOTE: Reprinted from *American Journal of Correction,* 26 (2) :12-17, 1964.

dividual to rehabilitation, for each person is a separate personality with a fascinating personal history uniquely his own and to which he adds each day. Personal goals can be changed or created, thereby altering the theme of the history being written by the individual. Intelligent understanding and sympathetic aid can be given to the individual to foster desirable and beneficial personality characteristics and sublimation of less desirable characteristics into constructive qualities.

Perhaps the most difficult and exasperating phase of the rehabilitative process is the initial approach. At the outset, newly committed prisoners are generally beset by a multitude of conflicting emotions and worries; they are frightened, in strange surroundings and unaccustomed to prison routine, they are resentful, hurt, separated from loved ones, and often harbor thoughts of revenge which may lead them to resent any manifestation of authority and to rebel against its exercise. At this state and until they become accustomed to their surroundings, fears somewhat allayed, and resentments given a chance to cool, it is probably best to interfere as little as possible and only as necessary with the individual. They should be treated kindly, courteously, and considerately, but with firmness, impressing upon them that they will not be treated unjustly and that their dignity as human beings will be preserved. Prisoners are quick to discern fair but firm treatment, to distinguish the difference between just and unjust measures of discipline, and to condemn and resent the unjust. Prisoners utilize overt manifestations of dishonesty, inequality, and injustices perpetuated by prison personnel to rationalize their own misbehavior, excusing their actions by believing that their misbehavior is no worse and perhaps not so bad as that of the offending official, in that the official purports to be honest.

If rehabilitation is the goal, then prison must not be used as a means of punishing offenders. Discipline, of course, is necessary, but it should not be used as a means of punishing infractions; instead, it should be used as a tool of the rehabilitative process, impressing upon the prisoner the need for law and order, the social benefits of law and order, the fairness of the rules, and that the rules are made for the protection and benefit of all concerned, both personnel and prisoners, not as excuses to inflict punishment upon prisoners.

When and how should the rehabilitative process of an individual be initiated? Certainly not until the individual has sufficiently controlled his emotions, fears, and resentment to enable him to discuss reasonably the cold, hard facts of the economic facet of crime as personally related to himself. Perhaps this is the best place to start, and the hard sell the most effective approach. Most prisoners who are sentenced to prison for crimes against property (including the narcotics vendors) are committed for crimes involving less than 2,000 dollars. On this basis, crime is a very unprofitable financial pursuit.

> *Case A:* Three men rob a liquor store, taking several bottles of liquor, cigarettes, and cash. Total value of property taken: $1,500; divided into three equal parts, $500 per man. Apprehended, tried, convicted, and sentenced to prison as the law prescribes on 5-to-life terms. They do an average of 3½ years in prison and 2½ years on parole. Profit per man per year in prison, $142.86. This, of course, assumes that the parole is not violated and he is not returned to prison for an additional period of time; $142.86 per year is a very poor return on the investment of time. Now, assume that these men were capable of earning $3,000 per year in gainful employment; 3½ × $3,000 = $10,500. $10,500 − $500 (share of robbery) = $10,000, which is the dollar loss for the 3½ years served in prison.
>
> *Case B:* One man cashes worthless checks amounting to $2,000 over a period of two months. Apprehended, convicted, and arrives in prison. Time set at 5 years with 2½ years on parole. Profit per year, $800. This is not sufficient to support a man in even submarginal circumstances. Potential earnings for 2½ years at $3,000 per year = $7,500 − $2,000 = $5,500, which is the man's financial loss for the 2½ years in prison.

Literally thousands of illustrations can be given from the files of any prison. It can be shown that crime, for most prisoners, on a strictly profit-loss basis does not pay.

To be considered along with and as a follow-up to the profit-loss factor is the factor of personal happiness. All prisoners express the desire to be free and to pursue their idea of happiness in an environment of freedom. Very often these ideas are in the form of unrealistic fancies such as high-powered automobiles, expensive female companionship, high night life, and deluding others into the belief that they are persons of affluence, thereby satisfying their own delusions of grandeur. This conception of happiness inevitably leads to overextension of finances and income which, together with a compulsion to maintain the image of "big shot" to their acquaintances, predisposes them to supplement their income through illegal and unacceptable devices.

Happiness is a relative term and there are varying degrees thereof. Individuals can be taught that continued overall happiness is preferable to short periods of lush, expensive living, which is not happiness but merely a poor substitute; that happiness is also found in the quiet serenity of familial companionship and that the excitement found in the boisterous, roistering company of intoxicated revelers, bar-hoppers, and back-slapping parasites whose friendship and loyalty lasts only as long as the ability to finance soirées endures, is not happiness nor even a good substitute therefor. Simple, acceptable, satisfying and economical substitutes can be found for the transient excitements and thrills of expensive night life. Personal recreational preferences should be explored in the individual to discover interests —recreational, beneficial, and constructive—leading to a richer, fuller, more satisfying, and happy life.

Comparison of the overall happiness in a prisoner's life with that of a brother or law-abiding friend might be helpful. The lot of a prisoner is an unhappy one at best, being denied, by the nature of his environment, the liberties and choices of pursuits so important to a satisfying life. While it is true that no life is one of unsullied bliss, it is equally true that the person pursuing happiness in an environment of freedom and liberty of choice is much happier, by and large, than the person in prison who is restricted in liberty, separated from loved ones, and with a minimum of choice. Which is better, short periods of unrestrained abandonment, followed by long periods of restraint and confinement, or a sustained life of freedom, relatively smooth and acceptably happy?

To each individual on earth, his own life is more precious than that of any other, therefore more valuable to himself. It must logically follow that the primary responsibility and duty of a man is to his own personal welfare, all other considerations being secondary.

Prisoners can be led to a reappraisal of their personal values.

Most individuals grossly underestimate themselves, not in extant capabilities, but in potential, latent capability. A person who is valuable to himself gives himself the best care, treatment, protection, and training possible, thereby enhancing his value to himself and to others. The skills and capabilities of any person can be improved and developed, thereby increasing the total value of the person.

More important, however, is the evaluation and high regard of a person for himself, of his pride in being a dignified, capable, sentient human being. No person should feel or be made to feel degraded, even though he is or has been. To the contrary, for men to act like capable, dignified human beings, they must be taught to feel like men, to know they are men, proud of their abilities and accomplishments, proud to be honest, capable, valuable members of society. Prisoners, in order to stress their personal worth and value both to themselves and potentially to society, should be constantly reminded by subtle and sincere means of their personal value, both to themselves and to others.

Most prisoners place great value on other prisoners' opinions of themselves. Can this desire for the good opinion of others be channeled into a desire for the good opinion of society in general?

Personal values must be personally assessed. A person is only as good as he believes himself to be. If he assesses himself as a thief and accepts and believes this assessment to be valid, he is a thief and will prove it by stealing. If he assesses himself as an honest man, accepts and believes this assessment, he is honest within his conception of honesty and will prove it.

Most prisoners have some admirable qualities, but sometimes these qualities are misapplied (i.e. loyalty to wrong persons or ideas). Redirection of these qualities can make them real assets to the prisoner rather than liabilities. An honest, ruthless reappraisal of personal values and worth is essential to rehabilitation and enduring adjustment to society. The pain of introspection and recognizing the unadorned truth, both good and bad, with absolute honesty, is rewarded by recognition of one's personal worth to one's self, and by recognition and admission of shortcomings and deficiencies, one can work to compensate for them and thus become a desirable member of society.

All men are not created equal insofar as IQ, aptitudes, potential, etc., are concerned. Some persons have high manual dexterity and poor aptitude for mathematics; some persons cannot thread a needle and are masters of administration. It would be highly impractical for a person with high manual dexterity and poor mathematical aptitude to attempt to become an accountant or for a person with poor manual dexterity and high administrative potential to attempt to become a watchmaker. It is easy to visualize the frustration and unhappiness inherent in these instances; however, it is surprising how many square pegs are driven into round holes.

Great assistance can be rendered in this area. There are presently available a variety of indices which accurately measure and chart individual potential. When such potential is charted, it should be fully and frankly discussed with the individual, advising him of his IQ, educational level, aptitudes, preferences, his needs, and the manner and means whereby his needs for development may be satisfied and followed with real assistance in development. He should also be fully and frankly advised of his limitations, both current (due to lack of training, education, aptitude, etc.) and saturation (the point beyond which he should not expect to exceed). It would be unrealistic to expect a person with a high mechanical aptitude, low spatial relations, and an IQ of 90 to become a precision tool designer; however, becoming a skilled lathe operator or automobile mechanic could be realized.

Full and frank discussion of potential and limitations can be of inestimable value, in that it encourages individuals to develop their latent talents, guides them into vocations where they may attain greatest height, skill, and recognition, and save years, perhaps lifetimes, of frustration, grief, and incompetence in working, competing, and failing in vocations for which they are unsuited.

Properly used and followed through, potential assessments and limitations can be a potent tool in the rehabilitation process.

Every individual has a code of morals as unique as his own personality. All prison employees have heard inmates proclaim their innocence and condemnation of certain categorical crimes. The sex offender may proclaim his moral superiority by uttering: "I'm not a thief"; the narcotics vendor justify by: "I never sold to anyone who did not want to buy and if I hadn't sold it to them someone else would have, and I never did steal from anyone"; the armed robber: "I'm no sneak-thief burglar"; the burglar: "I'm no rape fiend," etc., etc. Each category of criminals believes themselves to be morally superior to some other category of criminals.

It is commendable, of course, that a certain armed robber abhors sex crimes, sneak thievery, and narcotics offenses. This, however, does not make his personal moral code acceptable to the majority of society; he is a bandit, and society eschews bandits. Prisoners fail in their rationalizations to recognize that all prisoners have one thing in common: their moral codes are not acceptable to society, no matter what particular ingredient is lacking.

Reassessment of the moral code is vital to successful rehabilitation. What essential value (s) therein is lacking? The narcotics offender, for instance, may not fully realize the damage he aids and abets in inflicting on the addict's family, friends, and the potential value of the addict of which society may be deprived.

The total ramifications in the commission of any one crime are enormous. Suppose a service station is robbed. The bandit may believe that the only loss is suffered by the owner, more than likely a large company. But does the loss stop there? Consider first the individual robbed. He is held in terror at the point of a gun with the full knowledge that the next moment may be the last moment of his life, and his life is more precious to him than anything else on earth. That individual has suffered in the crime through mental anguish and, if he cannot prove noncomplicity in the crime, may be falsely accused of theft and lose his means of livelihood. Consider the owner, whether independent or a large company; the owner has been deprived of his lawful and just sales receipts, the cost of his wares, the taxes he must pay, the wages of his employees, the overhead and upkeep of the premises, and the profits he has lawfully earned by his labors. Consider the company which carries the insurance on the property; its loss is added to premiums paid by other policyholders, making insurance rates higher. The law enforcement body in the community must be expanded in order to cope with increasing crime rates, thereby increasing taxes upon the citizens to defray expenses. The damage caused by a crime is never a purely local thing. It ripples and spreads, affecting in varying degrees the economy of the nation.

In rehabilitation, a prisoner must reexamine his moral code, equate its deficiency with the deficiency he finds abhorrent in the moral codes of other, different-type offenders, and realize that all moral codes deficient in any ingredient which make them unacceptable are repugnant and will not be tolerated by society; that the possessors of these deficient codes, whether it be for sex, checks, burglary, or any crime, will be segregated from society and their freedom lost.

Religion is a sacred personal privilege and prerogative of which a person may elect to partake or eschew without fear of condemnation. Freedom to choose any religion, sect, or cult is unchallenged. The more popular religions are represented in prisons by chaplains and visiting ministers. Their services are available to all who wish to avail themselves of their benefits.

Religion, to a person who desires rehabilitation, is an asset. No matter by what name called, all religions advocate, in general, the same principles, and no religion advocates perpetration of crime. All religions advocate harmonious social living, e.g. the Biblical admonition to treat others as we would be treated by them, which in practice means that if you wish to be treated with kindness and consideration, then you yourself should first be kind and considerate of others.

The principles of religion, accepted and believed in, can assist in rehabilitation; however, although an asset, it is not a prime requisite to rehabilitation. Many honest persons are agnostic or even avowed atheists.

In recent years, correctional institutions have made great strides in establishing educational and vocational facilities. These facilities are of tremendous value to the uneducated, unskilled prisoner who is attempting rehabilitation. As education and vocational skills increase, so does personal confidence. Prisoners realize they are worth more, their earning power is increased, their confidence in their ability to compete in a competitive society is strengthened, and their need to assert their superiority by unlawful means is lessened. As the educational level is increased, there is a tendency to seek higher intellectual companionship, deserting the elemental environment instrumental in most incarcerations in prison. Proper, competent training in vocational skills give self-confidence and permits successful employment of new or increased skills in gainful competitive vocations.

These are tools whose importance to a rehabilitation program cannot be minimized.

Prison officials encounter great resentment and antagonism toward any manifestation of authority, sometimes presenting complex and extensive administration problems. Much of the resentment and antagonism is developed before prisoners are received in prison and, unfortunately, sometimes tends to increase during their tenure in prison. A major effort should be made to break down this resentment and antagonism, for it carries over from prison into society when the individual is released, and is instrumental in flouting the law and striking out at the resented image of authority.

As previously stated, these resentments and antagonisms are already well developed before prisoners are received in prison, but they need not remain so. Here again, perhaps, the cold, hard, brutal facts of life should be dramatically demonstrated, illustrating the fact that no person goes through life without being treated unjustly, brutally, and with total disregard of feelings, desires, emotions, or hurts; that every person suffers undeserved maltreatment in some form or other at some time in his life. Persons who are committed to prison are no different in this respect from the average law-abiding citizen; prisoners (although from listening to the relating of their woes they would have you believe so) are not martyrs crucified on the cross of injustice. Perhaps a minute percentage are innocent of the crimes for which they were committed. In this respect, however, they are no different from other millions upon millions of human beings who have been falsely accused and convicted (not necessarily of criminal activities) and therefore are entitled to no greater allotment of sympathy than the other wronged millions of people. History is replete with injustices massively perpetrated upon the innocent, i.e. the Nazis' slaughter of the Jews, the Inquisition, the martyred Christians.

Prisoners do not want to be treated unjustly, they do not want to be hurt; they do want people to feel sorry for them. The fact should be forcefully stressed that the victims who suffered injury at the hands of the person committing criminal deeds did not want to be treated unjustly, neither did they want to be hurt. But they were hurt by the conduct of the prisoner in total disregard of the unjustness to and fears of the victims. Does not the culprit, by actions of callous disregard of the rights, feelings, and desires of others, forfeit any claim to sympathy?

While these facts should be clearly and graphically illustrated for the benefit of the prisoner, it should be remembered that although retributive justice might demand like treatment, rehabilitation is the goal sought. The eye-for-an-eye philosophy increases antagonism and resentment. Justice might be tempered with understanding, and, yes, sympathetic assistance in training, educating, discipline, and constructive programs leading to rehabilitation. No sympathy whatsoever, however, should be wasted on the prisoner who whines that he was and is not being fairly treated and who seeks unearned sympathy simply because he is incarcerated in prison.

Very often, prison personnel find opportunities to assist inmates by suggesting activities which are beneficial, constructive, and time-consuming, thereby eliminating time otherwise spent in aggressions, self-pity, plottings, and senseless waste of time.

Sublimation of qualities and diversion into desirable channels can be helpful. The drive for personal recognition can be diverted from aggressions into education and vocational training to meet that need. The sexual drive may be sublimated by education and an understanding of the human male body and its needs. Sex is a powerful drive and is a problem to prison officials; however, an understanding of the male body, its functions and needs, may do much toward solving this problem. As has been suggested to newly received inmates, the human body, if left to its own devices, will care for its essential sexual needs through occasional nocturnal emissions.

Prisoners generally tend to mellow with time, becoming less and less willing to take chances, embark upon adventurous escapades, and to place themselves in perilous predicaments. Younger prisoners are more prone to boisterous demonstrations, sometimes creating much havoc, injury, and destruction. Older prisoners are usually more cautious.

Nothing but time changes the chronological age of a person; however, the mental and emotional age of a person may be rapidly increased to maturity.

A program of education, vocational training, building of personal esteem, self-respect, self-confidence, and competence will do much to mature a person, thus enabling him successfully to adjust and compete in our modern society.

CONCLUSIONS

Criminals cannot be rehabilitated without a personal desire for rehabilitation and voluntary cooperation in working toward that end. Rehabilitation is possible and feasible with the proper use of the tools now available. Rehabilitative facilities and tools should be utilized to their fullest extent by all concerned in the process.

While firmness is necessary in dealing with prisoners, a prisoner should be treated as a dignified human being and never degraded or be made to feel that he is an inferior person. Self-respect should be fostered. As he is treated, so will he respond.

NOTES AND REFERENCES

1. The author is a recidivist with a long tenure in prison, currently serving a life sentence for murder which is aggravated by an habitual criminal adjudication. Born June 12, 1916, in Detroit, Michigan. Attended school in Michigan, majoring in music. Served two separate 3-year sentences in Arkansas for robbery, one 5-to-life sentence in another state for first degree robbery, and the current sentence, on which 10 years have already been served. His present whereabouts are not known.

SECTION IV

THE IMPLEMENTATION OF CORRECTIONAL THEORY

L OPEZ-REY divides the field of penology into four major areas: administrative, scientific, academic, and analytic penology. The first listed is assessed here. In his opinion, it is the impact of the administrative structure which accounts for the various forms of treatment being far less successful than is claimed. He regards the growth of aftercare facilities, the primary purpose of which is to counteract deplorable institutional conditions, as an expansion of the penological function. It is the writer's contention that as long as obsolete criminal justice and prison systems are maintained, constantly expanding aftercare systems will be required. While directed principally to the British penal system, his remarks, with little modification, are generally applicable. The author closes with identification of ten fundamental questions, the resolutions of which require a radical transformation; these are crucial, if criminal justice is to be done and proper institutional treatment is to prevail.

Perusal of the 1954 article by Nelson will reveal that the "social lag" portrayed is no less extant now than 16 years ago. The offender has been largely ignored in the development of theories and programs for the care of troubled people—the nature of his behavior so threatens and irritates society that it tends to deny him the treatment necessary to resolve his problems. Nelson challenges both the correctional worker and society to close the "gulf" between what we know about crime and the offender, and what is actually done to prevent crime and to rehabilitate the offender.

"Prison rehabilitation is difficult to achieve, however, because most prisons are not primarily organized for this task," is the position of Stratton. As does Lopez-Rey, he views the matter of organization as the primary barrier to effective treatment. He points out that in many states, programs of correction are subject to the vagaries of politics and that many so-called innovations in "treatment" are ". . . humanitarian reforms." These are desirable of themselves and defensible on the basis of humanitarian principles, but they are not treatment. "They do not destroy the psychological wall between inmates and staff." The institution staff needs to be viewed by the inmate as representatives of an agency interested in him as an individual and intent upon improving his life situation.

Hedblom's article analyzes the rift between custodially oriented and treatment-oriented segments of the institution. The negative image of the inmate held by custodial personnel could, from a psychological point of view, be considered an unconscious commitment; since the custodial staff spends the largest amount of time with the inmate, it is the most susceptible to corruption. This leaves open the possibility that maintaining a negative attitude is defensive in nature and correctible by proper training and education. In the absence of such education and training, this unconscious commitment may be held as, and remain, an administrative necessity. The subtle manner in which the custodial orientation stealthily permeates the treatment attitude, thus emasculating its intended impact, is supported by Hedblom's data.

Administrative Penology (England and Wales)

MANUEL LOPEZ-REY

Like criminology, penology may be approached from various points of view, each giving rise to a different kind of penology. Historically, each kind of penology reflects a range of interests and aims as well as the prevailing humanitarian trends and scientific theories; each of these elements plays a different and occasionally opposing role. Among the contemporary kinds of penology the following seem to be the most important: administrative penology, scientific penology, academic penology and analytical penology. These terms are explained in my study *Analytical Penology,* to be published shortly by the International Penal and Penitentiary Foundation. The present paper will deal only with administrative penology. This is applied penology and as

NOTE: Reprinted from *British Journal of Criminology,* 5:4-35, 1965.

such represents the different penological systems in force in the different countries. Its main characteristics are that it is a governmental policy and that institutional treatment is still its predominant feature. Usually it is regarded as a progressive penology although, as will be seen later, the progress is more apparent than real. Despite the claims made, it still operates far too much according to the traditional trilogy—custody, security and control. This type of penology is mostly, if not exclusively, administratively conceived and organized and is the continuation of another administratively conceived function, the administration of justice. Consequently their respective servants, whatever their professional qualifications, are mostly administratively minded. As an administrative activity in each country, administrative or governmental penology is based on a system. This emerges little by little from the sediment left by successive policies and programs until it becomes by itself something deeply rooted, powerful, demanding and occasionally untouchable. Therefore the conception of penology as a social function, although often asserted, has not as yet entered deep enough into the structure of administrative penology—whatever is said to the contrary—in most of the existing prison administrations. The opposing force comes mostly from the system, in turn reinforced by a wider system of which the administration of criminal justice forms part. The result is that unless both systems are fundamentally changed, the improvements introduced do not modify them essentially.

The powerful impact of administrative penology explains why medicopsychological services, group therapy, or counseling and other forms of treatment are far less successful than is claimed. In actual fact, very often they are no more than "patch" remedies. It is the perdurability of the old system that more than anything else explains the continuous expanding, if not inflation, of the penological function. A typical case is that of the expanding aftercare policies, at present so deeply rooted that it would be regarded as penological heresy to say anything against them. However, the truth is that the origin of aftercare is to be found in the existence of past deplorable prison systems and that its continuation and expansion are confirmation that, if not deplorable, the present systems are in most cases fundamentally no more than the old systems artificially rejuvenated. Otherwise, an adequate administrative penology, instead of increasing aftercare activities, would have reduced them considerably. Another case of penological inflation is offered by group therapy or counseling. Unquestionably group therapy is a good method, especially if applied in better environments than those prevailing in the majority of walled prisons (incidentally there is no reason why it should not be used in open institutions as widely as in the closed ones), and therefore its use should be expanded. But it is another thing to advocate that as part of a penological service the prisoner's family should be submitted to group therapy.[1] More often than not, this penological inflation, like any other inflation, is an index of the failure of administrative penology to solve its fundamental problems. It would be unfair, however, to deny that administrative penology has achieved some success, but it would be no less unfair, particularly with respect to prisoners, to maintain that this success reflects the solution of the fundamental penological problems. This paper will deal with institutional treatment only, the reason being that it is in this form of treatment that the system is most firmly rooted. What follows is an example of the permanence of the traditional institutional system.

The Directory of State and Federal Institutions of the United States, Canada, England, and Scotland[2] enumerates, for England and Wales, 72 prisons with a total capacity of 21,263. No indication is given of the year of opening or average population. According to the Report of the Commissioners of Prisons for 1962, the number of prisons classified as local, special, central, regional, and corrective is 78, including the Grendon Psychiatric Centre recently opened. The discrepancy is due to the fact that in the Report, some of the institutions appear in more than one category. Out of a total of ten institutions, nine have a normal capacity ranging between 500 and 1,000, and only one—Wandsworth —has a capacity over 1,000. This picture is, however, greatly modified by the overcrowding or above-capacity condition of most of the local prisons in which the majority of the prison population is kept. Thus, out of 43 local prisons, no less than 27 were above capacity or seriously overcrowded in 1962. Among the latter and referring only to daily averages, the following examples may be cited:[3]

	Ordinary Accommodation	Daily Average Population
Birmingham	420	811
Bristol	269	447
Durham	665	1,019
Exeter	401	506
Leeds	559	998
Liverpool	830	1,393
Manchester	984	1,569
Pentonville	954	1,361
Wandsworth	1,123	1,606
Wormwood Scrubs	664	713

With some fluctuations, the prison population in England and Wales has been steadily increasing for a number of years. At the end of 1961, it was over 30,000, and at the end of 1962, slightly less than 31,700.

Among the different factors determining prison population, three seem to play a prominent role: (a) fundamental changes in patterns of life, especially when the materialistic aspect is unduly stressed, as frequently happens in welfare-state societies, (b) increase of the general population, particularly of young age groups, and (c) inadequate criminal justice machinery. All three have been operating in England for several decades.

At the end of 1961, over 8,000 men were "accommodated," three in a cell. Actually, this unsatisfactory situation is not new; it has been mentioned in Reports in the past and Sir Lionel Fox referred specifically to the overcrowding in local prisons as long as 12 years ago.[4] These prisons have a daily average of 18,130 (60.4% of the total prison population), of which 44.1 percent are put in groups of three in a cell. This means that 26.6 percent of the total prison population are "accommodated" in this way.

According to the 1962 Report: "Despite some increase in accommodation provided by the opening or development of new establishments, overcrowding has persisted in the local prisons and its attendant evils, so often described in previous reports, have again hampered attempts to establish a longer working week and modern training techniques." In spite of the hopes expressed, the statement reflects a situation that seriously disrupts all aspects of the treatment of prisoners, and that cannot be solved by the construction of new prisons.

When compared with American overcrowding, the English seems to be less serious, but figures do not tell the whole story, since other material conditions have also to be considered. In this respect, anyone with some experience of English prisons knows that, generally speaking, their material conditions including food, clothing, and bedding are below the corresponding ones in most North American, many European, and even some Latin American prisons. As for sanitary conditions, as a rule, the English cell is still in the chamber-pot era with the daily "slopping-out" parade as one of the first duties; supervising responsibilities of inmates and officers respectively is still a prominent feature of English prison life. It is in these poor sanitary conditions that three men are "accommodated" in a single cell in which they spend not less than 10 or 12 hours together every day with three chamber-pots or a single bucket. This situation does not conform with rule 12 of the United Nations Standard Minimum Rules, which states: "The sanitary installations shall be adequate to enable every prisoner to comply with the needs of nature when necessary and in a clean and decent manner." The fact that in each block, usually on the ground floor, better sanitary facilities are available, is not a satisfactory solution. This is confirmed by what Sir Lionel Fox so aptly said some time ago:

> In accordance with the Rules every cell is fitted with a bell and outside indicator so that the duty officer may be summoned in case of need. At the times when prisoners are locked up there is a minimum of staff on duty, and after 10 p.m. only one with a cell-key; it may be inferred that, particularly in large prisons where several flights of steps may have to be climbed and considerable lengths of stone landing traversed to reach a distant cell, the prisoners come to understand that the unnecessary ringing of bells is unwelcome.[5]

This traditional sanitary practice is still a feature of newly constructed prisons. Thus Everthorpe Hall Prison, built in 1958 and the first to have been built since 1910, lacks individual sanitary facilities other than the chamber-pot.[6] The reasons advanced for maintaining this primitive system were also traditional: one, that better facilities were too expensive, and another, that prisoners would cause constant stoppages as they did in Pentonville in 1842. As regards the former, of a total cost of 600,000 pounds the wall of the prison apparently cost no less than 100,000 pounds and this, ironically enough, has become an anachronism, since Everthorpe has always been used as a borstal rather than as a security prison.[7] In any case, the result is a useless wall and no adequate sanitary facilities. As regards the second type of reasoning, it is rather surprising that after well over a century it is assumed that the prisoners of a well-developed and affluent society will behave more disgracefully than their counterparts in some less developed and poorer societies where individual modern sanitary facilities are becoming the rule.[8]

In order to solve the overcrowding problem—which is different from that of reducing the prison population—the government has embarked on a large construction plan, the specific data of which are not easy to find.[9] According to the data available, it seems that the main purpose of the plan is to provide accommodation. The envisaged cost is about 25 million pounds, and when completed in 1967 no less than 160 penal institutions (old, new and remodelled) will be available. The hope is that the halcyon days when no cell contained more than one prisoner may one day return.[10] Assuming that nothing intervenes to increase the average annual growth of 1,525 inmates since 1956, in 1967, accommodation for well over 37,000 will be required. If the proportion 5 to 1 between prisoners and staff is kept, no less than 7,400 officers, against 6,329 on December 31, 1962, will be needed, as well as accommodation for them, salaries, allowances, traveling and removal expenses, and eventually superannuation.

Although well-intentioned, policies of accommodation without at the same time substantially altering the existing prison system will not yield the expected results. Experience shows that overcrowding is more the sequel of obsolete prison and criminal justice systems than of a lack of space. As long as these systems remain untouched, the situation will be fundamentally the same. The fact that since 1948 several Criminal Justice Administration Acts have been adopted has not essentially altered the

obsolete structure and functioning of criminal justice. As for prison matters, the reforms introduced have not fundamentally
changed a no-less-obsolete prison system. In this respect, it should
be noted that the series of official reports produced by committees
and councils in charge of finding solutions have never gone beyond the stage of suggesting arrangements within existing situations or systems.[11] The result is that although some progress has
been made, it is mostly peripheral.

The following significant examples are given in support of the
above statements.

1. The classification of penal institutions has only a formalistic
administrative character, since a local prison may be used as a
regional prison, a corrective training prison, a borstal, or a central
prison, while the latter may in turn function as a local or regional prison, as a borstal, or as a corrective training prison. The
usefulness of this type of multipurpose institution is dubious in
view of the aims of contemporary penal treatment. In the writer's
opinion, the multipurpose institution should be abolished. Among
other disadvantages, it gradually reduces the availability of open
spaces which are sought for a variety of mushrooming annexes
and services and because quite often the most severe form of
treatment eventually pervades the others, particularly when shortage of staff requires that some of them work alternatively in different sections. Typical examples of this type are Brixton, Hollo-
way, and Wormwood Scrubs. It is difficult to assess to what extent custody, security, and control chores are increased, as well
as routine work, and at the same time other activities are jeop-
ardized. In any case, the shortcomings from an effective treatment
point of view, as well as for the organization of work, are obvious.

2. The cell-block system is the type around which the English
prison system still revolves. The latest example is Blundeston
where the existence of small dormitories is overshadowed by four
four-story cell blocks with the traditional system of sanitary facilities on the ground floor. As practiced in Anglo-Saxon countries, the
cell-block system is an unhappy vestige of the Pennsylvania and
Auburn systems, although in different degrees both systems are
based on abstract puritanical conceptions of reformation and
not on a human appraisal of the offender.[12] As long as men are

forced to spend more than a third of their time in cells, their treatment, working conditions, attitudes, discipline, cleanliness, etc., are seriously handicapped while custodial routines inevitably expand. Furthermore, by its own physical characteristics, even if modernized, the cellular system constitutes a serious handicap for a better understanding between prisoners and staff. It is no wonder that English prisoners welcome the three-in-a-cell system in spite of its inconveniences. What is needed is the small two-story building for a maximum of 20 or 30 inmates with several dormitories and only two or three cells. Contrary to widespread opinion, this system is cheaper than the present one, among other things because it presupposes that no more than 30 percent of convicts need to be sent to closed institutions. Actually the five- to eight-bed dormitory system acts in many respects as a rudimentary group therapy treatment and very probably would reduce the need for this form of treatment—so acute in the American and British systems in which the corroding cellular system prevails. In any case, in dealing with human problems, it should be kept in mind that human capital is far more important than economic capital curiously so wasted under pretenses of economy by perpetuating the cell-block system.

3. There is a gradual reduction of the size of the cells under the assertion that they are used for sleeping purposes only.[13] Anyone familiar with prison life and regulations knows that this kind of reasoning is merely an expression of wishful thinking, inasmuch as in the security prisons, which still constitute the majority in England and Wales as elsewhere, prisoners spend half their time in the cells. The practice of providing cubicles for sleeping purposes only wrongly assumes that as soon as the prisoner gets into his cell he will automatically lie down and fall asleep. But prisoners as human beings require a certain amount of space of their own and not only for sleeping. The tragedy is that the shrunken cell is inevitably used to "accommodate" three prisoners because, by sticking to obsolete policies, the administration is seldom able to solve periodic or chronic overcrowding. This kind of "treatment," that by itself handicaps any rehabilitation process, makes necessary other forms of medicopsychological treatment which would be less necessary if the accommoda-

tion provided were motivated a little more by penological considerations and a little less by financial reasons.

4. In England and Wales, as in the United States, the majority of prisoners (about 90%) are kept in closed institutions. This explains why, while the latter are more often than not chronically overcrowded, the open institutions are quite below capacity. In justification of the obsolete policy, it is usually said that the selection of prisoners for open institutions is a difficult task and that there are limitations in the use of these institutions. But little progress can be made unless difficulties are overcome, and in any case barely 10 percent of English prisoners are sent to open institutions, while Finland, a far less affluent society, is keeping 41 percent of her prison population in open institutions.[14] The impression is gained that in England and Wales, open institutions are used more as the last stage in a progressive system than as the institution to which prisoners are sent directly. Although this "terminal" use is accepted by the United Nations recommendations on open institutions—a term much preferable to that of semi-secure institution at present current in official English terminology—the same recommendations are in favor of their direct use.

5. An excessive number of offenders are sent to prison for short periods of time. In 1961, slightly over 67 percent of all prisoners were sentenced to six months or less. This reflects a bad criminal policy for which the prison administration is not responsible. The Second United Nations Congress held in London in 1960 recommended the gradual reduction of short-term imprisonment and invited governments to ensure the enactment of legislative measures to this effect, as well as to undertake scientific research so as to determine for what persons short-term imprisonment is unsuited. It is to be regretted that among the listed research projects undertaken by the competent House Office Research Unit, as well as by the Universities, none is devoted to this crucial question.[15]

6. Finally, the increase of prison population as well as the growing routine functions of custody, security and control are partly caused by the excessive number of untried prisoners, many of whom are not convicted later or if so are not sent to prison.

In 1961, the total number was 33,545, of which 14,213 or 42.4 percent were not sent to prison on conviction. Here again, the situation is the direct consequence of a bad criminal judicial policy, of which the prison administration is one of the victims. The situation improved slightly in the second half of 1962, apparently as a result of the application of certain provisions of the Criminal Justice Administration Act, 1962. The reduction—about 300 —is undoubtedly welcome but unless it reaches higher figures, the situation will remain practically unaltered.

The problem of prison labor in England and Wales remains unsolved, as in the United States and in the majority of countries. The guarded style of current reports confirms this unsatisfactory situation, which is still approached as a purely administrative problem and not as one that can only be solved by considering prison labor as part of free labor and of the national economy. In this respect, the conclusions of the United Nations London Congress already mentioned are unequivocal. The administration approach has been maintained in the report *Work for Prisoners* and seems to be supported, at least indirectly, by the Commissioners of Prisons in the reports for 1961 and 1962. As an explanation for not going into the problem of the remuneration of prison labor as discussed by the United Nations London Congress, the Advisory Council on the Employment of Prisoners, in the above-mentioned report, says that the question of whether prisoners should be paid normal wages raises wide penological and social issues which it would take a long time to study thoroughly. It further says:

> Since our advice on prisoners' earnings was needed urgently, we decided that the most valuable work that we could undertake in the circumstances was to consider what changes, if any, ought to be made in prisoners' earnings without, at this stage, going into the possibility of a fundamental alteration in the scale of earnings.

The foregoing reflects the traditional policy of avoiding issues and radical changes and recommending instead rearrangements that leave the problem intact. After the new scheme of earnings in 1959, a further one was adopted in 1962; its so-far-satisfactory results will be short-lived, since social problems cannot be solved by such arrangements. Prison labor must be regarded as a social problem because of the number of persons affected, who are not only the prisoners, and the political, social, and economic aspects it raises.

Following the traditional pattern, the Advisory Council recommended that the earnings should be regarded as "pocket money," that an average prisoner working reasonably well should earn not less than five shillings a week, and that the scale of three to ten shillings would allow a considerable number of prisoners to earn about eight shillings a week. Pursuing this unrealistic approach, the Advisory Council maintains that these earnings will provide a powerful incentive to prisoners to do the best they are capable of and enable them to buy a modest quantity of such goods as are available to them and to make small savings towards such things as Christmas presents for their families (paragraph 86). Finally, after declaring themselves satisfied that as pocket money ten shillings a week is an adequate maximum, the Council states that while some prisoners would no doubt put a higher amount to good use, for example, by saving part of it for discharge or by remitting money to their families, many prisoners would merely dissipate it (paragraph 100).

Can anyone seriously believe that prison work and the so-called prison industries may be organized on such flimsy economic and psychological foundations? Against the unrealistic advice of the Advisory Council, another official report says: "We think it undesirable that a man should leave the prison gates to face the challenge of a new life in freedom, and all the problems of resettlement, with nothing but a few shillings calculated to provide his bare subsistence on the journey home."[16]

In 1951, the average amount earned by a prisoner was about three shillings a week—an exceptional worker might earn four shillings, but more would be rare.[17] In 1962 and 1963, it was just as rare for a prisoner to make more than six or seven shillings a week. Even assuming that all prisoners able to work make eight or ten shillings, the problem remains unsolved. The fact is that it has taken no less than twelve years to increase the average by two shillings—up to five shillings a week. At this rate it would take about ninety years before they can earn 1 pound a week.

The historian of prison reforms will discover that in England

and Wales the determining force behind the periodic small increases in earnings is not rehabilitation, the reduction of aftercare responsibilities or any other lofty aim but simply the price of tobacco. Anyone familiar with British prisons is amazed at the important role that tobacco plays in the daily life of prisoners and indirectly in the running of the prisons. The Advisory Council admits the tobacco motivation; when referring to the 1959 increase it says: "The increase in the minimum rate was generally welcomed, apparently by both prison staff and prisoners, and the only criticism we can make here is that it seems to have been over due at the time and has not been overtaken by the increase in the price of tobacco following the 1960 Finance Act" (paragraph 83).

With respect to other fundamental aspects of prison labor the following table is significant:

	1949		1961		1962	
Daily average population	20,043		29,025		31,063	
Available for employment	16,932		26,218		27,890	
Available for Employment						
Manufactures	10,158	(59.9%)	12,500	(47.7%)	13,085	(46.9%)
Outside work	996	(5.8%)	600	(2.3%)	594	(2.1%)
Farms	538	(3.2%)	1,388	(5.2%)	1,455	(5.2%)
Works Department	1,622	(9.6%)	2,918	(11.1%)	3,100	(11.1%)
Domestic	3,618	(21.3%)	7,350	(28.04%)	8,177	(29.2%)
Vocational and industrial training	—		1,462	(5.6%)	1,479	(5.3%)
	16,932		26,218		27,890	

Although some progress has been made, this is offset by the recess in some areas. The fact that in 1962, 29.2 percent were used for domestic purposes as against 21.3 percent in 1949 is, from a penological point of view, a setback. No doubt the increase may be partly explained by the increase of the prison population, but more than anything it demonstrates the inability of the prison system, and more particularly of the State-use system, to cope with a situation which was certainly not new. This also explains the low percentages of men assigned to vocational and industrial training in 1961 and 1962; that in 1962 out of an increase of 1,672 men available for employment, only 17, or less than 1 percent, were given such training and only 566, or 33.8 percent, were employed in manufactures, while no less than 50.5 percent were used for domestic occupations (Appendix No. 5, 1962 Report).

The artificial character of prison labor is further demonstrated by the fact that in spite of continuous efforts, mailbag production and repair is still the main feature of all prison manufactures. In 1961, of 9,743 employed in this branch in one local prison, no less than 40.7 percent were occupied in this way; in 1962 the proportion was 41.2 percent. It is even more unsatisfactory that although some machines are used for this type of work, hand-sewing is still practiced because if only machines were used, some of the prisoners would have nothing to do. More recently, a new modality of work called metal recovery, which consists in cable stripping, engine dismantling, breaking down meters, etc., has been introduced. The expansion of this unskilled type of work has been recommended by the Advisory Council on the Employment of Prisoners because it requires very little training, little capital expenditure, and little workshop space. The Council added: "We should like to see recovery work substituted for all unnecessary hand-sewing of mailbags." Nevertheless, in 1962, 1,164 or 11.5 percent of the total inmates available for employment in local prisons were so occupied. If to mailbag sewing and metal recovery are added other unskilled occupations such as making brushes, mops, mats, heavy canvas work and wood chopping—leaving aside the dubious content of Miscellaneous with no less than 731—about 62 percent of the working force are used for low-skilled work. As for the other 38 percent, most of them do semiskilled work, of which tailoring, with 1,005, constitutes about 10 percent of the total. The number of printers in 1961 and 1962 was 51. The reason given for the low figure is that it takes time to train a printer. This is true, but it is hard to believe that in more than 10,000 prisoners, not one was already acquainted with the trade. Actually what such low figures show is the inability of the State-use system to provide skilled jobs. Finally, it is significant that only 1.2 percent and 1.3 percent of the 1961 and 1962 prison budgets respectively were allotted for all prisoners' earnings, including borstals and detention centers.

The foregoing shows that in spite of continuous efforts and

its excellent record for administration and organization, the English prison service is unable to improve prison labor conditions as long as the State-use system is applied. In spite of all improvements, this system is out of date and unable to satisfy contemporary, political, economic, and penological needs. The discriminatory attitude of Trade Unions against prisoners and prison labor should also be mentioned. Apparently they have not yet realized that everyone has a right to work, to favorable working conditions, to equal pay for equal work, and to just and favorable remuneration for himself and family—or that quite a number of prisoners are regular workers. Obviously prison labor raises certain difficulties, but these should not be construed as insurmountable obstacles. As already stated, prison labor is part of free labor and should be integrated with the national economy. Unfortunately, this discriminatory attitude is reinforced by that of a number of administrators who claim that the organization of prison labor as part of free labor would disrupt their well-established administrative systems with the introduction of new ones and that if deductions for food and clothing are to be made from proper prison labor remuneration, this would practically amount to the present system of gratuities which has fewer accounting complications. This reasoning, which I have frequently heard at international gatherings, shows the type of mentality still prevailing in many prison administrations.

The prison staff in England and Wales—with all its professional and in-service training—is compelled, by the force of circumstances created by an obsolete system, to perform almost exclusively custodial functions. Accordingly, prison regulations point far more to this type of function than to those more in accordance with the social character assigned to prison personnel by the United Nations Standard Minimum Rules. The more obvious results of the existing conditions are widespread frustration, lack of understanding, greater antagonism between prisoners and staff and an excessive number of cases of indiscipline. In spite of these unfavorable circumstances, it is to be noted that handcuffs and anklestraps were never used in 1961 and only once in 1962, although in both years some serious disturbances took place.[18]

The prevalence of custody, security, and control functions as well as the lack of work and other serious shortcomings led the Prison Officers' Association to submit a memorandum to the Home Office in November, 1963, in which, among other things, it is said that members of the prison service

> . . . should play a responsible part in what should be the main aim of any penal system, the rehabilitation of the prisoner. Today, however, people who join the service full of high ideals of doing something to help others soon become disillusioned and even bitter and cynical. . . . The day's chore of unlocking the men and locking them up again differs very little from the work of the turnkey of the last century, and the present administration of the service does nothing to help eradicate the feeling of frustration which pervades the working life of the prison officer.

After referring to prison work as something usually dull and unimaginative lasting not more than 22 hours a week, it continues . . . "After serving a sentence under these conditions a man's senses are dulled and he leaves prison knowing only one thing —how to live in a prison." Even if the situation is overstressed in some respects, there is little doubt that the memorandum reflects the functioning of an inadequate prison system and in any case the frustration of the staff.

Although it has a brilliant tradition, the present organization of aftercare in England and Wales is quite unable to cope with contemporary requirements. If any doubt were left about this, the data included in the last report on the matter would certainly dispel it.[19]

The staffing of prisoners' aid societies and their potential caseloads clearly show that these societies—supported almost exclusively by public funds—constitute a penological pretense. As examples for 1962, the following will suffice: Royal London Society, which is by far the best, staffed with a potential case load of 11,000, had six whole-time and two part-time aftercare officers. Others, with potential caseloads ranging from 3,000 to well over 5,000, had a maximum of three or four whole- and part-time officers. As for social workers appointed by the National Association of Discharged Prisoners' Aid Societies, suffice it to say that in prisons with an average daily population of well over 1,000, the maximum available is three. In other words, for a total daily average prison population of over 30,000, including borstals and detention centers, the number of social workers is 64. According to existing regulations, the number of persons in 1962 potentially to be under compulsory or voluntary aftercare was approximately 12,400 and 54,000 respectively. Obviously the latter figure is the maximum and not the actual number of persons who wished to be helped by aftercare services. As for compulsory aftercare, the figure does not necessarily mean that all persons received effective assistance. If these figures are taken together with those referring to the availability of ways and means, including financial means, the conclusion is that the situation is, to say the least, far below a satisfactory level. This is not surprising, inasmuch as aftercare always reflects the condition of the prison system it is intended to supplement.

In April, 1961, the Advisory Council on the Treatment of Offenders was asked to review the situation and consider whether any changes were necessary or desirable and to make recommendations. The report submitted, although interesting in some respects, leaves the question of aftercare unsolved. The arrangements proposed are of dubious practical value. The dissenters' memorandum attached to the report is, with good reason, very critical of the vague and somewhat inorganic recommendations made. According to the dissenters,

> The proposed scheme gives no worthwhile center of direction at any level. A false step at this stage would be difficult to retrieve. But it would be equally disastrous if the first step were so feeble and faltering that it achieved no more than half measures and allowed further procrastination. This is a lesson of the Maxwell Report. Interest and enthusiasm would wither and hopes of real advance would recede.
>
> There has been enough tampering with after-care over the past fifty years. Next to the local prisons it is the weakest link in our system for dealing with offenders. What is needed now is a bolder vision—and a scheme with some guts in it. Then we could be content to proceed by stages.

If credence is to be given to the information published on the discussions on the matter in the House of Lords in December, 1963, the impression gained is that the general consensus was that the system of voluntary societies was rapidly running down and that the State should take the responsibility for the provision of aftercare. On the other hand, most of the interventions made, particularly those in favor of extending aftercare services as much as possible, also give the impression that there was some confusion about the implications of such an extension. An extremely good point was made, however, when it was said that the most remarkable thing about the report was a major omission; the Council appeared to think that the condition of the prisons had nothing whatever to do with aftercare.

The growing trend for an expanding aftercare service is determined by (a) a prevailing obsolete criminal justice system that still sends all but a minority of offenders to closed prisons, (b) a no less obsolete prison system that, although rejuvenated more or less scientifically, is unable to provide adequate treatment and appropriate material living and working conditions, and (c) the widespread belief that all prisoners must undergo a process of rehabilitation of which aftercare is an essential part.

It is not possible to examine in detail each of these points here. Suffice it to say that as long as obsolete criminal justice and prison systems are maintained, constantly expanding aftercare will be required because of the growing number of prisoners and the disintegrating impact of existing living, working, and treatment conditions in the majority of institutions. As for rehabilitation, as previously stated, not all prisoners need to undergo the process through individual or special forms of treatment, and even less are all prisoners in need of aftercare. What is required is both a decent penal system according to which a minor part of offenders are sent to maximum security institutions and far better living and working conditions for all prisoners. With respect to the distinction between voluntary and compulsory aftercare set up a priori by law according to the age of offenders, their different categories, the type of institution, etc., this system is penologically wrong as well as expensive—in fact it is not feasible, as experience has already demonstrated.[20] Certainly it is against the principle of individualization which demands that every form of treatment be determined by the individual circumstances of each case and not by the fact of being part of a group or category according to statutory regulations as is the case nowadays. Another important aspect is that as far as possible, aftercare should make use of the already existing services of assistance, employment, health, etc. What is here suggested is to reduce to a minimum the differences of treatment between nonoffenders and ex-offenders for social-psychological as well as financial reasons. Usually, aftercare services stress the distinction, and this is resisted by ex-prisoners, particularly after the unsatisfactory living, working, and treatment conditions in the prisons. Briefly, instead of periodically enlarging aftercare, mostly because of erroneous ideas about treatment, rehabilitation, and penal function, all this reinforced by sentimental attitudes, it should be restricted to individual cases. Only in this way will the service become effective. In any case, it is illusory to imagine that compulsory treatment can be provided automatically to almost 65,000 ex-prisoners every year. Instead of trying to do this, the money should be used to improve prison labor remuneration. Prisoners should be trained in constructive work and be decently paid so that they are not always in need of assistance. A good penal system reduces aftercare to a minimum.

FINAL REMARKS

The foregoing shows that in one of the most highly developed countries, the fundamental prison problems are unsolved and that the old features of custody, unsatisfactory living conditions, and widespread idleness are as strong today as they were a hundred years ago. Although rejuvenated, the prison system in operation is still essentially of the nineteenth century and reflects a criminal justice mostly of the same period.

The differences between England and Wales and some less-developed countries are, *mutatis mutandis*, only of degree. Nevertheless, while in the latter there is a correspondence between general low standards of living and prison conditions, in the former prison conditions are far below the standard of living. By prison conditions, I understand those affecting the most important aspects of the prisoners' lives, i.e. living and working as well as treatment. Although special services and programs as well as recreation facilities are necessary within reasonable limits, their multiplication has unfortunately created the impression that prisoners, if not pampered, are better treated than nonoffenders. To the experienced observer, this is not so, since in many cases these services merely hide the failure to solve the main problems. In any case, to be successful, special services and programs, including recreation, have to operate within the framework of satisfactory treatment services and programs, which are scarce at present.[31]

The following are the fundamental questions:

1. The necessity of reducing to a minimum the number of persons sent to prison to await trial.
2. The use of short-term imprisonment only in exceptional cases.
3. The integration of prison labor with free labor and the national economy.
4. The organization of adequate general treatment services and programs.
5. The reduction to a minimum of the closed cellular prison and the increase of small- and medium-sized open and semi-open institutions.
6. The reinforcement of the prisoner's relations with his family and facilities for the satisfaction of normal sexual needs.
7. Better prerelease preparation and better and greater use of parole.
8. The treatment of prisoners regarded as part of the criminal judicial function; the present organization and functions of the prison administration reduced to a minimum as a separate service.
9. The transformation of the prison personnel into a service in which administrative and custodial functions are reduced to a minimum and social functions increased to a maximum.
10. The organization of adequate statistics on institutional treatment.

The time for "administering" criminal justice and institutional treatment is over. A radical transformation is required if criminal justice is to be done and proper institutional treatment to be given. Certainly the latter will never be achieved by penological intellectual pursuits so widespread nowadays. Although they may satisfy the participants of national and international gatherings, they cannot hide one of the most outstanding contemporary failures: that of the institutional treatment of offenders.

NOTES AND REFERENCES

1. See Fenton, Norman: *The Prisoner's Family* (A Study of Family Counselling in an Adult Correctional System). New York, The American Correctional Association, 1959.
2. Compiled by The American Correctional Association, New York, 1963.
3. Unless otherwise specified, the data are taken from the following sources: *Reports of the Commissioners of Prisons for the years 1961 and 1962,* H.M.S.O.; the *Directory* referred to in note No. 2 above; *Crime in the Sixties* by Beryl Cooper and Garth Nicholas, 1963; and occasionally from *Criminal Statistics, England and Wales,* 1960, 1961 and 1962, H.M.S.O., London.
4. See his excellent book *The English Prison and Borstal Systems,* London, 1952, p. 104.
5. See *Crime in the Sixties,* p. 106.
6. The U.S. Bureau of Prisons in *Recent Prison Construction 1950-1960* refers to this lack of facilities by saying that Everthorpe cell blocks do not contain the expensive individual plumbing characteristics of American prisons (p. 86).
7. This expensive policy of building solid walls has been corrected in Blundeston, where only a fence has been erected.
8. With respect to Everthorpe, the Ministry of Works insisted that the sanitary facilities provided on the ground floor were ample. See its note issued as a comment on the interesting paper "The First New Prison—But Is It New Enough?" written anonymously and published in *The Architects' Journal,* December, 1958. A similar system as far as sanitary facilities are concerned has been followed in Blundeston. Regarding sanitary and other conditions in English prisons, recent books written by ex-prisoners are illuminating. For a really scientific study of the conditions prevailing in Pentonville, see "The Experience of Imprisonment" by Terence and Pauline Morris, in *The British Journal of Criminology,* April 1962.
9. See "The Building Programme," chapter IV of *Penal Practice in*

a Changing Society, H.M.S.O., 1959; the respective paragraphs of the 1961 and 1962 Reports; *Crime in the Sixties* already cited; the letter with annexes of October 28, 1963, sent to the Home Secretary by The Howard League for Penal Reform, and statements made at the openings of new institutions.

10. See 1962 Report, p. 12.

11. Among others the cases of the Report of the *Interdepartmental Committee on the Business of the Criminal Courts,* and *Work for Prisoners,* both published in 1961, and *The Organization of After-Care,* 1963, are typical. In contrast, the papers prepared by the Home Office are remarkable for their directness and high quality. See especially *Penal Practice in a Changing Society* and *Murder,* published in 1959 and 1961 respectively.

12. Montesinos always opposed the Philadelphia and Auburn systems as contrary to the reinforcement of human will—the pivot on which, according to him, reformation must be based. The main tenets of his system were: (a) varied and constructive prison labor available all the year round and remunerated, (b) reduction to a minimum of the system of punishment and rewards; the greatest of the latter was to become foreman of a workshop, and (c) the principle that the prison receives only the man but not the crime, which is left outside. (La prisión solo recibe al hombre, el delito queda fuera.)

13. In 1842 at Pentonville, the size adopted was 13 ft × 7 ft × 9 ft high, giving 819 cubic feet of air space. At the time, labor was cellular. Later, the size was reduced to 10 ft × 7 ft × 9 ft high, giving only 630 cubic feet of air space. The reason given was that work was done outside the cells, but the truth was that work was not always available and quite a number of prisoners were kept in overcrowded cells. When Everthorpe was constructed as a security prison, the same poor prison labor conditions were prevailing; nevertheless under the same pretense, the size of the cells was further reduced to 7 ft long × 3 ft 6 in wide and 7 ft high. The fact that Everthorpe was and still is used as a borstal does not alter the conclusion that the reduction was actually determined by economy reasons.

14. See Soine, K. V.: *Open Institutions in Finland,* included in the volume of studies to be published by the International Penal and Penitentiary Foundation in memory of Sir Lionel Fox.

15. See corresponding appendixes in 1961 and 1962 reports. However, mention should be made of the study, *The Short-Term Prisoner,* 1963, by Dr. R. G. Andry, financed by the Home Office and the Nuffield Foundation and directed by Dr. H. Mannheim under the auspices of the London School of Economics and Political Science.

16. See *The Organization of After-Care* already cited, paragraph 186, in which it is recommended that "national assistance, where it is due, should be paid to the offender before he is discharged, so that when he leaves prison he has sufficient money to meet immediate contingencies." Needless to say, this remedy still leaves untouched the problem of prison labor.

17. See Fox, Sir Lionel: *op. cit.,* p. 199.

18. It should also be noted that while in other countries guards with little or no training decide by themselves on the application of methods of restraint, in England and Wales regulations require that they be applied by direction of the Medical Officer or with his concurrence.

19. See report on aftercare cited in footnote 16.

20. The tendency to extend compulsory aftercare according to statutory categories was already evident in the report of the Advisory Council on the Treatment of Offenders *The After-Care and Supervision of Discharged Prisoners,* H.M.S.O., London, 1958.

21. These services and programs can hardly be organized where the cellular system prevails. This is not only the case in England and Wales but also in Belgium where the "cellular inheritance" from the nineteenth century is extremely heavy, and in Canada, France, Italy, Germany, the United States, etc.

The Gulf Between Theory and Practice in Corrections

ELMER K. NELSON, JR.

Spokesmen for the correctional field have long urged public acceptance of rehabilitation as a substitute for punishment in dealing with the offender. It is said that society may obtain improved answers to old problems by shifting the focus of remedial efforts from the crime to the criminal.

NOTE: Reprinted from *Federal Probation,* 18 (3) :48-50, 1954.

PUBLIC INTEREST IN ALTERNATIVES FOR PUNISHMENT

Today, for numerous reasons, public interest has become alive to the commonly advocated alternatives for punishment. The popular press has sensed this new concern and published a significant volume of material concerning prison riots, criminal careers, and varied correctional programs. We have entered the impatiently awaited era in which rehabilitative approaches will be allowed increasingly to demonstrate their claimed superiority over coercive methods. For this reason, it is important that we ask a self-searching and seemingly heretical question, namely: Has there evolved within corrections a sound and consistent body of principles by which to guide the forthcoming development of programs for the rehabilitation of the offender? Few workers in the field would be so naive as to answer with an unqualified affirmative. Despite our insistent clamor for a "positive approach," we have yet to achieve a working definition of the term.

BRINGING THEORY AND PRACTICE TOGETHER

The major assumption of correctional treatment possesses much validity, but we have only begun the hard task of creating interaction between theory and practice so that each is modified freely and constructively by the other. The literature and teaching of corrections suffer from a tendency to deal with ultimate objectives rather than the means by which these ends may be attained. Correctional administrators, on the other hand, tend to become cautious individuals—necessarily more mindful of avoiding the explosion of today than embracing the new horizon of tomorrow. The penal disturbances of recent times have clearly indicated the abortive nature of treatment efforts which are not soundly integrated with custodial functions.

What are the main obstacles to more satisfactory merger of theory and practice in corrections? This problem could be discussed extensively. Separate articles could be written about the stale penal traditions which create a social lag, the forces which interfere with communication between the various kinds of workers who deal with the offender, and the difficulties involved in orienting professional workers to settings in which the use of authority is a basic and necessary element.

THERAPEUTIC PROGRAM IN
AN AUTHORITARIAN SETTING

To the writer, however, one factor seems more fundamental and all-inclusive than any other in accounting for our difficulties in implementing correctional theories with workable programs. This factor is the absence of a consistent approach to the offender, an approach in which the function of controlling dissocial behavior is combined harmoniously with the task of "treating" the individual who manifests such behavior.

There continues to be great confusion and indecision regarding the adaption of therapeutic programs to authoritative settings. We have identified the damaging use of authority as a prime factor in the causation of delinquency, and yet many correctional workers are in an anomalous position of repeating the very misuses of power which originally contributed to the maladjustment of offenders under their supervision. The modern prison is organized about a dichotomy of custody and treatment in which there is only minimal awareness of the ways in which custody may be a part of treatment and treatment a part of custody. Correctional workers tend to gravitate toward one of two extremes in their attitudes toward the offender—a punitive extreme and a permissive extreme. The resulting use of authority may be more closely geared to the emotional involvements of the worker than the treatment needs of the offender.

These differences of approach frequently lead correctional staffs to work at cross purposes with each other. The rigidly strict guard may become harsh in dealing with an inmate whom he considered to have been pampered by the institutional social worker. A probation officer, feeling that the judge has been unduly severe in a given case, may lend subtle support to the probationer in nourishing resentment against constituted authority. The problems of the delinquent must surely be reinforced by these confused uses of authority which are not helpfully related to his need for treatment and therefore strengthen his inner conviction that society is insensitive to his problems and basically unreasonable in its expectation of him.

HELPFUL USE OF AUTHORITY

It is true that the effective use of authority is recognized as part of correctional treatment in a growing number of programs to-day, but in the best of these there remains a lack of clarity on how to incorporate this principle into activities in which the of-fender is vitally involved. For example, how do we determine whether a disciplinary action directed at an inmate is punitive (a detrimental use of authority) or firm (a helpful use of au-thority)? Does the answer to this question lie in the degree of severity of the action, the emotional state of the authority who imposes it, or the interpretation of the individual who re-ceives it?

We may obtain more definitive answers to such problems only through a partnership between theory and practice in which each gains ready access to the insights discovered by the other, and a process of cross-fertilization of ideas constantly enriches our understanding. This is the medium through which we eventual-ly may overcome our tendency to view the offender from a suc-cession of narrow and specialized perspectives—a police view, a legal view, a custodial view, a treatment view. We cannot hope to convey a coherent conception of the correctional process to the public until some common denominator is found for these diver-gent approaches to the offender.

NEED FOR UNIFIED CORRECTIONAL FIELD

Perhaps these inconsistencies will be resolved in the end by the recognition of corrections as a legitimate field in its own right, an entity which is more than the sum total of the disciplines and occupations which constitute its working parts. But the concept of a unified correctional field appears more than mildly objec-tionable to many who have a vested interest in handling the of-fender in a segmented fashion. The police officer feels threatened by any viewpoint which presents the delinquent as other than an enemy of society. Most lawyers act in terms of the classical in-terpretation of crime, in which the offender is seen as a free moral agent who must pay a suitable penalty for his wrongs. Many social workers hold that corrections should be considered a phase of social welfare, governed by principles generic to that field and not justifying an autonomous existence of its own. The psychiatrist and psychologist are prone to believe that their task of dealing with human beings should not be affected significantly by the setting within which they work. Other specialists within the correctional field defend their separate domains with equally earnest zeal—the chaplain, the teacher, the librarian—all are chary about making a close identification with the field in which their techniques are applied.

It is characteristic of humans that they make a concerted effort and become less concerned with contradictory interests when faced with an urgent and important problem which affects their collective welfare. Wars and depressions serve to illustrate the operation of this principle in the sphere of political action. But we have been loath to grant that crime is a social affliction of sufficient scope and urgency to command a unified approach on the part of those immediately responsible for its prevention and control. Recent statistics which reveal a relentless increase in delinquency, particularly with youthful offenders, should divest us of any complacency previously held in this matter.

The criminal has been largely ignored in the development of theories and programs for the treatment of troubled people during the past half-century. The dissocial behavior which characterizes the delinquent has so threatened and irritated social groups that they have tended to deny the offending individual treatment for his underlying problems, a procedure somewhat akin to refusing medical care to one afflicted with an infectious disease.

THE CHALLENGE DEFINED

The challenge which faces the correctional field has become more and more sharply defined. The social scientists have formulated theories which provide substitutes for the punitive handling of offenders. The public exhibits a tentative and uneasy willingness for these ideas to be translated into action. The question is: Can correctional workers develop a strong sense of professional identity through which (as a result of collaboration) theory and practice may be reconciled with each other in more discriminating ways than prevail at the present time? This may best be accomplished by thinking and planning in terms of the total correctional problem rather than superficially isolated parts of it. In such a context, we may discover that custodial functions (which set limits on the activity of the delinquent) and treatment functions (which strengthen the individual for more successful activity) are mutually consistent aspects of the same process.

Prisoner Rehabilitation—Confluence or Conflict

JOHN STRATTON

Prisons are built to serve the functions of punishment, deterrence, removal, and rehabilitation. Historically, prisons have primarily focused upon the first three; only in recent decades has rehabilitation become a major concern.

In prison, men were expected to suffer for their misdeeds. As an instrument of punishment, the prison is a very effective device. It produces many subtle pains. Deprivation of freedom and of many pleasures that most of us take for granted cause a great deal of discomfort and psychological pain for the offender.

Prison is expected to deter individuals from breaking the law. Deterrence is thought to operate in two ways: (a) It operates upon the offender, the person exposed to imprisonment. On the basis of his experiences, he is thought to develop the notion that "crime does not pay." (b) Persons who have not broken the law are thought to be encouraged to stay honest by knowledge of the penalties others have paid for law violation.

The effectiveness of the prison as a source of deterrence is difficult to evaluate, but available evidence indicates that it is not highly effective. Punishment in general has not been proven by itself to be an effective deterrent. A partial explanation for this can be offered. Punishment, to be effective, needs to be both certain and swift. Imprisonment and the other types of punishment

NOTE: Reprinted from *The Correctional Psychologist*, 3 (2) :8-12, 1967.

imposed through our judicial systems are frequently neither swift nor certain.

The prison serves to remove individuals from society and it does this relatively effectively. We read only infrequently of men escaping from prisons. Most men who are placed in prison are seldom able to commit crimes against society while they are there. Occasionally they will commit crimes against fellow inmates, however.

A crucial point is that men are released from prison. Most men are not relegated to prison life permanently. The vast majority of men who are sentenced to prison return to society. Unless they have experienced changes in their attitudes and values, they present the same problem to society upon their release as when they were first sentenced. This, then, raises the question of rehabilitation.

Prison administrators today are more concerned with rehabilitation than they have been in the past. They have come increasingly to realize that the men placed in their charge will reenter society and that they have a responsibility to do something to make these men safe for society. Consequently, a greater emphasis is now placed on rehabilitation. It is difficult to attend a correctional conference where this subject does not arise. Prisoner rehabilitation is difficult to achieve, however, because most prisons are not primarily organized for this task. Evaluations of a variety of prison systems lend support to this statement.

There are individuals who contend that prisoners who make successful postrelease adjustments do so, not because of rehabilitation efforts, not because of their experiences, but in spite of them. We have all heard, I am sure, the point of view expressed that a prison is more a training school for crime than it is a rehabilitation agency and the analogy drawn between reformatories and grade schools, and penitentiaries and high schools preparing individuals for lives of crime. The situation is not that extreme, but it is true that many prisons are not particularly suited for rehabilitation activities.

Donald Gibbons, in a recent book, *Changing the Lawbreaker,* has written a very insightful and stimulating chapter entitled "Obstacles to Treatment." He details the barriers to rehabilitation that exist within the correctional structure. These barriers are probably well known to most persons in corrections. They have probably confronted them at various times. Gibbons breaks these barriers down into two basic types. He discusses bread and butter problems and problems inherent in the social organization of correctional programs. The bread and butter problems are those to which we are probably most sensitized—problems like legislatures not providing sufficient funding to pay adequate salaries or to initiate new programs.

Adequate salaries are necessary to attract and hold adequate personnel. It is difficult to obtain and hold well-trained people in prison work, since there are so many other positions that pay better. It is noteworthy that so many good people are attracted to careers in corrections in spite of this difficulty. I am constantly amazed at the number of capable, devoted people who are in this work, people who could be doing better financially in other areas.

It is difficult to develop adequate programs without good personnel, well-trained individuals who will stay with the programs. It is difficult to develop programs without equipment and facilities. Frequently, when there is a budgetary cut, it is the treatment and treatment-related programs that are affected first.

Some individuals must be kept out of society. It seems to be the primary charge of the prison to restrain the individual first and to rehabilitate him second. But quite obviously he has to be changed or society faces the same problem upon his release that it faced before.

Another bread and butter problem discussed by Gibbons is the "political problem." In many states, high-level correctional positions are tied to politics and every time there is a change in administration, new personnel are appointed. In these situations it is often the case that individuals are selected not on the basis of ability but on the basis of commitment to a particular political organization. This problem is becoming less salient in most states, however.

Still there are other political problems that exist: outside interference in policy matters, overriding authority, etc. These are bread and butter problems, problems that every correctional administration faces, problems that can be more or less resolved with time and effort.

The problems in the second category, difficulties inherent in the social organization of the correctional program, are less easily dealt with. They exist even after the bread and butter problems have been resolved. These problems involve such things as conflicts regarding the degree of emphasis to be given the various functions of the institution. There are, as I have pointed out, different goals that correctional institutions serve. The goals are sometimes not completely compatible with each other, e.g. rehabilitation and restraint. To maximize rehabilitation, it is sometimes advisable to run a "loose" institution, to cut down on custody procedures. This could result in more escapes. The function of withholding the individual from society would then be less capably served.

Conflicts occasionally develop between correctional personnel who are more oriented to the holding aspect of prison and those who are more oriented to the rehabilitation function. The prison has both jobs to do and this creates a dilemma. How can rehabilitation and restraint be maximized at the same time? Compromises can be made, but they are often unsatisfactory to the parties involved. This is a basic problem and not easily resolved.

An even more basic conflict exists between inmates and staff. To maximize rehabilitation, there needs to be interaction of a positive nature between inmates and staff. In many systems, however, this does not occur. Instead, a wall develops inside the prison—a psychological wall between inmates and staff. They perceive each other as enemies. The staff is charged with controlling inmates, manipulating and restraining them. Inmates try to resist this control and manipulation. Frequently their goals are quite dissimilar to those of the prison staff.

Men do not come eagerly to prison, welcoming the opportunity for treatment that confronts them. They do not commit themselves to prison when they find themselves engaging in deviant activities. Many inmates are oriented to resisting any influence the prison might attempt to exert on them. It is difficult to overcome this orientation.

It is my contention that prison staff, both custodial and treatment, are important agents of resocialization or rehabilitation. They are the only noncriminal individuals with whom inmates have daily contact who carry prosocial orientation. The majority of an inmate's social interaction is with other inmates, many of whom may hold and articulate antisocial values. It is unlikely that an inmate will adopt prosocial attitudes if he is constantly exposed to individuals who support and defend different modes of illegal behavior. It is the prison staff who are in the most strategic position to help develop attitudes supportive of law-abiding behavior. In many cases, however, there are structural barriers to effective interaction and communication.

Some administrators feel that interaction between staff and inmates beyond the minimum required for running the institution is dangerous. Friendships could develop and the friendship role could take precedence over the staff-inmate relationship. There are other arguments offered for minimizing contact between staff and inmates as well, but if rehabilitation efforts are to be optimized, these contacts have to exist. The inmate needs to see the staff not as an enemy who is out to "get" him but as representatives of an agency which is interested in him as an individual and in improving his life situation.

In spite of the problems and obstacles, prisons do develop treatment programs. They do develop procedures and tactics to modify those conditions that have produced criminal behavior in the individual. Treatment programs should not be confused with humanitarian innovations, as is frequently done.

Prison administrations frequently introduce changes like continuous feeding or allowing inmates to talk to each other in the mess halls or in the corridors, allowing them to walk out in the middle of the corridors rather than next to the walls, making living conditions in the cells better, providing recreation, taking them out of stripes and putting them into work clothes, etc. These are not really, in the strict sense of the word, treatment programs; these are humanitarian reforms. They are desirable in themselves, they are defensible on the basis of humanitarian principles, but they are not treatment.

There is an important reason for making this distinction. Occasionally a prison system will implement humanitarian reforms which will be perceived by the public, by the press and sometimes even by individuals involved in correctional procedures as treatment. They will note after an elapse of time that these innovations do not bring about an appreciable change in the amount of recidivism or of misconduct in the prison. They then use this information as an argument against treatment.

One of the few statements heard from inmates in positive evaluation of particular prison systems is, "they treated me like an individual," "they treated me like a human being," "they treated me like a man, rather than like an animal, rather than a nonentity." Humanitarian reforms may help prisoners maintain conceptions of themselves as human beings and as men. This is important if rehabilitation is to occur.

The term "rehabilitation" is also used in reference to specific institutional programs. Educational programs, religious programs, and vocational training and employment programs are often labeled as treatment programs. These programs are important in rehabilitation—there is little question about this. There is, for example, documentation of the importance of economic factors in postrelease adjustment. We know that not being able to get jobs, not having job skills, or not having attitudes that will facilitate work adjustment play an important role in individuals coming back to prison. We know that education also plays a part, not only to the extent that it improves job getting and job holding ability, not only to the extent that it improves the individual's potential for social mobility, but to the degree that it improves his concept of himself as an adequate individual. It is highly probable that a person in a society where most people can read and write who cannot do these things feels somewhat inadequate. This may cause adjustment problems. While education, vocational training programs, etc., have obvious significance, they are not the totality of treatment.

It might be argued that offenders can be "rehabilitated" by exposure to these programs alone. If true, this statement points out the importance of classification systems in corrections, a classification system that can be utilized for treatment decisions. Men are classified in prison primarily for custodial purposes rather than for treatment purposes. A classification system is needed that will group men into categories on the basis of the kinds of treatment from which they can most benefit. Offenders who are basically prosocial in the orientations, who are situation offenders, or who have gotten involved with the law because of economic pressures may be relatively easy to rehabilitate. If they develop skills and the ability to hold jobs, they may avoid reincarceration because those factors that "pressured" them toward illegal behavior have been modified. On the other hand, there are offenders in prisons who are not oriented to working legitimately. These individuals will probably not be rehabilitated through education or through the development of job skills. It is not enough for these men to develop the skills and abilities to obtain and hold jobs. They must have their value orientations and their attitudes changed. A man who is dedicated to burglary as an occupation will not be rehabilitated by learning new job skills. Learning how to operate an electric welder or acetylene torch will not, in all likelihood, lead to rehabilitation. The end result will probably be a more highly skilled burglar. A man is not likely to get a job and work hard just because he knows how. His attitudes have to be compatible with this kind of activity.

In the same way, an illiterate sneak-thief can be taught to read and write. Unless his attitudes have changed, the best that might be accomplished is to turn a sneak thief into a check-passer. For rehabilitation to occur, there has to be a change in value orientation. This fact must be recognized.

Vocational training programs, employment programs, and educational programs are important. But it must be recognized that for some inmates, they are sufficient for rehabilitation, for others they are an important element, for still others they play no role at all. Individuals, both in correctional work and outside, have criticized vocational training, education, and other similar programs, saying they do not really rehabilitate. This is, in part, true—they do not in and of themselves. There has to be attitude change along with change in skills. So rather than discard these programs as sometimes we are urged to do, we have to be more careful regarding what kind of inmates are placed in them. Certain categories of offenders, in addition to programs of this nature, must be exposed to programs oriented to changing values.

In prison systems across the country, only a small number of programs that are primarily oriented to value changes can be identified—programs like psychotherapy, group therapy, or milieu management. These terms have negative connotations for many people, as they are often interpreted as coddling prisoners. Basically there has to be some kind of manipulation of the individual's psychological life and environment if he is going to be rehabilitated. I am not suggesting that every inmate be subject to psychotherapy. I suspect that very few would benefit from this. I am suggesting that programs need to be developed and implemented where inmates are exposed to prosocial values and encouraged to accept these values. This may be done through maximizing staff-inmate contacts or through special group sessions with inmates discussing their problems with select staff members.

There are a variety of approaches that might be attempted. I say attempted because there is no one approach that is guaranteed. Different institutions have tried different programs with varying degrees of success. Their efforts suggest that by selecting inmates for programs tailored for their own specific problems, that some reduction in recidivism results, i.e. a smaller number get into further difficulty with the law.

That is an operational definition of rehabilitation—the person does not come back. Rehabilitation should not be thought of as complete character reformation. It should not be thought of as the elimination of all "vices"—smoking, drinking, swearing, chasing women, etc. This is asking a great deal; more, perhaps, than most of us would be willing to give up. If inmates can behave in such a way that they do not come in further contact with the law, then operational rehabilitation has been achieved. The best place for rehabilitation to occur is outside the prison.

The prison is not and probably never will be an ideal structure for rehabilitation. Daniel Glazer, in an article published in "Key Issues," described his notion of what prisons would be like in the distant future. It was an idealized treatment situation. It is unlikely that Glazer's ideal prison will exist in our lifetime.

This does not mean, however, that advances in rehabilitation programs should not be expected.

As indicated above, rehabilitation seems to best take place in the free community, and the success of the prison in rehabilitation is tested once a man returns to the community. Many inmates experience difficulty in reentering free society. The problem is often one of social reintegration. This is because the prison is basically an isolating institution—it isolates man from society, prosocial values, his family, and his friends. Letters and visits occur relatively infrequently. The longer a man is in prison, the fewer letters and visits he receives. He is isolated from society and then suddenly he is thrown back out into society to face the problems of a free man. A kind of "cultural shock" can take place.

Many inmates will say upon release that they are going to go straight, that they have been rehabilitated. They know right from wrong, they know that prison is an undesirable spot and they will never come back. They are going to get a job. They are going to get married; or if they are married, they are going to settle down with their wives and raise a family. They talk about the kind of job they are going to have a year from now or two years from now, their own little business, etc. Their expectations frequently are unrealistically high. They frequently are not aware of, or are not willing to recognize, many of the problems they are going to confront. When they come face to face with these problems, they are not able, in many cases, to adjust to them, and they fall back into violating behavior. They expect their family to accept them; the family does not accept them. They expect to be able to get a job; they are not able to get a job. These things lead to postrelease failure.

Programs are now being introduced that reduce the degree of isolation of the inmates—programs which optimize his contact with society. One example is the work release program. Certain selected offenders will have the opportunity while they are serving their sentences to have contact with the social world in which they are going to have to exist after they are discharged. They will have an opportunity to live up to responsibilities that they perhaps have not lived up to before, an opportunity to develop self-conceptions of themselves as worthy individuals and to internalize prosocial orientations. Prison tends to derogate a man, to tear down his self-conception. It develops in him a notion that he is "no-good," that he is a criminal, that he is undesirable, etc. Initially this may appear defensible. It is unrealistic, however, to turn him back into society with this kind of orientation and expect him to make a successful adjustment. The work release program is one way of counteracting derogation. There is still derogation, there is still punishment, but there is also some effort to improve the inmate and his self-conception.

Halfway houses represent another approach. A man close to release may be placed in the community under supervision, halfway between the free world and the prison. He continues to receive guidance and support in his efforts to cope with the problem of adjusting to the role of "free man."

These programs probably aid in the rehabilitation of offenders. I say "probably" because they have not been thoroughly evaluated. Furloughs, allowing selected individuals to go home on special occasions or a short time prior to release in order to line up a job may also facilitate the adjustment of offenders. I want to emphasize the importance of selectivity here; you cannot place any man in one of these programs and expect him to benefit from it or for him to operate within its confines. There must be selectivity. Certain men can benefit, certain men cannot. The problem of deciding whom to expose to which program is a crucial one.

Ruth Cavan has stated that approximately half of the men sentenced to prison spend 2½ years or less there. She suggests that many of these men would not have needed to go to prison because they might have benefited from probation.

Probation has been used cautiously in many states. There are those who argue that this practice could be used more extensively. This does not mean turning men loose with a slap on the hand. Perhaps some probation programs work this way, but probation programs, to be effective, must involve close supervision of the offender—treatment efforts, not just release.

One other approach that might be mentioned is a kind of modified probation. This particular approach has been tried on juveniles. Individuals are sentenced, not to an institution, but to a program whereby they work under supervision in selected jobs with other offenders. They participate in discussion sessions periodically, perhaps two or three hours a week. There is an effort to build up among the individuals who are participating in this program a primary group, a group of friends who together develop prosocial norms, values, and attitudes supporting law. When these individuals are released from supervision, it is assumed, or hoped, that the group will continue to function as a prosocial support system. It is hoped that these groups will act as insulators or barriers against further criminal activity.

I want to conclude with a warning note. Some of these programs I have mentioned are very appealing, e.g. work release and halfway houses. If they are developed, they should be set up in an experimental way. Certain individuals should be exposed to these programs; other individuals similar to those exposed should be left out of the programs. After a period of time, comparisons should be made between those exposed to the program and those not exposed, so effectiveness can be evaluated.

There is a tendency in corrections when a new program is adopted to expose everyone to it who is eligible. This is understandable. If you have something you think is going to work, you want to expose everyone who can benefit from it. But if this is done, no way of evaluating the success or failure of the program exists. Many times, programs are implemented, kept in practice for a while, and then dropped without any real assessment of their impact. This does not facilitate the correctional process nor contribute to knowledge about corrections.

An Examination of Conflicting Ideologies

JACK HEDBLOM

This article is concerned with a problem that is considered to be of crucial importance in its effect upon the prisoner, both in his adjustment to prison life and his rehabilitation in preparation to returning him to society. It is a problem that is intimately connected with all aspects of prison social structure and arises from the existence of two conflicting ideologies in a penal insti-

NOTE: Reprinted from *The Prison Journal*, 43 (2) :10-19, 1963.

tution. These ideologies are, respectively, a treatment ideology and a custody ideology. Each ideology is reflected in the paradoxical position of the American prison system. On the one hand, treatment leading to the eventual reformation of the offender is a state ideal. On the other hand, there exists an emphasis on security and protection of the public, as well as a belief in the punitive purpose of a prison. Should the prisons punish or reform? The problem is yet to be resolved.

The problem is reflected in the basic social structure of the institutions themselves, since basic staff units in the institution are the treatment and custodial employees. These two units often work in opposite directions due to different aims and values. In the literature of sociology, the conflict has been examined extensively in recent years.

The first complete study of a prison community was reported by Donald Clemmer in 1939.[1] His work did much to stimulate the growth of sociological analyses of aspects of the institution. Much of this literature documents and discusses the conflict existing between the custody and the treatment personnel in an institution. It discusses the subtle negative attitudes of the custodial staff for the professional staff and the concomitant attitude held by the professional staff that the core functions of the custody staff prevent any effective treatment program.[2] Further, it might be indicated that the images of the inmates as held by custodial staff and treatment staff differ considerably. The image itself could well be formed by the function of the individual in terms of custody or treatment role. Theoretically both the treatment role and the custody role should play an important function in terms of the rehabilitation of the inmate. In their essay, "Resocialization Within Walls,"[3] McCorkle and Korn indicate that probably the most important individuals involved in the problem of personality reconstruction are the custodial staff. Certainly the custodial staff spend the largest amount of time with the inmate. The effective role expectation can be indicated, if not measured, in the instance of the work programs existing in the institutions. Due to a lack of incentives in the work programs existing in some institutions, as well as the inmate's inability in many cases to choose the type of work he is to be actively engaged in, work levels in prison industry are low. According to McCorkle and Korn, these low work levels induce custodial attitudes in the supervisory personnel that explain this low level of performances on the part of the inmate to his current institutionalized situation. The prevalent attitudes of work supervisors toward convict labor, according to McCorkle and Korn are (a) the convicts are inherently unindustrious, unintelligent, unresourceful, and uninterested in honest work and (b) they are, generally speaking, a worthless lot who have never learned and can never learn good work habits.[4] This is a form of rationalization that absolves the supervisory staff of any responsibility for the prison system's inability to reform or for the low work production rate. These two expectations on the part of the custodial staff or the teaching staff foster in the inmate the inability to adjust in a noninstitutional job on the outside.[5] The custodial officer is aware of his susceptibility to corruption, which in turn leads to an attitude of distrust and above all apprehension pertaining to the inmate body. The most obvious method of avoiding personality entanglements and perhaps corruption is the rigid reliance upon the set patterns of rules of a given institution. By this formula, all men are treated the same, punished or not punished to exactly the same degree. The system is "fair" and at the same time it removes the sense of individual responsibility from the shoulders of the custodial personnel. The professional staff member, on the other hand, must necessarily become involved on a personal basis with the inmate population. In this sense, the type of contact the treatment personnel have with the inmate differs distinctly from that of the custody personnel. Many of the treatment personnel would tend to feel that the overemphasis on the routine and the rigidity of rules is harmful to the basic dogma of treatment. It is natural that the disagreement with this system could be construed to constitute a threat to the basic security of the custodial officer.[6] While the custodial personnel have a rather pat theory for handling the inmate population, there exists little or no consistency in a theory of correctional treatment. The very eclectic nature of the actions of the treatment personnel themselves have led to confusion and misunderstanding on the part of the custodial staff.[7]

The primary purpose of an institution is that of custody.[8] Francis and Johnson ascribe this attitude to those engaged actively in custodial work. They refer to it as "custodial ideology." The differences in training between the custody and professional staff are extremely important in the understanding of the rift existing between the custodial and treatment personnel. According to Ohlin,[9] the recent addition of professionally trained psychiatrists, psychologists, sociologists, and social workers in the prison regime has produced a rather marked difference in function between the administrative and custodial staff and the treatment personnel. "This cleavage has resulted from what has been perceived as a basic conflict between the custodial and treatment orientation toward prison work."[10] Attempts at compromising this rift is essentially harmful to the inmates in the sense of further adjustment to society. "In some situations the most common form of accommodation between the custodial and the professional staff is one in which the professional staff mediates between the custodial staff and the inmates to effect greater institutional security. The professional staff makes diagnoses and classifications that are exploited primarily from a security standpoint."[11] Thus, from many standpoints, there are actual differences existing between the custodial and the treatment staff of any given institution. It is little recognized that the overemphasis on the custodial system itself places limitations on the treatment staff that the treatment staff themselves are not completely aware of and so do not adapt techniques to service their essentially unique situation. The custodial staff on the other hand, expects the treatment staff to function adequately and satisfactorily within a system for which techniques have not been devised and so maintains that the lack of efficiency in the treatment program is rather the result of the treatment people themselves, rather than the inadequacies of the techniques of the treatment personnel.

It is interesting to note that in view of the aforementioned readings, little or no evidence of research could be found relative to ascertaining the attitudes of administrators toward the treatment function or the effects of these attitudes upon the inmate's possible rehabilitation. Even less research has been done relative to measuring the extent or the existence of a differential ideology maintained by either the custodial staff or the treatment staff. The research to be reported here is such a study.

This study hypothesizes that custodial personnel will exhibit a greater commitment to a prison's custody function than will the treatment personnel, and the treatment personnel will exhibit a greater commitment to a prison's treatment function than will the custodial personnel. It is hypothesized, also, that images of criminals and criminal behavior held by treatment and custodial personnel will be supportive of their respective roles.

All those who are engaged in teaching or guidance functions were classified in this study as treatment personnel, while all those who were engaged in security functions were classified as custodial personnel. The warden was not included, since his was the only position that formally crosscut the two basic delineations. Treatment personnel included all teachers, both academic and manual, cooks, cook's assistants and store keepers. The custodial personnel included all guards and supervisors of guards. Each of these basic types was characterized by a target statement which was meant to state succinctly all functions of the various types involved.

To the ideal custody type, the most important aspect of a penal system is security. Constant surveillance of the inmate is necessary at all times. Escape is always an imminent danger, and each prisoner represents to the ideal custody type an escape risk. The importance of routine and the smooth functioning of the prison should be paramount in the thinking of the custody type. For this line of reasoning, immediate reprisal is necessary for each infraction of the rules. This is because, to the individual custodial personality, routine is primary to the custodial function. The inmates themselves are there to be punished, since they are in prison because of a moral wrong. The inmates represent to the custodial personality an enemy. This is a generalized enemy and not necessarily related to an individual inmate. Because of the relative social positions in the prison community, the custodial personnel manifest a feeling of superiority in relation to the inmate. It is felt that concomitant with this is maintained, consciously or unconsciously, the idea that for one reason or another, the treatment program is not at all effective. The inmate's previous deviance is used by the custodial type as a rationalization of extreme control of the inmate. A reliance upon rigid rules for the maintenance of order is maintained as well as a belief that any deviance from these rules would result in chaos.

The formalized role expectation of the custodial type strongly emphasizes security and routine. Personal job security for the custody type depends upon a lack of disturbance in the prison routine. Therefore, consciously or unconsciously, he is necessarily dependent upon the aforementioned characteristics.

The ideal treatment type exists virtually as the antithesis of the ideal custodial type. The most basic theoretical concept maintained by the hypothetical ideal treatment type would be that criminal behavior, like normal behavior, can be explained in terms of behavioral science and constitutes no moral anomaly. Basic to this idea is that all deviants themselves can be helped to adjust their behavior patterns to the norms of society. This implies that the basic motivation of the penal system should be reform and not punishment. The penal system within this framework should be tailored to the needs of the prisoner and its routine subordinate to the needs of the inmate. Here is a direct criticism of the definite sentence. And so the routine of the prison in its effect upon the inmate is harmful, since it does not prepare the inmate for his eventual return to society. The emphasis upon personal choice and the development of a sense of responsibility incorporated in the minimum-security institution makes this institution preferable, from the standpoint of reform, to the maximum-security institution. The majority of inmates do not represent an escape risk to the treatment personnel; thus, to the treatment personnel, the entire prison system is based on a set of false premises. Rehabilitation potential, to this type, should not be based upon the seriousness of a committed offense but rather in terms of an objective evaluation. It is more important, then, to prevent crime than to punish criminals.

A questionnaire was devised to measure the degree of staff commitment to each of the aforementioned ideologies. The questions were developed from the major tenets of each target statement of ideologies. Persons committed to each ideology would, in turn, through their answers, indicate their commitment. One half of the questionnaire consisted of statements that a custodially oriented person would answer affirmatively, "Strongly Agree," the other half of the questionnaire consisted of questions that a treatment oriented person would answer affirmatively, "Strongly Agree." In addition to this, the prison personnel were tested as to their image of the criminal. The image questions were a dimension of questions concerned with treatment or custody orientation. They were developed through the use of the same characterizing statements used to develop the questions measuring the commitment to custody or treatment ideology. It was felt that the image held of the criminal would compliment the commitment to the custody or treatment ideology. By this line of reasoning, a person committed to the custodial ideology would have a custodial image of the inmate. As outlined previously, this is essentially a negative image. The treatment image of the inmate would be positive in the sense of not viewing the inmate as an enemy and believing in the possible reformation of all inmates. It cannot be stressed too strongly at this point that the negative image of the inmate held by the custodial personnel would essentially be an unconscious commitment. The commitment to the custodial function of the institution would be equally unconscious.

The scale used to indicate agreement or disagreement with the questionnaire statements was a five-point Likert Scale. Its dimensions range from "Strongly Agree" to "Agree" to "Undecided" to "Disagree" to "Strongly Disagree." Number values were assigned from one to five. The test was scored unidirectionally so that a high total score would indicate a treatment orientation and a low total score would indicate custody orientation. The Likert Scale was chosen, since it offers several advantages over other attitude measurement devices, the most important being that with an increase in the number of responses in a questionnaire, the reliability of that questionnaire is also increased. The "Undecided" category removes the "forced choice" aspect of the scale, giving the individual taking the test an opportunity to express confusion or indecision.

The initial questionnaire, when completed, contained 87 statements about aspects of prison work in relation to the dimensions previously discussed. In this form, it was presented to the Rhode Island Training School for Boys to discover whether or not the measuring instrument would discriminate between a treatment and a custody group and to discover which items discriminated to the greatest degree.

PRETEST AND VALIDITY

The pretest group was chosen by the superintendent of the Rhode Island Training School for Boys from his staff of 90. He chose the individuals making up the two groups on the basis of his personal knowledge of the individual's commitment to custodial ideology or treatment ideology as outlined in the type statements used to develop the questionnaire. This means was used as a method of validating the measurement instrument. It was felt that if the questions discriminated between these two pretest groups in the appropriate directions, a shortened version should discern in similar directions. The test and the pretest group were comparable, in the sense that the pretest group consisted of teachers and counselors and custodial people and the test group also consisted of teachers and custody personnel.

The final study was done at the Rhode Island Adult Correctional Institution at Howard. It is a maximum-security institution. The data was collected by having each man on each force take the questionnaire individually at his post. The only preparation each man was given prior to his taking the test was the researcher reading the printed instructions. They were told that names would not appear on the questionnaire.

Since the entire population was included in the study, any difference found between the custody group and the treatment group is real and significant.

TEST RESULTS AND INTERPRETATIONS

The custody scores on the treatment-custody continuum range from 42 to 75. Their image scores range from 45 to 75. The treatment group, on the other hand, on the treatment-custody score range from 42 to 89, while their image scores range from 45 to 71. A comparison between the average scores on the T C continuum for both groups reveals differences in the expected direction.

That is, the treatment group had a more positive image of the inmate and ideologically placed less emphasis on the importance of the custody function. On the T C continuum, the custody-group average score was 60.25. The treatment-group average on the T C continuum was 64.46, indicating a greater commitment to the treatment ideology than manifested by the custody group. The average image score for the custody group is 54.76, while the average image score for the treatment personnel is 57.06. This is, once again, a difference in the predicted direction indicating a greater commitment to the treatment image—a more positive image of the inmate. Where the T C score and the image score show a positive correlation (.453) for the custody group, there is no correlation (.098) between the T C and the image score for the treatment group. This could well indicate that the treatment-custody score is a separate element from the image score. It could also indicate that there is a greater agreement between the image of the criminal and a commitment to custody image in the custody group than in the treatment group. It was felt that neither the raw scores nor the correlation figures adequately defined the relationship differences between the two groups. In order that these relationships be further defined, the extreme scorers on the image scale and the T C scale in both groups were compared. In the custody group, those who scored lowest on the T C scale had an average of 3.2 years more experience than do average of the 10 high scorers. The average age of the groups were all but exactly the same as were the figures for average years of education. The differences in average T C score, however, are indicative of differential commitments. The differences in image score indicate that the groups, i.e. the 10 high scorers and 10 low scorers on the T C continuum, are more in agreement as to what the criminal is than how to deal with him in a prison setting.

Another comparison between the 10 high scorers on the image scale and the 10 lowest scorers on the image scale in the custody group indicate differences in the aforementioned comparison. The high scorers on the image scale (high score indicating commitment to a more treatment image of the inmates) have 7.4 years experience in prison work. The low scorers have an average of 9.4 years in prison work. This difference of two years complements the low scorers' difference of 3.2 years on the T C scale. These figures could well support the hypothesis that extended service in prison work will result in a commitment to a custodial ideology and a negative image of the inmate. There is only a difference in average education of .2 years. The low image-scale scorers prove to be 12.2 years older on the average than the 10 high scorers on the same scale. Those who scored higher on the image scale in this group also scored higher on the T C scale than the 10 low scorers on the image scale. It would then seem that those who hold a more positive treatment image of the criminal also are more treatment oriented on the T C scale. The manifest difference on the T C scale is 12.4, while the difference on the image scale is 19.0.

A comparison between the two high-score groups discussed to this point, that is the 10 highest scorers on the T C and image continuums, indicates more similarity than dissimilarity between them. Those who scored very high on the image scale have 2.3 fewer years of experience and 1.9 average fewer years of education. Their T C scores are, however, within 3.6 of each other and their image scores are within 5.0 of each other. When these differences are compared with the differences between the high and low scorers in each group, the similarities become more apparent.

A comparison of the low-scoring groups on each dimension indicate small differences in the same direction. The low-score T C group scored 7.5 points lower than did the low image-scale scorers on the T C scale. The latter, however, did score lower on the image scale in the amount of 5.4. Both low-score groups scored lower on both the scales than did their corresponding high-score groups. These findings seem to support the hypothesis that the image of the criminal is indeed a dimension of a commitment to a custodial ideology.

A comparison of the high and low scorers in the treatment group on the same scales renders results in the same directions. The high and low scorers in the treatment group were chosen on the same basis as the high and low scorers in the custody group. Since the size of the treatment group is significantly smaller than the custodial group, only five cases were chosen from each extreme.

The high scorers on the T C scale in the treatment group

manifest 3.8 fewer years experience than the low scorers on the same scale. The low scorers, on the other hand, manifest 1.8 years less education than the high scorers. Their average age is also 1.6 years less than the high-score group. These figures indicate that it is those members of the treatment group with lower educational levels that are less treatment oriented than those members of the treatment group with more education. The high score group on the T C continuum tended to be older on the average than the low scorers. This difference was 2.6 years. In comparing the high score group's average 80.0 on the T C scale with the low score group's average of 51.8, the difference of 28.2 indicates a greater variation within the treatment group than within the custody grouping of high to low scorers. Those who score high on the T C scale also tend to score high on the image scale in the treatment group. The image score for the high scorers on the T C scale in the treatment group is 2.0 higher than the same score for the custody group. This indicates a difference in the predicted direction in relation to the stated hypothesis. The low scorers for the custody group, on both the T C scale and the image scale, are lower than the same scores for the treatment high and low scorers. This, once again, is a series of differences in the predicted direction.

A comparison within the treatment group between the high and low scorers on the image scale indicates that the low scorers have 6.1 years more experience in prison work than the high scorers. The educational level for the high scorer is, however, .6 years higher on the average. Their educational levels are similar, yet there is a difference in average age of 7.6, favoring the low-score groups. This figure tends to complement the differences found between the ages of the high and low scorers on the image scale within the custody group. As can be seen in Tables I and II, there is a difference of 25 points between the T C score of the group representing the low image-score within the treatment group. This difference indicates that those in the treatment group who score high on the image scale also score high on the T C scale. In addition, those who score high on the T C scale score high on the image scale. The average T C and image score for the treatment group, including both high and low dimensions, are higher than the corresponding scores for the T C and image scale.

CONCLUSIONS

These differences in scores shown in Tables I and II indicate differences that are both consistent with the stated hypothesis and the differences found between the basic treatment group and the custody group tested at Howard.

It can be stated tentatively, that hypotheses 1 and 2 have been supported by the findings of the study, although it is impossible, due to space, to report all of the findings of the study here. Custodial personnel do exhibit a greater commitment to prison custody function than do the treatment personnel, and the treatment personnel are more committed to a treatment orientation than the custody personnel. The images of the criminal as held by the custody and the treatment groups do differ, and they are supportive of their respective roles.

TABLE I

COMPARISON OF HIGH AND LOW SCORERS ON THE
IMAGE SCALE AND T C SCALE CUSTODY GROUP

Variable	High T C Scorers	Low T C Scorers	High Image Scorers	Low Image Scorers
Average years of experience	9.7	12.9	7.4	9.4
Average years of education	11.1	11.4	9.2	9.4
Average age in years	38.9	38.7	35.8	48.0
Average score on T C scale	71.8	48.3	68.2	55.8
Average score on image scale	59.8	51.2	64.8	45.8

TABLE II

COMPARISON OF HIGH AND LOW SCORERS ON THE
IMAGE SCALE AND T C SCALE TREATMENT GROUP

Variable	High T C Scorers	Low T C Scorers	High Image Scorers	Low Image Scorers
Average years of experience	6.2	10.0	6.4	12.5
Average years of education	13.2	11.6	13.4	12.8
Average age in years	42.0	39.4	34.4	42.0
Average score on T C scale	80.0	51.8	82.0	57.0
Average score on image scale	62.8	55.4	63.6	57.0

The study suggests several directions for further research. Although there existed differences in the predicted direction, the differences were small enough to indicate either an atypical population or the presence of an unknown factor. If there exists an unknown factor, it is not indicated in the literature of the field. It is also possible that the treatment personnel undergo an institutionalization process. By institutionalization is meant that the individual will begin to adopt the norms and values of the social institution he is associated with. As a possible result of this hypothesized institutionalization process, the treatment personnel become committed to the custody function of the institution. The comparison made between the high and low scorers on both the image and the T C scale, for both the custody and the treatment group, indicate that all of the low-scoring groups have more experience in prison work than the high-scoring groups.

There are several practical applications for a study of this kind. If it can be shown that there exists a conflict area between the custody and the treatment groups in an institution, then it must be assumed that this conflict hampers the function of both groups. If the test with further application were shown to be valid and reliable, personnel could be chosen in accord with desired orientation.

Further uses for this questionnaire, presupposing a reliable and valid instrument, might use it as a measure of effectiveness of a training program aimed at developing a commitment to a treatment or a custody ideology. In further relation to training sessions for the personnel of a penal institution, the questionnaire could serve to indicate to the personnel of an institution just where they stand and why they feel as they do.

NOTES AND REFERENCES

1. Clemmer, Donald: *The Prison Community*, Boston, The Christopher Publishing House, 1940.
2. Vold, George B.: Does the prison reform? *Annals of the American Academy of Political and Social Science*, 293:42, 1954.
3. McCorkle, Lloyd W. and Korn, Richard R.: Resocialization within walls. *Annals of the American Academy of Political and Social Science*, 293:88-89, 1954.

4. *Ibid.,* p. 92.
5. *Ibid.,* p. 93.
6. *Ibid.,* p. 95.
7. Francis, Roy C. and Johnson, Arthur L.: Some theories of penology. In Roucek, Joseph S. (Ed.): *Sociology of Crime.* 1961, p. 258.
8. *Ibid.,* p. 260.
9. *Ibid.,* p. 267.
10. Ohlin, Lloyd E.: *Sociology and the Field of Corrections.* New York, Russell Sage Foundation, 1956, p. 15.
11. *Ibid.,* p. 15.

SECTION V

DISCIPLINE: THE VALUE OF SANCTIONS

THE setting of limits is inevitable if society is to function in the interest of all. The particular type of social system which an institution constitutes processes those persons whom society has excluded as rebels against conventional authority. Coming to grips with the problems presented by such malcontents is the reason for the existence of institutions; to do so in such a way as to avoid further coalescing of antisocial attitudes demands the wisest use of authority. Fink discusses authority with regard to each segment of the present criminal justice system. As Dean of a school of social work, whose students function in direct contact with the varied segments, he offers a viewpoint unencumbered by minutiae. The smothering effect of arbitrary authority can be destructive to correctional intent; or the wiser use of limit-setting can develop, support, and sustain those prosocial attitudes existing in every inmate. His emphasis on the necessity for "change from within" urges officers to implement discipline in such a manner as to lead the inmate to see authority in its rational senses.

Glaser focuses the use of authority as a most practical medium of communication; i.e. the systematic use of discipline can serve correctional ends. He suggests that discipline need not be especially severe but should be as certain as possible—and as swift. The accumulation of unnecessary and even destructive rules, which get at the symptoms of defective morale only, rather than at the causes, subverts the use of discipline and renders it ineffectual. Lack of clarity regarding the necessity of extant rules, existence of unwritten rules, and the whimsical application of rules defeats the purpose of discipline. The implementation of useful discipline requires a point of view which, according to Glaser, can only be developed through professional training.

Wallack has long been regarded as one of the most innovative wardens in the correctional system. His interest in training covers over 30 years. As early as 1937, he initiated a training program

222

which was mentioned by Gill as one of the nation's most successful. His comments may seem rather biting, but over 25 years of
experience as warden of a penal facility permits him this prerogative. That incarceration must be viewed *as punishment* rather
than *for punishment* is the necessary viewpoint, if penal facilities
are to be rehabilitative. "If I were to be convinced that harsh
and even brutal treatment would accomplish these goals, then I
would say that the end would justify the means. . . . The history
of prisons bears out the fact that brutal punishment, be it physical or psychological, results only in producing a more confirmed
criminal with stronger antagonism toward the very society we
avow to protect." It is the author's considered opinion that discipline must be an "orderly, reasonable process." When disciplinary processes consist of the enforcement of rules that are neither
clear, understandable, nor reasonable, Wallack contends they will
be initiative-sapping, character-decimating, and provocative of
criminality.

Those who decry punishment view past offenses as relevant
only insofar as they uncover the need for treatment. Without condemning the justice of punishment, Spitzer notes that it is a
proper technique of social control—when applied appropriately
and in the right situations. In his discussion of the use of punishment, he attempts to place it in perspective in the rehabilitative process as an instrument rather than an end in itself; it
need be neither retributive nor vindictive, but can be truly corrective.

Authority in the Correctional Process

ARTHUR E. FINK

As one starting point in a discussion of authority in relation
to the correctional services, it may be useful for us to consider
the all-pervasive place of authority throughout our lives. Certainly, if we reflect upon it a bit, we can recall how early we begin to become aware of authority in its many manifestations. We
may encounter this early in our family situations, especially in
relation to our parents—the limitations that are imposed and
our struggles against what we are obliged to do and the prohibi-

NOTE: Reprinted from *Federal Probation*, 25 (3) :34-40, 1961.

tions about what not to do. These rules may not make very much sense to us, nor are we overly enthusiastic about respecting them, but little by little, each of us in our own way, make some kind of working accommodation to them. We have met authority and we will never be without it as long as we live.

AUTHORITY IN THE SCHOOL AND COMMUNITY

Then our little world of the family opens to a larger world of the school and the community and we experience authority as it is expressed by other persons and imposed by other rules. Certainly the teacher and the principal, with all of their professed willingness to help us, seem to resemble our parents and to have a liberal assortment of prohibitions, commands, and regulations with which some of us begin to have trouble. Sometimes, some students have so much trouble that it seems necessary for school officials to take restraining action or, in aggravated situations, to disassociate such youngsters from the school system. Regardless of what action the school takes, all students have experienced its authority and some have come into uncomfortable conflict with it.

COMING TO TERMS WITH AUTHORITY

In the larger community, of which the school is only one part, the adolescent—we will assume for the purposes of our discussion he or she is that far along—meets many more rules, limits, injunctions, indeed laws. Here, again, there will be varying adaptations to these demands, not unrelated to the degree of success achieved in earlier encounters with authority. In some instances, these earlier difficulties may be so unresolved that action may have to be taken by an agency known as the juvenile court. The man or woman who presides over the court insists he wants to help and this sounds just like what some other people have said; in fact, the judge is painfully reminiscent of those other authority figures—parents, teacher, principal—and he seems to have even stricter rules than they did.

With all due respect to parents, teachers, and principals, it may be observed that perhaps for the first time the youngster had had to come to grips with authority, that literally and actually he is face to face with authority as he and the judge look at each other. In all likelihood the judge knows something about him already, for another person who looks familiar and who is in the same room has prepared some material which, too, sounds familiar. One of the large tasks of the judge will be to set in motion the process by which this youngster can begin to get help in coming to terms with authority, as he, the judge, acts on behalf of and as an agent of the community and as he, at the same time, acts for the welfare of the boy. Nor are these purposes contradictory; rather they are integral aspects of the very service for which the court was created and for which it continues to exist.

Let us assume that the judge, having examined the material the probation officer has prepared and making his own analysis of the youngster and the difficulties he is having, decides to place the boy on probation. Here, again, the boy faces authority—authority of the community, of the court, of the judge, and now the authority of the probation officer. Like the judge, the probation officer has a service: primarily serving the community but also serving the offender in such a way as to conduce to his welfare. As he begins to work with the boy, the probation officer may encounter considerable resistance. This may take the form of silence or mumbled and unintelligible replies; resentment and sullenness; a blaming of his troubles on other people; or an aggressive hostility expressed against the court, the judge, and the probation officer. The disciplined probation officer will recognize and understand these various manifestations, seeing them as some of the many ways in which human beings in trouble try to keep from having to face their own part in their difficulties. The probation officer who not only represents authority but is authority must get past this shielding front and must help the boy to begin to take hold of what he can do about himself.

Not infrequently as the boy begins to open up and to permit communication between himself and the probation officer, he may press for a relaxing of the authority which the probation officer is exercising. To some people it may seem to make good sense to ease up on the use of authority—after all this boy has had a hard time at home and at school, other people have been too strict with him, and besides that he is only a boy as yet. To other people it may seem very important to bear down on this boy, to let him feel the full force of society, and to teach him a lesson this early. The competent probation officer may see it differently. As he gets to know the boy, he becomes aware that while there has been authority in the family and in the school, the boy has managed, by one means or another, to avoid coming to terms with it. Perhaps there has been too much strictness, or not enough, or a too erratic use of it. The probation officer's job will be to take this boy as he is where he now is, and to help him with the reality of the struggle he is now having with authority.

This help which the probation officer offers the boy around authority is ineffective when presented in lecture form. It takes on meaning when it is handled with respect to specific items, such as the conditions of probation. For an apparently simple example, I will quote from an actual record.

> For the time being, he would be obliged to observe a 10 P.M. curfew and attend school daily. Carl balked at this. He was 16 and didn't want to go to school. We talked about this, Carl complaining that he wanted to work and I pointed out that I wondered if he would really be satisfied with that and wondering, too, if he could really be self-supporting. The factor most impressive to Carl, however, was learning that although at 16 he had a legal right to stop school, in the eyes of the law he was still a minor and could not leave home without his parents' permission. . . . Carl looked most unhappy and fumed for awhile. I suggested he think about these things at his next interview. The remainder of the time was spent preparing Carl for his Mental Hygiene Clinic examination. Carl did not like the idea at all. . . . I explained why we felt a psychiatric examination was important and made arrangements for a later interview with him. He left the office in a very disgruntled frame of mind.
>
> Carl came in on time for his next appointment. I was greatly encouraged by this interview because for the first time Carl was really able to talk back, almost to the point of arguing. True, everything he put out was negative and hostile, but it does show he can be reached. He even shed a few tears which he didn't try too hard to hide this time. We talked in spurts for well over an hour and Carl did not appear ready to bolt as on previous occasions.
>
> He was angry about his Mental Hygiene Clinic examination because I thought he was "crazy." As we struggled with this and finally cleared it up we got to talking about "trust." Carl did not even trust his mother, why trust the court?

There are a number of comments that can be made about these fragments of interviews with Carl that bear on our discussion of authority. For one, authority can be dealt with most effectively, especially with an adolescent who heretofore has not come to terms with it, in small bits. To tackle authority in all of its manifold aspects and in its totality would be overwhelming for Carl—indeed would be meaningless. To relate it to such tangible requirements as school and a curfew provides him with something he can handle, or can refuse to handle. He can then know what he is doing and can be held to his part in it by his probation officer.

Taking on Responsibility

This leads to another aspect of authority—namely, the responsibility which the individual carries in relation to it. The imposition of authority from above or from the outside is not effective alone. It is only as the individual who encounters authority takes some responsibility for what that authority means to him or does to him that any beneficent action follows. As long as Carl can keep himself untouched—really untouched inside of himself —by any authority so long can he continue to resist the demands of society and go his own way. However, when authority impacts upon him in small but not unmeaningful areas of his living, then he must come face to face with it and carry the responsibility for dealing with it negatively or positively. If he deals with it negatively, he can still keep it outside of himself and respond to it destructively; if positively, he begins to internalize it and lets it begin to operate constructively in his life.

The Struggle With Limits

Another aspect of authority relates to the struggle that all of us, including the offender, have around limits. We push against limits and yet we would be terrified without them. They are essential to growth, to change, and to all aspects of living. Many years ago, Kenneth Pray remarked about the need for such limits.

> These limitations are not only ineradicable facts of life to which . . . we are bound to adjust . . . they are, in fact, the very bases upon which we discover our own capacities, for we must have something

to struggle against in order to find ourselves, to achieve selfhood with all its satisfactions. Without these limits, we are lost in a tidal wave of surging impulses, none of which is better or more satisfying than any other.

It is the probation officer's job to understand this and to work with the delinquent in his struggle with limits, for by so doing, he, the probation officer, is enabled to offer the constructive possibilities of authority.

Necessity for Change From Within

Let us assume that Carl and his probation officer are working together satisfactorily and let us take up with Bill who has made such little use of probation that the judge has felt obliged to revoke probation and place Bill in a training school. The judge has no illusions about the training school—he will not expect miracles—but he does hope the more controlled setting of the training school will provide Bill with the opportunity to settle down a bit, to take a look at himself, and with the help of a trained worker to take steps toward bringing about some change within himself. Bill may not have learned yet to live within limits, nor to have come to terms with authority; and he has probably managed to hold off any genuine change within himself. He may resent the rules of the institution and may start out breaking as many of them as he can. He may defy authority as it is embodied in the person of the superintendent and members of the staff. These are all matters which he and his worker will need to do something about.

At the one extreme, the response of the institution may be to bring the full force of its total power to bear upon Bill and to flatten or crush him. The other extreme would be based upon feeling sorry for Bill and all his misfortunes and to cushion the impact of the institution upon him. It is here suggested that neither of these extreme measures is likely to prove useful. In the one instance, Bill's unresolved struggle with authority may be sharpened and intensified still further. In the other—the easing up—it would be a disservice to Bill because it would be relieving him of his own share of responsibility for the situation in which he finds himself. There is a useful service somewhere in between the two.

Bill needs to feel the power and the authority of the institution as something that can be used helpfully in relation to his problems. As mentioned earlier, this is not gotten over to Bill via the lecture method but around specific situations as they arise and as Bill handles them and as he can talk things over with his worker. In this process, undoubtedly Bill will make mistakes, but with the help of the worker he can learn from those mistakes. If he is overprotected he does not have the opportunity to test himself against the reality in which he is and hence can gain no benefit from the experiences. Throughout all of this —this mean between two extremes—it is essential that change shall come about in Bill. This is something that Bill must do and be responsible for; it is not something that another person, not even the worker, can do for him.

AUTHORITY AND THE MAN IN PRISON

As we did with Carl, let us do with Bill—let us move on to another kind of situation in which we can examine authority in relation to the correctional process. Let us assume we are dealing with an adult offender who has been on probation, whose probation has been revoked, and who is now in prison. Many of the foregoing remarks also apply to the man in prison. Perhaps they apply in greater degree by reason of not having been worked out earlier in life: The struggle with limits; coming to terms with authority; taking on responsibility for one's self; and the necessity for genuine change.

One of the hardest jobs the prisoner has is to get himself into prison. To the layman this must sound like double-talk; of course the man has gotten himself in. However, a closer examination of these words—or perhaps more strictly speaking what is behind the words—reveals there is such a thing as being in prison physically and another thing which is being in prison psychologically. In the latter sense, this means facing what it is that has gotten him there; not merely the act or acts for which he was tried, convicted, and sentenced but essentially the kind of person he is that has gotten him to this pass. From the start it will be the worker's job to help the inmate face all of that. Many, if not most, prisoners may feel that they have been sent to prison unjustly. It is not uncommon for the inmate to insist it was someone else who committed the offense; or that the other person got off with a light sentence; or if he was the only one involved that he was not given a fair trial; or that he drew a "bum rap." There are an infinite number of ways of denying one's involvement of being in prison, and it is frequently in this kind of situation that the worker must start. His first job may be to help the prisoner to face the real fact that he is in prison, that he has gotten himself there. This will be necessary before the worker can help the prisoner get something out of the prison experience, and ultimately to be ready to get himself out of prison, able to stand on his own feet, and taking responsibility for himself.

Some prisoners may express their disinclination to face being in prison by open defiance of the prison's rules. This aggressive behavior may be a way of a prisoner denying he is in prison. True, he knows his body is behind walls and in a cell, but he is unwilling to face his real self in his predicament. A competent worker recognizes what is going on within the prisoner, recognizes as an employee of the prison that rules must be obeyed, and sees the prisoner's responses as offering an opportunity to look at himself, to struggle with limits, to come to terms with authority, and to bring about some change within himself.

Another prisoner may, right from the beginning, bend all his efforts to getting out by legal recourse. Again, the skillful worker will see this as a way of not facing being in prison. Here the worker's efforts will be directed to helping the prisoner to express, largely by words and feelings, his responsibility for himself and his part in being where he is. It will not be until the prisoner can be helped to get past this point that he can begin to use what prison has to offer and really prepare himself for release.

Another way of getting out is by escape, and understandable to the layman as this desire may be, it still has meaning to the prison worker as a refusal to face one's self and the situation one has brought about. Nor do prisoners customarily discuss their intentions with staff workers, but on at least one occasion this happened. After bringing this to the attention of the appropriate prison official, the worker recorded his account of the experience. A portion of this is excerpted here for the purpose of illustrating some of the points of our discussion.

I asked him how he was feeling now about being here and about wanting to be out on the "street." Was he still thinking about escaping? He did not look at me; instead he stared at his hands, looking very dejected. He said he still thinks about it; he cannot help but think about it. Every night he thinks about his family and how much he feels his place is with them. The agonizing slowness of time makes him want to scream sometimes at night. He would feel better if he could do this, but he is afraid they will send him to state hospital if he does. He feels his life is being wasted in here. His rightful place is with his wife and child. He thinks about getting out a lot. I told him I knew that getting out was important to him and I wanted to see him get out but not by means of escape. I wondered if he knew what escaping would mean to his wife. What would she think about it? He said he has never really asked her directly, but he knows she would disapprove. He told me he thinks he is going to try to be with her for their anniversary. I wondered if he were successful in getting out, how long did he think he could stay out. He knows what he would face when he came back (if he came back alive), then how about the next anniversary, and the next one, and the next one, and the ones after that. How long could he expect his wife to wait for him if he received additional time?

Despite having access to a hacksaw, this prisoner did not escape nor try to escape; the prison officials took the situation in hand and nothing happened. The important consideration for us here was that a worker could help the prisoner to face something of himself; could help him to take some responsibility for himself; could help him in his struggle with authority; could help him to be "in" prison so that he, the prisoner, could in time really get himself "into" prison, and then to begin working toward bringing about the kind of change within himself that would enable him to move toward getting himself out of prison. The getting "out" here means only getting his body out but within that body or person, enough inner change happening so that he could take responsibility for himself and for what he thinks and does so to keep him as a self-respecting and useful citizen— useful to himself and to other people too. Indicentally, this particular prisoner did serve out his minimum term, had his difficulties in prison, but was deemed ready for parole supervision and was eventually released. He may not have been a new man at the time of his discharge, but he was certainly a changed man because he has used the prison experience to do something different about himself than had been true previously.

Another way that a prisoner may have of not facing himself and his situation is to want to escape from it by way of self-annihilation. The worker records, later, the following incident with the same prisoner.

> Another long silence followed and then he remarked that if he were man enough or had courage enough, he would take his own life. I inquired if he really felt it took a man to do that. He nodded. I said that if he really wanted to solve all of his troubles, that would be the easy way to go about it. It did not take courage.

It is to be hoped that these several excerpts will give substance to the points about helping the offender in struggle with authority. Obviously this is not done by the lecture method nor by telling the prisoner what he ought to do. He knows what he ought to do. The help consists of working understandingly with the prisoner, enabling him to get certain things out of his system, and confronting him with his own share of responsibility for what he is and what he does. It consists in helping him to make the decisions about himself. He has to make them; another person, no matter how gifted, cannot make them for him.

What has just been said about the man in prison is just as true of the woman in prison. Here in North Carolina we have become familiar with some of the constructive possibilities of working with women offenders after they are committed to Women's Prison. Each year, students from the School of Social Work have carried on their field work training under the supervision of a qualified staff at Women's Prison. All of the points that have just been discussed about the offender are very real in the working experience of these students—the struggle with limits, the coming to terms with authority, the necessity for inner change, and the taking on of responsibility for one's self. Not infrequently, it is around this last point that students have the hardest time. As they work with women prisoners, they become increasingly aware of the tendency on the part of the prisoner to put the blame on someone else or something else. One of the hardest jobs the student has (assuming she has learned it to the same degree within herself) is to help the prisoner to admit to herself the share she has in her own difficulties. It is quite understandable that the student may have genuine feeling for the predicament the prisoner is in, especially if there are children in the home outside. However, the student learns, and usually the hard way, that it is no service to the prisoner to get caught up in her difficulties and to overlook the necessity to help her face her own responsibility. It is only as the prisoner can be helped to come to this— to really get herself into prison—that she can begin to use the opportunity prison offers and thus move step by step toward ultimately getting herself out of prison.

AUTHORITY AND THE MAN ON PAROLE

Now let us look at the last of the situations in which as professional workers in the correctional field we are engaged, namely parole. Again, we will have to make some assumptions. The man who is on parole has encountered authority in its many forms from his early life onward. More recently he has been in prison, and the judgment has been made that he is ready to leave the institution and to make a go of it on parole. No more than any other person can he avoid the demands that will be made upon him as he tries to live and work in a kind of modified liberty. Indeed, by reason of all that he has gone through—the behavior that got him to a court and then to prison and the person that he is—he may have a more difficult time working out his salvation than other persons.

The parolee finds that even though he is out of prison, there are rules to go by. Many of these seem restricting, and even though he may have learned something from the prison experience these restrictions may prove irksome, if not at times downright frustrating. As with all of us, the struggle between the inner and the outer goes on interminably. The rules about working, supporting one's dependents, the kind of company one keeps, the limitations on travel, etc., are explicit. Does one conform to these requirements only as they are insisted upon by the parole officer with all of the force of the law which he embodies; or does the parolee act upon the basis of some change within himself that has been going on for some time? I am willing to suggest that it may make a great deal of difference as to how the parole officer goes about his job with the parolee.

The way the parole officer works will depend to a great extent upon his convictions about people—his respect for them as human beings, with all of their shortcomings; his appreciation of the uniqueness of each person with whom he is working; his belief in the capacity of people to change; and his conviction that true change must come from within. As he works on these premises, he can approach each of his parolees as individuals who have difficulties of a serious nature and who need help in getting themselves straightened out and know that he has the skill to help. He, too, must believe in the rules and must realize that his helping is within the bounds set by the rules.

Suppose we take a simple and not unusual situation which is taken from the actual record.

> Much of Jim's troubles come from his not having found himself and in not being sure of what he wants. This was particularly true about his job. He was also aware that he needed to find companionship and affection. He remarked, "I guess I want what I have never had." He seemed to see the point when I said most of his trouble was in his own attitude toward people, his unwillingness to trust himself and others enough to give them friendship. We talked of ways of solving the problem constructively and of his other choice of escaping from his troubles as he had before into vagabondage and crime.

An examination of this excerpt reflects a willingness on the part of the parole officer to talk things over with his parolee. There was a back and forth quality about his intercommunication. The parole officer was giving Jim the chance to talk over some of his difficulties and enabling Jim by what he was saying and doing to come to decisions about himself. He was quite willing to have Jim engage himself in his own problems and to hazard some of his (Jim's) own solutions.

Several months later, Jim brings Marie to his conference, and his parole officer records some of the interview as follows:

> Jim then reminded me that he has mentioned Marie to me as the girl with whom he was going and added that her mother objected

strenuously to him. Marie smiled and nodded agreement. It quickly became apparent that they were in love and Jim said they hoped to be married. However, the chances for it did not look so good because of her mother's opposition, and Marie was only 19. I said it must seem pretty tough if they were fond of each other and wanted marriage but found it blocked. What did they propose to do? Jim said they would have to wait until Marie was 21 unless her mother changed her mind. He added, "Of course, we could always go over the state line." I asked him what he thought of this last remark as a solution. Jim replied it would be a risk, since he was on parole. I agreed, saying I too thought it would be a great risk. He might get away with it but if he didn't he would have a lot of time ahead of him.

Here, again, the parole officer could involve Jim in his own thinking and consequences. It might appear to many uninformed people that the simplest thing would be to impress upon Jim what he could do and what he could not do. This we all know as the ordering and forbidding technique, but we also have doubts about the lasting effect of decisions made along that line in contrast to the value of decisions made by the individual in a self-responsible way. This requires of the individual that he face up to himself, that he recognize the limits within which he has to operate, that he be fully aware of the authority that surrounds him, and that he make his own decision upon the basis of change that has taken place within him and carry responsibility for the decision he has made. These are the identical points that have been stressed throughout these pages and are as applicable to the man on parole as to any of the other persons about whom these remarks have been made.

CONCLUSION

In conclusion, I refer again to Kenneth Pray. It will be recalled that earlier I quoted some of his remarks about limitations. Written in the middle 1940's, the wisdom in them is as firm today as yesterday. Referring to freedom, Mr. Pray insisted it was a relative term when he said:

> There is no absolute freedom anywhere in this world and there ought not to be. None of us has absolute individual freedom; none of us believes in it; none of us would know what to do with it if we

had it. Some structure of authority, defining and enforcing the necessary limits upon individual personal responsibility and conduct, as
a condition of social cooperation, is an indispensable basis of any
kind of life in any society. Such authority is essential in the prison;
it is essential in the outside community.

Within these essential limits of social cooperation, freedom for every individual to make his own choices and judgments, to take responsibility for his own life, is not only an invaluable right of personality, it is an inevitable and immutable fact of life. Every individual will ultimately take and use that freedom whether we like it
or not. That is to say, in the last analysis every individual will behave as he himself wants to behave, for his own reason, to attain
his own ends. . . . We may, of course, while he is within our immediate influence, get him to behave outwardly the way we want him
to behave—sometimes under practically physical compulsion; for a
somewhat longer time, perhaps, through fear of painful consequences of acting otherwise; for a still longer time, probably,
through hope of ultimate reward such as an earlier release from
confinement. But when he leaves our sphere of power—and all prisoners will ultimately do so—he will act as he himself, deep down inside, wants to act.

Several times it was remarked that the method of lecture or
admonition was not especially effective in helping the offender
to deal with himself or the difficulty he is in. Yet for many people it seems so natural to tell others what they ought to do or
not to do and then to assume that others will do what they are
told simply because they are told. And when it comes to working
with the offender who has not yet come to terms with authority,
it seems to make even more sense to tell him what to do or even to
direct his life for him. I am moved to observe that such an approach, if not downright harmful, is of limited usefulness or of
no use at all, because it is based upon a misleading notion of
human behavior. The worker in the correctional field is likely to
be far more effective if he can engage the offender in the process
of doing something about himself. Basic to this process is the
quality of the relationship between the helper and the helped,
whereby the one enables the other to express ideas and feelings
and even actions, and to which the helper responds in such a way
as to increase the opportunity for the offender to take an additional responsibility for himself.

Thus as we bring to a close our discussion of authority in the correctional process, it is essential that we be convinced of its usefulness; indeed of its indispensability. We need to value it, as much for the worker in corrections as for the person being helped. But we need to see, also, the other aspects as they are related to the use of authority, namely, the use of limits, self-responsibility, and inner change. By our understanding of these and our skillful use of them, we thereby offer to the offender the opportunity to realize more fully his own capacity as a human being to live satisfyingly and constructively.

How Institution Discipline Can Best Serve Correctional Purposes

DANIEL GLASER

Discipline probably has received less detailed analysis in correctional literature than any other major aspect of correctional administration. Yet in warden's conferences, and in informal discussions among officers, we find concrete questions of disciplinary practice being raised repeatedly. Perhaps the literature is scant because there is less agreement as to preferred practice in this area than in any other sphere of corrections. This justifies our endeavoring to specify some of the issues involved in prevailing arguments and to assert what are believed to be the most important principles applicable to these issues, such an effort aiding in resolving differences or in leading to carefully controlled tests of alternative practices.

We usually agree in summarizing the purposes of correctional institutions as first, custody and secondly, rehabilitation. A certain amount of conformity to institution rules is essential to each of these purposes. The term "discipline" is used in this article in its narrowest connotation as that which is done to those inmates who violate rules. It is assumed that discipline is intended to reduce further violation of rules.

Discipline, defined as dealing with rule violations, is only one aspect of the institution's efforts to gain conformity to its rules. It might be called the negative aspect. The positive aspect includes inspiring, persuading, rewarding, keeping inmates occu-

NOTE: Reprinted from *American Journal of Correction*, 17 (2) :3-6, 22, 1955.

pied, keeping them relatively happy, and otherwise directly encouraging and facilitating their conformity to the rules. We often call these positive aspects "morale promotion." Psychologists advise that positive methods are more effective than negative methods in procuring desired behavior. Nevertheless, the need to deal with some rule violations arises in all institutions, even in those with the best morale promotion programs. But our topic raises the secondary question. What methods of discipline, while coping with violations, least impair morale promotion?

THE OFFENSE OR THE OFFENDER?

One issue which underlies many disagreements on handling concrete cases is whether discipline should be based on the offense or the offender. We generally agree that if positive efforts to inspire rule conformity are to be effective and if officials are to exercise a rehabilitative influence, inmates have to conceive of the administration as fair and interested in the individual inmate's welfare. This interest is used to justify disciplinary rules which are flexible and which are administered on a very personal basis, reflecting an effort to understand why the offender violated institutional rules. Discipline is then based on the reasons for the infraction—the personalities and situations involved—rather than on the infraction itself. This approach reflects the ideal of individualized treatment which dominates American corrections and which is manifest in the indeterminate sentence, classification, and parole. While understanding why an inmate misbehaves is essential in classifying and counseling, it may be argued that flexible discipline inspires a conception of the administration as unfair and seriously impairs inmate morale and the effectiveness of rehabilitation programs. Three types of arguments may be directed against such personalized discipline, and in favor of striving for standard penalties for each infraction meriting a penalty.

First, inmates do not understand the personal considerations on the basis of which an administration imposes different disciplinary actions on different inmates for ostensibly the same rule infraction. Therefore, personalized discipline may have an adverse effect on the positive program of the institution. The more severely penalized inmates are considered unfairly treated, and more lenient disciplinary actions are interpreted, even by the beneficiaries, as a sign of the officer's incompetence—that he has been "conned"—or as more evidence of unfairness. Such reactions to apparent inconsistencies in discipline spread rapidly through the close-linked inmate social system of an institution and seriously weaken respect and regard for officials, handicapping their rehabilitative efforts.

Next, in the prevailing inmate belief systems, apparent favoritism in discipline is taken as evidence that stool pigeons are encouraged, whether they are or not. Incidentally, if stool pigeons are cultivated, they are much less useful as informers if favorable disciplinary treatment enables other inmates to identify them. At any rate, where inmates sincerely believe a stool-pigeon system is deliberately encouaged, their conception of officials as moral cynics creates an almost insurmountable obstacle to morale and rehabilitation promotion.

Finally, impressions from experience with those infractions for which penalties have become very standardized in certain institutions suggest that if all infractions were reduced to a standard list to the greatest possible extent, with fixed penalties for each, discipline would be considered fair simply because it would be impersonal. Complaints would be more against the code of penalties than against the officials administering the code. We are assuming that any such disciplinary rules would be binding on the officials dealing with the infractions as well as on the inmates, so that both would generally know in advance what an inmate "has coming" when he breaks a rule. We will discuss later the problem of determining the most desirable rules and the most desirable penalties. The main argument here is that for those rules for which objective codification is possible, codifying the rules and penalties make discipline more impersonal, makes officials less resented, and therefore aids them in their morale and rehabilitation promotion.

Objection to making disciplinary practice primarily a function of the offense, not the offender, arises in practice from such impressions in individual cases as: "He's such an ornery character we ought to give him the works." "He's been pretty good lately, let's give him a break." "This is the third time he's broken that rule, our usual penalty isn't enough for him." Sometimes, even with a standard disciplinary code, an officer's prejudice or vengeance makes for capricious enforcement, as when he says: "We can't give much on this, so we'll get him on that." A less appropriate charge is then made for the sake of imposing a more severe penalty. But these reactions, by reducing the impersonal nature of disciplinary practice, impair relations between the administration and all of the inmates, even though they may appeal to the emotions of the disciplinarian. One may well doubt if there is any net gain for rehabilitation, custody, or rule conformity in unnecessary deviation from impersonal discipline.

Some flexibility is unavoidable, insofar as infractions cannot be standardized. Such flexibility may be limited to some extent, however, by an endeavor to specify degrees of certain subjective infractions such as insolence, with penalties confined to those forms which are indisputably clear and dangerous. Such an effort at specification, of course, is more appropriate in instructions to officers than in rules for inmates. Flexibility in treatment of different inmates committing the same infraction may be rendered impersonal to the inmates, however, by promulgating rules on standard increases in severity for each successive infraction within a given span of time. There are limits, of course, to how far such increases can go, and continuous administrative segregation for special study and treatment usually is necessary when these limits are reached.

CERTAINTY AND SEVERITY

One fairly well established criminological principle is that the greater the severity of a penalty, the less the certainty of conviction. A second fairly well established principle is that increasing certainty of conviction usually reduces infractions more than increasing severity of sentence. These principles suggest that discipline need not be especially severe but should be as certain as possible. Any standardization which can be introduced into disciplinary action increases the certainty that an inmate will receive a particular penalty. He may still gamble on not being caught, but he cannot gamble on conning the disciplinarian or on catching him in a good mood in order to be less penalized.

The history of discipline in many institutions shows cycles which begin with increases in severity of punishment whenever there are increases in rule violations. In this way, over a period of months or years, punishment gets more severe. As a consequence, however, there is likely to develop increasing reluctance to report all cases, and there is likely to be a tendency to impose the higher penalties less uniformly on those cases which are reported. Thus punishment becomes less certain, and discontent grows among inmates and staff. Finally, some reductions in severity occur, often following a shake-up in key personnel. Now the cycle of increasing severity begins again.

Such cycles in discipline are especially common in institutions for juvenile and youthful offenders, and in women's institutions, where irregular waves of infractions and crackdowns seem more frequent. This cycle probably accounts for the frequent observation that punishments are more severe in institutions for juveniles than in institutions for adults. An administration faced with an increase in rule infractions should first try to determine and remove the causes of the increase. Only if infractions remain disturbingly high after this has been done and after the detection and reporting of infractions has achieved maximum certainty is it likely to be beneficial to even consider increasing severity of penalties. Codification of rules and penalties, insofar as possible, prevents ready reflection of moods and fears of officials in disciplinary practice.

WHAT RULES ARE NECESSARY?

If we are concerned with certainty that rules will be enforced, we must ask what rules are necessary. There is a tendency for institutions to accumulate rules—never to drop them. It is easier to pass a new rule affecting the symptoms of defective morale than to get at the cause. Eventually there are many marginal rules which are enforced only haphazardly. Examples include most limitations on talking, silent insolence, and profanity. By having rules which are only enforced half the time or less, do we accomplish any useful purpose in those cases where we attempt to enforce them? Is it not true that personal prejudice and vengeance in officers are encouraged by maintaining rules which no official is expected to enforce consistently? I suspect that we hamper enforcement of those rules which we consider important by maintaining rules of minor importance, for which enforcement is uncertain and capricious. In the course of codifying institution rules, it may be well to drop many marginal rules.

Elimination of unimportant rules greatly improves inmate-staff relationships by making the staff seem less petty. If the staff members can spend less of their time as policemen, they are able to habituate themselves more to serving the positive programs of the institution through acting as teachers, leaders, counselors, and within limits, friends, to the inmates. Indeed, in the long run, conformity to some standards of conduct may be increased by eliminating poorly enforced rules with respect to such conduct. Federal officers report favorable consequences from major reduction in rules, such as reducing the periods and places in which inmates are forbidden to talk.

> Perhaps a clue as to the types of rule which are important can be gained from some studies of industrial relations. My colleague, Professor Gouldner, found that for those rules which are originated primarily by outsiders to an industry, such as antismoking regulations originating by insurance companies, joint violation is supported by informal sentiments among both management and workers.

On the other hand, rules originated and justified by only one party are persistently violated by the other, and efforts at enforcement are a source of continuous tension. Rules originated by both parties, however, such as the promulgations of a management-worker safety council, gain compliance, and employees who violate them offend both their fellow workers and management.[1]

Without getting involved here in such issues as the dangers or benefits of giving inmates a voice in prison management, I think we can say that in order for a rule to be effectively enforced without impairing inmate morale and rehabilitation, the rule must be readily justifiable to both inmates and staff as essential to the smooth operation of the institution.

There are several types of rule which are unavoidable. First of all, of course, rules against felonies will have inmate and staff support. Felonious infractions usually handled by institution disciplinary systems range from sodomy to attempted murder, from larceny to attempted escape, from forgery to criminal destruction of property or criminal negligence. Rules against those misdemeanors which are widely prosecuted in the free community also receive wide support in prison. However, misdemeanor and felony, such as petty and grand larceny, should be distinguished clearly. Rules against masturbation are foolish. Rules against indecent exposure might be defended, if clearly defined, but even their necessity may be doubted. Vaguely defined designations or misdemeanors should be avoided, and acts which are more distasteful than dangerous or seriously demoralizing might be left to control by the informal sentiments of the prison community.

A second type of rule which is enforceable is a rule which is clearly necessary for institution routines. I am not one of those academic criminologists who believe that there is an inverse relationship between rehabilitation and regimentation or between rehabilitation and degree of security. Such views are an oversimplification of the correctional facts of life, in my opinion. Inmates know that secure custody is the first demand which the law and the public make of the administration. They know that they have to be counted regularly and that this is least troublesome for all concerned if they are up for count. They know the risks and that there are restrictions on movement for each grade. They also know that the movement of many men is accomplished most effectively if the men are in lines.

> It was my impression from close personal contacts with inmates at an institution sometimes called America's tightest, that necessary routines are not resented, especially if they are promulgated clearly and unambiguously. Inmates who impair these routines arouse the wrath of other inmates as well as the staff. For those rules which are clearly necessary for essential routines, infractions generally are clear-cut. They are especially easy to codify specifically, standard penalties are especially appropriate for them, and they may be enforced with a minimum of fuss and dispute.

A major problem in all institutions is fighting. I believe that it is an unreal conception of human psychology which sees all persons as having a fixed fund of aggression which they must express. The evidence marshalled for such simple frustration-aggression hypotheses has been given the contrary interpretation by some psychologists, that aggression is one of several methods of solving problems and that any method can become habitual if it is encouraged and other methods are discouraged.

The habit of meeting problems by aggression is often a major factor in the misdemeanors and other difficulties which inmates get into in the free world, as well as in prison. Rather than encouraging this habit by having them put on the gloves and engage in grudge fights, it may be appropriate that fighting be penalized with some severity. The aggressor in the fight can be defined as he who makes the first attempt at physical violence—not verbal violence. Where the aggressor can be clearly established by officials, he can be punished more severely than the defendant, the defendant being completely excusable if it is clear that he made every possible effort to avoid the fight. However, in the usual case, where the aggressor cannot be established clearly, it is appropriate that there be a standard penalty for all involved. The person who knows he was on the defensive will blame the aggressor, not the administration, for his being punished, provided that the rule is standard. It has been my observation that such a policy in time causes inmates to learn to avoid fights which they never would have avoided before coming to prison and that these new habits serve them well after they leave prison.

UNWRITTEN RULES

Some institutions proudly report that they have no rules except, of course, for a few rules on crucial routines, such as safety rules in shops and some rules on the movement of men. Investigation soon reveals, however, that new inmates must spend many days learning exactly what is expected and what is not allowed. There are innumerable rules, but the rules have never been written down.

There is a danger under these circumstances that each officer will become a law unto himself. That which is permissible with one is forbidden by another. The administration loses some control over its institution in this way. While a certain amount of variation in the treatment policies of different officers may be desirable as an asset in classification, there is a constant danger of it growing to the point where it is a threat to morale, rehabilitation, and even custody. Diversity in the policy of different officers in an institution has been reported as a factor in several riots.

Lack of clear official formulation of rules is an especially major problem where high standards cannot be maintained in recruiting employees and where there is rapid turnover of officials. It is also more serious where there is not a highly developed inservice training program for employees. Institution disciplinary officers or boards will always provide some definition of the rules by their treatment of individual cases, if these officials are consistent, and if, except for standard increases in penalty for repeated infractions, they fix penalties on the basis of the offense rather than the offender.

Insofar as the actions in disciplinary cases are the only means of communicating rules and penalties to officers and inmates, much unnecessary tension results. The morale of an officer is lowered if an infraction which he considers serious seems to be regarded lightly by the disciplinarians. Some react to this by not reporting infractions which should be reported, while others make excessive charges in order to avoid having their complaints treated lightly. By being "out to get" the inmate for whom their previous complaint was disregarded, such officers impair inmate-staff relationships, harming morale and rehabilitation programs. Damage to these programs is further increased when, in order to preserve officer morale, the disciplinarians feel obliged to treat every infraction which an officer reports as meriting a penalty. Many of these several types of tension in inmates and staff can be reduced insofar as institution rules and penalties can be communicated clearly to everyone and are administered consistently.

WHAT PENALTIES BEST SERVE CORRECTIONAL PURPOSES?

Having reduced rules to an essential minimum and having stated them as clearly as practicable, we are left with the question, what penalties are most appropriate when the rules are violated? There are no easy formulas, but a number of principles merit consideration:

First, penalties which are certain need not be severe.

Second, standards of severity are a function of traditions in a penal system: sudden increases from traditional levels of severity will cause resentment, while sudden decreases in severity will be interpreted as meaning that the administration attaches little importance to the rule infraction.

Third, there is need for much active imagination in the development of new types of disciplinary action. The familiar hole, the prison within most prisons, represents a minimum of imagination. A basic principle for a new type of disciplinary action should be that the inmate should not be kept idle and brooding for protracted periods. Giving the inmate a special task to complete may be more desirable, in many instances, than merely imposing a period of restriction of movement or activity on him. Constructive tasks, preferably of some training value even if a chore, may help the inmate develop the attitude and abilities which can further his conformity to rules as well as his rehabilitation. Ideally, of course, the task should be a useful challenge, permitting him to feel he is earning respect again. Of course, traditional types of penalty probably will be necessary for those who refuse to accept the challenge. But days and nights of idleness and boredom in isolation may further incapacitate the inmate for adjustment to the demands of the institution's program, as well as to the demands of noncriminal life outside of prison.

Fourth, if the penalty involves no activity of positive morale and rehabilitative value, it may be appropriate to minimize the period in which the inmate is kept out of constructive activities. If, as with repeated infractions, one wishes to make a penalty more severe, greater effectiveness may result from increasing the number of penalties which are imposed (or pleasures denied) for a given period than from simply prolonging the period in which given penalties must be endured. Hastening the termination of punishment status hastens the moment when positive measures for promoting morale and rehabilitation can be renewed.

Fifth, there is need for systematic research on the effectiveness of alternative disciplinary practices and policies. Most of the principles which I have set forth must still be regarded only as reasonable hypotheses, at most—not as established facts. As reasonable hypotheses, they merit testing. A prerequisite to scientific testing is accurate recordkeeping on infractions and penalties. Another asset to research may be to require that officers record the principles on which they base important disciplinary rules and decisions.

While many persons deplore punishment, none have practical solutions for punishment for every situation where punishment is used. Where one can show penalties do not further the rehabilitation of him who receives them, it may be worth investigating whether the penalties further the rehabilitation of the rest of the inmates or whether the penalties are essential for other ends than rehabilitation, such as custody and morale. Correction is more an art than a science at present, but it is an art in which alternative theories and techniques may receive scientific test. It is an area of research which is too important to warrant further neglect.

A POSTSCRIPT ON DISCIPLINE[2]

My 1955 article, "How Institution Discipline Can Best Serve Correctional Purposes," was based on experience primarily in maximum-security prisons. These were in a state system where many employees, at all levels, still procured their jobs more through political patronage than through merit. In these institutions, an effort was made by the wardens to maximize the social distance between staff and inmates. Officers were regularly suspended for becoming too familiar with the prisoners, and these suspensions were publicized on the staff bulletin board as a warning to others. In what passed for staff training, it was stressed that "you can't trust an inmate." A frequently voiced justification for these policies was the fear that inmates would inveigle themselves into friendship with guards in order to get favors, including the passing of contraband or some opportunity to escape. Posted in all staff dining halls of this state's prisons was the picture of an inmate of several decades earlier. The caption under the picture related that this man had been a guard, but was sentenced to a long prison term for bringing in a gun to an inmate in exchange for money, the gun resulting in a shoot-out in which several people were killed.

Experience in quite different prisons was the first of three major influences changing my views on discipline since 1955. Some of these other prisons were in the United States federal system, some in California, and some in Scandinavia, although I found sharp contrasts in practice between different units in each of these systems. In those where discipline impressed me most favorably, social distance between staff and inmates were minimized.

The second influence altering my views on discipline was B. F. Skinner's operant reinforcement approach to the psychology of behavior change, the validity of which has been most conclusively demonstrated in recent years. Especially relevant is its evidence that if behavior which once was gratifying disappears because it is punished, it will recur whenever the punishment ceases, unless alternative behavior has been as rewarding in situations similar to those in which the deviant behavior previously occurred.

The third influence was the new clinical psychology of O. Hobart Mowrer, which indicates: (a) that much deep-seated anxiety and compulsion comes from a person's having committed acts that he regarded as wicked, even though his defense against acknowledging his guilt to himself may be to commit the same acts more flagrantly and (b) that these emotional disorders do not change by his merely verbalizing insight but by his engaging voluntarily in compensatory good behavior that gives him a better conception of himself.

In *The Effectiveness of a Prison and Parole System,* I referred to the 1955 article as arguing for a "definite penalty hypothesis," to which I proposed two alternatives. One, the "flexible rules hypothesis," is based on the contention that ". . . objectionable behavior by men in prison is so diverse that no set of rules could encompass it without being long, complex, and difficult to apply, or so arbitrary that it would arouse resentment by dealing similarly with highly diverse acts." The second alternative I called the "constructive penalty hypothesis," and based it on the contention that ". . . administration of disciplinary penalties is most effective if it minimizes alienation of the rule-violating inmate from staff and maximizes his alienation from supporters of his infraction;

promotes in him a clear regret over having committed the infraction; but provides him with perception of clearly available opportunities to pursue a course of behavior which will restore him to good standing in the prison and give him a more favorable self-conception than he has as a rule violator."[3]

I call these three principles hypotheses because we are in crying need of rigorous research, preferably controlled experimentation, if we are to know with more certainty which principle works best in which circumstances. My inferences from what we now know about prison life and human psychology and sociology, however, are that each hypothesis provides useful guidance, but in different circumstances.

Limits and Strategies with Definite Penalties

The definite penalty approach of the 1955 article probably is most effective in two types of circumstance. The first is where the infraction is very standard and relatively unambiguous. Examples include not putting tools away, not cleaning up a cell, taking more food than one eats, oversleeping, and so forth. There is least alienation of inmates from staff if everyone knows what penalty one "has coming" in these cases. If penalties are imposed uniformly, neither favoritism nor prejudice can readily be inferred from them.

The sociologically astute prison administrator gets an elected inmate advisory committee to decide on the standard penalties for each very standard infraction, preferably specifying an increasing severity for each successive violation in a given span of time. If inmates fix the penalties, staff cannot be blamed for their severity. Indeed, experience suggests that the warden probably will need to use his veto power occasionally, because inmates tend to be too punitive. Besides, increased certainty rather than severity is what makes a definite penalty effective, after a distinctly discomforting level of severity is reached.

It should be noted that the "definite penalty" principle and what is designated above as the "constructive penalty" alternative are not necessarily incompatible. One can regularly impose definite penalties that are of a creative type. For example, Guthrie's contiguous cue principle in learning theory suggests that the most effective way to get a person to remember to put his things away is to have him spread them out and put them away again repeatedly, simulating as closely as possible the actual conditions in which he is careless, rather than simply imposing an unrelated discomfort. Having a person who litters pick up litter in a larger area, having a spiller do mopping, or a breaker do mending, may all be more relevant than denying the culprits movies for a week, or locking them up.

Another effective strategy at times is to impose penalties on all inmates in a unit for poor housekeeping, carelessness, or some other types of misbehavior by any member of the group, combining this with unit rewards for outstandingly good conduct records by all members. This makes the inmates share staff interest in getting deviant individuals to conform. Care must be taken, however, to see that a consequence of group penalties for misconduct by one or only a few group members is not "kangaroo courts" and excessive punishment of the deviants by other inmates.

Sensitivity to possible mass reactions is needed in all discipline, to avoid staff's endeavoring to enforce excessive rules or to impose what may properly be conceived as inordinately humiliating or childish penalties. Such misjudgment may do more harm to the prison's disciplinary "climate," by alienating inmates from staff, than it achieves by inducing conformity to some rules. Above all, the prison administrator must realize that order in his institution, as well as disorder, are collective conditions reflecting widely shared views and feelings. Much individual misbehavior is symptomatic of collective conditions in inmates and staff and not merely of the mentality of the individuals who are caught.

The second type of circumstance appropriate for the definite penalty principle is that in which higher prison administrators believe that the judgment of their subordinates in inmate discipline cannot be relied upon. The amount of flexibility delegated to staff is necessarily a function of the confidence correctional administrators have in them. This is not so much confidence in their honesty as trust in their perceptiveness, their communication skills, their ability to avoid being "conned," and at the same time, their sympathy, understanding, and freedom from prejudice in dealing with inmates. It is lack of such confidence which warrants efforts to maximize social distance between inmates and staff and to make penalties as definite as possible.

While considerable social distance between staff and inmates may be inevitable, some prisons now attempt to minimize it rather than maximize it. Instead of discouraging fraternization between employees and prisoners, they encourage it. I have been in Danish prisons, both for youthful offenders and for adults, where each staff member is expected to try to get close to a limited number of prisoners, and each prisoner is encouraged to try to develop friendships with a few staff. In one youth prison in a rural area, staff were often taking inmates home for Sunday dinner, and they kept in touch with them after the prisoners' release. Practices somewhat similar are found in some American prison camps.

Although this sort of relationship cannot occur in all prisons, and perhaps not for every inmate in any prison, one general principle applies in all prisons. This is that inmate influence on other inmates, while always appreciable, varies inversely with staff influence on inmates. Lack of ready access to staff, on an informal basis, increases the power among prisoners of the inmate politicians and manipulators who are long enough in the prison to be "inside dopesters." These are often the most criminally oriented and sophisticated connivers, who are frequently in prison jobs where they can—or pretend to—put in a good or bad word for inmates, alter records, advise inmates on their probable fate at the hands of staff, pass contraband successfully, and cultivate a network of obligations and fears among other inmates. The more accessible, friendly, and reasonable are the staff, the less becomes the power in the inmate community of an "inside dopester," and the less intense are the "inmate code" and the "rat complex" in the mentality of the prisoners.

Certainly, the fixing of very definite upper limits of penalty for any inmate infraction is a safeguard against staff abuses. Fixing maximum penalties for various broad categories of misbehavior reduces the risk that unusually sadistic or prejudiced staff might impose penalties so cruel and unusual as to discredit and embarrass the prison administration. But while maximums are desirable in any prison, other advance fixing of penalties seem inappropriate wherever one has the following circumstances: (a) a category of infractions in which separate cases are highly diverse in the type and intensity of personal or group emotion they express and (b) a prison where the maximization of inmate-staff communication is encouraged. It will be noted that these are the exact opposites of the conditions where definite penalties were said to be most effective.

GOALS OF FLEXIBLE PENALTIES

Certain types of disciplinary problems are in some instances the most serious that an institution experiences and in other instances are not very disturbing. Examples are fights among inmates, possession of contraband, insolence toward staff, and refusal to work. Because of this variability, these are the infractions least adequately handled merely by the automatic imposition of the same penalty for every case. It is appropriate for the staff to assess in each of these separate events the intensity of the emotions expressed, whether these feelings are momentary or enduring, how many persons they affect, what causes them, and how they may be altered. This means that such events should be, first of all, occasions for improved communication.

When people are angry, communication is likely to be least adequate. If, when an infraction occurs in which people are angry, it is expected that a particular penalty will be imposed regardless of what, if anything, is said by anyone involved, communications will usually be especially poor. If, however, the penalty is uncertain and is not necessarily determined immediately, communication consequent to the infraction may be especially revealing and useful, provided the staff involved are skilled in making it useful.

In the prisons in which I believe discipline is used most constructively, it is expected that any serious assault among inmates, clearly disruptive rebelliousness towards staff, or major contraband activity, will lead to all prisoners involved being placed in isolation. What happens thereafter, however, is not predetermined. A variety of staff personnel—custodial, officers, psychologists, chaplains or others—talk to the isolated inmates after they have cooled down, discussing what happened, probing as to why it happened, and trying to reach consensus on what might be done to prevent such events from recurring. The visits are prolonged, abbreviated, repeated, deferred, or altered, according to what seems most conducive to useful communication. The objective of this communication is not to determine how long the inmate should be kept in isolation as a penalty but to decide what he might do and what staff might do to correct the conditions that caused his difficulty.

Ideally the staff disciplinary group includes both line personnel in daily contact with the offender and high-ranking officials. Therefore, it is empowered to make changes in assignment as well as to impose penalties. This "Adjustment Committee" is sometimes a subcommittee of the institution's Classification Committee, or in a large institution it is the Classification Team for the unit where the infraction occurred, augmented by a few more senior staff. Involvement of line staff who know intimately the situation in which the offender's difficulties develop is essential if the causes of the infraction are to be understood by higher officials.

Serious or persistent infractions, when they occur, should be regarded as clues to the rehabilitative needs of the inmates involved or to the correctional deficiencies of the situation in which they occur. They may reveal the disruptive games that people play, deficiencies of social perception and judgment, or merely excessive self-centeredness and lack of consideration for others. They may reveal serious sexual or identity problems that a person is trying to solve. And they may reveal these things in staff as well as in inmates. Another argument for mixing of different staff ranks on Adjustment Committees is the guidance it can provide to higher officials on lower staff selection and training.

The easiest—but often least adequate—solution to a disciplinary problem is to transfer the inmates involved to other assignments, other housing, or a new schedule, thus eliminating the situation where the misbehavior occurred. Often the inmates are eager to have this done, for they blame their difficulties on others or on the situation. Although such changes may sometimes be constructive, they may more often be a misguided expedient. The shallowest explanation is often to blame an event on other people or on circumstances, rather than on oneself. An even more serious deficiency is to equate mere blame with explanation; little understanding is provided by calling a person or a place bad, instead of identifying, when relevant to the misbehavior, diverse intentions, specific misjudgments, ineffective responses, shortsighted or self-centered perspectives, and sources of reinforcement which perpetuate these acts. Only by trying to go beyond blame to analysis can one be well equipped to correct profound misbehavior.

Constructive discipline is concerned with increasing the ability of prisoners to cope effectively and legitimately with the provocations to anger, fear, selfishness, or desire they encounter, not just in prison, but also in postrelease life. It tries to help them find gratification, including a favorable view of themselves, in socially acceptable alternatives to misbehavior. Alcoholics Anonymous, Synanon, and other organizations stressing service to others are often an aid in this, and hence may contribute to discipline. Unless both insight and corrective action are achieved by offenders, the causes of their disciplinary infractions will persist, even though a definite penalty may succeed in making the infractions less frequent or more successfully concealed during imprisonment.

Constructive discipline progresses from developing with the prisoner a shared insight into the causes of his misbehavior, to challenging him successfully to correct them. Ex-convicts, ex-addicts, and ex-alcoholics are especially effective in this. Such correction often begins when the inmate sincerely apologizes to those he has done wrong, and if possible, make restitution or repairs the damages he has done. Correction is concluded very significantly, however, only if the offender on his own goes further by doing good for others through acts opposite to those of his offenses, which are committed not so much for overt reward or praise as for his own covert gratification. How far along this rehabilitative trail staff can move inmates is always problematic, but only if staff recognize such ultimate goals in discipline can they devise tactics to move in the direction of these goals.

NOTES AND REFERENCES

1. See Gouldner, Alvin W.: *Patterns of Industrial Bureaucracy.* Glencoe, Illinois, Free Press, 1954.
2. This concluding section was specially written for this publication by Dr. Glaser.
3. Glaser, Daniel: *The Effectiveness of a Prison and Parole System,* abridged edition. Indianapolis, Bobbs-Merrill, 1969, pp. 120-121.

What Price Punishment?

WALTER M. WALLACK

"Ten years at hard labor in the state penitentiary!" Who is that judge kidding? Does he really believe that hard labor of itself is punishment in prisons today? The pendulum has swung in a mighty arc since such phraseology applied to our prisons. If vengeance is our motive, if breaking the body and spirit of an offender is our goal, how better can we accomplish this than by condemning him to idleness, uselessness, purposelessness?

Prisons were first designed to hold the slothful, the debtors, the derelicts, the misdemeanants, the prostitutes, and the mentally afflicted. The punitive prison evolved from this humble beginning and provided among its other refinements hard labor. By design, as much as from necessity, hard labor was cruel, back-breaking, and man-killing.

To incarcerate rather than exterminate a man for the slightest offense may be regarded as a step up the cultural ladder. But the emphasis was still on punishing the body. Little or no thought was given to any other aspect of his being.

"HARD LABOR" OR CONSTRUCTIVE WORK?

Hard labor in the workhouses came to be espoused by the thinking men of former times as providing the most efficacious milieu in which the errant one might meditate his wrongdoing while, incidentally, his keepers grew rich on his earnings. Indeed, at one time the offender paid for the privilege of being em-

---

NOTE: Reprinted from *Federal Probation,* 25 (1) :3-7, 1961.

ployed under such an arrangement, and the keepers in turn paid for the privilege of being keepers. Crime marched on in spite of the system.

There is very little hard labor performed in any prison today. Such as does exist is safeguarded to be doled out by the spoonful. Coal piles, where they are still shoveling the stuff by hand, constitute one of the rare hard-labor details. So does an occasionally hand-dug ditch, under supervision one hopes. But these jobs, along with others requiring an abundance of muscle, are few and far between. The hours devoted to them are negligible when one thinks in terms of years of confinement. It is hard labor to be sure, but for the most part performed in an easy way. By comparison WPA labor was back-breaking.

So why are judges sentencing convicted offenders to hard labor? Simply because to do so is one of the ideas that from the first has prevailed in the administration of justice, namely, that hard labor is punishment. Our judges, even with tongue in cheek, are bound by the archaic criminal code and will be so bound until such time as statutes may be rewritten. One wonders if legislative bodies know there is little or no hard labor in prisons today. There was a time when hard physical exertion and long hours was a prime factor in the lives of nearly all men, either convicts or free citizens. Within the minds of many of us lingers the memory of our sometime sunrise-to-sunset wielding of axes, hoes, shovels, forks, picks, and other hand tools. Hard labor can be punishment. However, we seem to ignore the fact that physical labor has gone from prisons to a greater extent than it has from free life. Even "make" work has all but disappeared. Nor shall we shed a tear over its demise. "Busy work" with no purpose, no objective, is little better than no work at all.

So, hard labor as penal punishment scarcely exists any more. But the penal institution is per se an instrument of punishment. Surely, there is no worse punishment than being deprived of one's liberty. Doubtless it was the disappearance of labor for punishment that resulted in the introduction of other physical punishments in prison administration—at least it was conducive to that result. Punishing the body while ignoring the concomitant destruction of the psyche saw, and still does see, the infliction of brutal, unusual, and inhumane practices in our prisons. It is this concept of penal punishment that informed penologists deplore. Such practices have proved beyond doubt that they are not only anticorrectional but that they contribute mightily to strong antisocial feelings on the part of prisoners; feelings that will be directed harmfully toward society and the individuals who compose it whenever there is opportunity. Thus the intelligent penologist accepts imprisonment as punishment, not for punishment. To him, imprisonment is punishment. He seeks only to exclude from it those practices and conditions that of themselves counteract whatever possibilities there are for the rehabilitation of offenders against the law. This is not a soft, unduly sympathetic attitude at all. There is in it no desire to forget the criminal's victim, nor to let him go free to continue his depredations. We do not know yet anything better to do with criminals than to imprison them while trying to do something for them that will result in their no longer harming society. Mistakes will be made. But that is no reason for abandoning the logic that experience has brought us.

Today idleness is the curse of most prisons. There were many abuses under the system when prisoners could be employed at contract labor jobs and also produce goods for sale to the public, but we have gone so far in the opposite direction that we are making it virtually impossible to offer an "on-the-job" type of training which will fit these men to take their places in the labor ranks of society. Prison tools and equipment may not always be up to date, but most of them are not to be classified as antiquated and could be used to better advantage. By and large, prisoners want to work. Our curtailed working hours, in some states limited by law, are not producing good work habits. We are demoralizing those who came to us with good work habits already established. Labor unions and manufacturers have made it impossible for prisoners to offer any competition, and "state use" laws have kept work at a bare minimum. Of course, the good prison administrator will avail himself of every opportunity to provide constructive work for his men, but there is not enough to go around. Enforcing idleness upon a man is inhumane punishment. I believe that we are destroying many men in this manner. We should forget all about the question of work for punishment and restore it plentifully in its proper dignity as a positive value in penology.

BRUTAL TREATMENT PRODUCES CONFIRMED CRIMINALS

Recently I was lightly "quoted" in *Newsweek* as saying "Only the dumb clucks get into jail. . . . Punishment just wrecks people." Such "scholarly" pronouncements were the outcome of what I considered to be a thoughtful discussion with the author. No doubt the "quotes" were intended to appeal to the less erudite among the readers, and the box was intended to call further attention to the authenticity of the statements. Too bad that the spotlight scanned the scene so briefly. To think I had the center ring and was left standing on my head. Perhaps with two feet firmly planted on the ground, I can now say what I really believe.

I am for anything that will eliminate crime, do away with criminal behavior, produce law and order, or put an end to recidivism. If I were to be convinced that harsh and even brutal treatment could accomplish these goals, then I would say that the end would justify the means. But such has not been the case from the early days of the first prisons to modern times when incidents of real cruelty have brought on violence, destruction, and bloodshed. The history of prisons bears out the fact that brutal punishment, be it physical or psychological, results only in producing a more confirmed criminal with stronger antagonism toward the very society we avow to protect. It would be difficult to prove that public executions did or did not cut down the number of crimes punishable by death, but we know that such crimes continue to occur. I admit it was a sure cure for recidivism. The maiming of culprits found guilty of stealing failed to eradicate the pickpockets and highwaymen, although their mutilated bodies were displayed for all to view. It is almost impossible to make a case for or against punishment or the fear of it as a crime deterrent. Obviously, we do not know how many uncaught criminals there are. We do not know how many people refrain from crime because they do not want consequent loss of social status if caught, not to mention confinement as an additional

hazard. We do know that nothing has deterred those who are convicted every day by our courts.

MANY ARE VICTIMS OF A LIFE OF PUNISHMENT

There are some far-out theories that all criminals are suffering
from mental illness. For the most part such beliefs are pro-
pounded by theoreticians who have seldom had more than a cur-
sory glimpse of a prison. I do not subscribe to this theory, but I
know that some of our offenders are mentally, emotionally, and
physically sick. Therefore, we are inflicting another punishment
if we deprive them of proper medical and psychological care.
And we are increasing the burden upon society if we turn them
back into the community in the same state or worse than when
they entered our prisons.

The case histories of many of our prisoners will reveal that
they had been the victims of a certain kind of punishment
throughout their lives. Too often the mother of a young offender has thought to absolve herself of all responsibility by declaring, "I never could do anything with him. He's just like his old
man." She has threatened and beaten. She hates the old man and
she hates him too. Nor is the other side of the coin any brighter.
"He was such a good boy. He never got in trouble before." He
was a good boy as long as he did not get into anybody's hair at
home. He was good—he stayed out from underfoot. He found
his amusement on the street, with the gang, out of earshot. And
sometimes he brought home money. Never mind where he got it
—he was generous.

To be poor is punishment to some, especially in the midst of
plenty. To be poverty stricken would be regarded by anyone as
punishment. Life for some is filled with this kind of punishment and the resentment deepens and the frustrations grow. All
too soon, society will feel the repercussions of these resentments
and frustrations and will demand that punishment be added to
punishment believing that this alone will cure the evil.

Nor are the poor and ignorant the only victims of punishment.
How often we hear, "He came from such a fine family. They
gave him everything." But did they? Did they give him love and

understanding and an attentive audience? Or did they give him a car and spending money and too much freedom to roam about to find his "kicks" in the latest most sophisticated style? Was he forced to make decisions on his own when he desperately wanted advice from his socially overburdened parents? The rich can be underprivileged too.

DISCIPLINE OFTEN CONFUSED WITH PUNISHMENT

Punishment in the guise of discipline has played some part in the lives of most of us. It ranges from the this-hurts-me-more-than-it-does-you type administered to the beloved young fry through the adolescent you-can't-watch-TV-for-a-week stage and persists in some of our adult reactions to other adults. But can it be that the matter of degree of discipline or the intent to punish is the important factor? Again it seems to me that discipline must be an orderly reasonable process. The recipient of the discipline must be able to accept it as such. To be sure, we all rebel and become resentful to some extent when our own notions of the discipline demanded of us are in conflict with those of the disciplinarian. But we do not become antisocial or vicious because we regard ourselves as being so punished. This must be because we have been endowed with good heredity and our lives have been channeled by stabilizing forces.

We have today the depressing sight of many men idling away their time in prison who should never have been sent there in the first place. Some should have been committed to hospitals for medical and psychiatric care. Others should have been kept in the community under adequate probation supervision. Many are confined in maximum security prisons who could better equip themselves for a normal life on the outside by being in an open-type institution with its superior training facilities. We are hamstringing our parole authorities by loudly abusing them when they err in their judgment of a man entrusted to parole. Not all human action is predictable and not all parole boards can be composed of Solomons. Deplorable as the results of an error may prove, we will make some mistakes or we will be confining many men beyond the time that they might safely be released.

There is a keen awareness among those of us who deal with

crime and criminals that our first duty must be to the society which has been the victim of crime. But I submit that there is no contradiction in our wanting to treat criminals fairly and humanely and at the same time feeling the greatest compassion for their victims. Only a very small percentage of our prison population will spend their natural lives in prison. It seems to me that we would be doing society a greater disservice if we lost sight of the fact that we have these men—call it rehabilitation or reeducation or retraining or whatever. Only by employing all the tools at our command can we hope to offer society better protection when these men return to freedom. We do not want to be found guilty of aggravating the antisocial behavior which brought them into conflict with society in the first place. We are not condoning their acts when we treat them as human beings. Even the mad dog is not put on the rack. Can we treat our fellow men with less dignity?

Detractors of our viewpoint are by no means few. We find them in high places as well as among those whom we expect to be limited by lack of information and vision. They cry for punishment and declare that we are encouraging future criminals by providing those we have in our charge with such luxuries as psychiatric care. Modern open institutions have been likened to country clubs and one might infer that the waiting list is long. In 30 years of prison experience, I have yet to hear of an inmate who committed his crime because he yearned for living in such style. However open the institution, it is still a prison. And it is still punishment because it means loss of liberty.

Many among us are alarmed unnecessarily at the proposals offered by some armchair penological philosophers for dealing with our admittedly increasing number of criminals. Hospitals are not going to take over the care of all criminals. Prison doors will open only by degree as experience proves the desirability of such measures. And then it shall lag the proof by years. Some prison doors will never open. There will always be a need for some maximum security, but even here we need not add further punishment if we mean by that cruelty and debasement.

Discipline is as necessary for a prison as it is for a well-ordered free society. But all too often the word "discipline" has been confused with punishment. I consider the end result of discipline in the prison to be no more nor less than the orderly presence of the inmates. The rules and orders of the institution must be clear, understandable, and reasonable. When they become confusing, lacking in purpose, and designed to humiliate, they tend to sap initiative, decimate character, and create antagonism to authority. We must impose penalties for the infraction of rules, but I believe these penalties should be regarded as just that and not a subtle way of punishing minor faults. We do not want to make the mistake of deliberately converting discipline into punishment. Our problem is to achieve good, reasonable discipline which will provide the best possible atmosphere for dealing constructively with a man. Discipline in prison should never be a process of getting even with the rule breaker or even the recalcitrant. Rather, and this is drawing the line very fine, it should be a means for dealing with all prisoners firmly and fairly for positive control. The method must be firm enough to secure and maintain orderly control. But the degree to which this is exceeded is to that extent destructive to discipline.

WE ALL NEED TO DO OUR JOBS BETTER

Those of us in the business of dealing with crime would welcome more help in the field of crime prevention. Who knows how many now serving time might have been put on the right track before it was too late? I do not, but I suspect that there are many as I interview prisoner after prisoner and verify their stories. Somewhere along the line someone goofed. Just as preventive medicine has taken its rightful place in our ordered scheme of life, so should crime prevention.

I maintain that among us in free society today are some very clever diabolical criminals who continue to elude their astute pursuers.

One may say with much truth that by and large it is the least clever of our lawbreakers who are caught—the dumb clucks, if you please. We need quicker detection of crime, faster apprehension, swifter and surer administration of justice. Some of our prominent cops and supercops who rail against the way prisons are run, probation applied, and parole enforced, should look closer at their own bailiwicks rather than constantly seek to draw attention away from their own shortcomings by destructive criticism of penologists. I would be the first to say that we have some excellent law enforcement in this country, but none of it is as good as it could be and sadly there is not nearly enough of it. We all need to do our jobs better.

We have to accept the fact of punishment for convicted law breakers. There is no point in quarrelling with this. Rather our concern must be that it is constructive. Crime and criminals we shall always have with us. Our task is to find ways and means for reducing the incidence of offenses. Toward that end we shall constantly have to ask: What price punishment?

Punishment Versus Treatment?

PAUL S. SPITZER

The last century, and particularly the last few decades, have produced in our society a questioning, even skeptical, approach to traditional ways of thinking and behaving. The spectacular rise of technology and the concurrent loosening and shifting of values and social institutions have in great part contributed to this process and, in turn, have been stimulated by it. An especially striking trend has been the valuation of newness for its own sake and perhaps an overreadiness to discard the old, regardless of its inherent merit, whatever that might be.

NEW BROOMS SWEEPING THE FIELD

Nowhere has this tendency been more apparent nor more productive of conflict than in the ways in which society has viewed offenders against the public good and in the ways in which it has dealt with them. The professional practice of corrections is a relatively new field, and its practitioners are new arrivals. They have entered swiftly into an age-old social-problem area and have briskly proceeded to propose the clearing away of the accretions of the centuries. Among the debris, they found the basic concept of punishment[1] and the myriad techniques by which human ingenuity has implemented it. This survival was declared to clearly

---

NOTE: Reprinted from *Federal Probation,* 25 (2) :3-7, 22, 1961.

represent the unenlightened primitive past and as such, it had to go.

This declaration is not simply the revulsion of the tender-minded against brutality. In a time when exploding populations and generalized bigness are said to be rapidly reducing men to interchangeable units, many voices are being heard pleading the cause of the individual who is being robbed of his individuality. They say that human dignity, in danger of being fatally compromised, is among the most vital attributes of free men. This dignity is injured, so goes the argument, when one person is subjected to the degradation of being punished by others, whether privately or in the name of the public good. More specifically, it is said that the offender remains human, whatever his offense, and as such is unique and uniquely valuable. All men gain by his rehabilitation, they assert, and this is accomplished, in the last analysis, by love not hate. Punishment to them is vindictive and retributive. Both the punished and, less obviously, the punisher become victims of hate, and society suffers. Thus they conclude that punishment is a positive evil.

TRADITIONAL ARGUMENTS FOR PUNISHMENT

In addition, the rational justifications for punishment are decried as fallacious. One such justification holds that by punishing the offender, he and others who see his example are deterred from further offenses. However, evidence is produced to show that punishment, as such, is actually irrelevant to the incidence of crime. Much of this evidence is wholly convincing. Another justification holds that society itself is injured when a crime occurs, and the offender therefore owes a debt to society which is paid when he is punished. The opponents of punishment declare this argument to be meaningless, since in no way is the offense undone when the offender suffers. His victims may feel better, but this is the direct result of the satisfaction gained from sanctioned aggression and cruelty toward another who has injured them, not because the wounds of the original offense have been healed in some mystical way.

One of the oldest arguments for punishment states that the identical injury should be done to the offender as was done by him. This might be called an argument for symmetry. The offense, in a manner of speaking, has unbalanced a system which in the nature of things should be balanced. The taking of an eye for an eye redresses the balance. Since this is not really a rational justification, it cannot be successfully refuted by reason. Rather, it is dismissed as an outgrown relic of the childhood of the race, no longer worthy of adult attention.

Another contention is that punishment is intimately associated with the entire development of human civilization. It is an institution which affects and is affected by all other aspects of society and can be understood only in context. To rip it from the social fabric would be to leave the rest in tatters. Perhaps of more immediate relevancy in this regard is the statement, obviously true, that some fraction of the people believe in punishment and demand that offenders be punished. Any authority which ignores or defies this demand does so at its peril. Since this describes a condition rather than justifying it, no refutation is possible or necessary. When the inference is drawn that the condition justifies its own continuance, it becomes open to the same criticisms as any other alleged social evil.

Finally, what might be described as justification by appeal to ultimate authority is employed by some. Punishment holds an undeniable place in the Judaeo-Christian tradition as well as in other major religious movements. Its proponents, here, contend that it is the wish to God that offenders be punished, since as possessors of free will, they chose freely to violate His moral law. The very simplicity of this contention underlies both its strength and its attractiveness. The only questions that need to be answered are those of whom to punish and how, not if or why. Only the naive bother to ask how the will of God is known with such certainty. The more sophisticated, however, point out that the severity of the Old Testament has been tempered, if not superseded, by the charity of the New. In dealing with the offender, they say, a better authority would be that of the Sermon on the Mount.

There are other justifications for punishment and other counters to them, but the above arguments are among the more important. They illustrate the points which are (a) the contention that punishment is not only positively wrong but that it does not even accomplish a good end by a possibly dubious means, and (b) that punishment, in very large measure, has served the immediate satisfaction of the needs of the punisher alone. Any benefit to the offender or to society in the larger sense has been of minor importance and negligible incidence.

Having demonstrated to their own satisfaction that punishment is futile as well as brutal, many, and possibly most, correctional workers of the new persuasion propose to substitute various positive treatment methods. These are all designed to further the goal of rehabilitation of the offender. Rehabilitation is obviously desirable in a society which still holds the preservation of the value of the individual among its ideals. Punishment, it is contended, is irrelevant to this end as well as undesirable for the reasons advanced above. Therefore, punishment has no place in a modern correctional program. This is the usual conclusion, and "punitive" has become a thoroughly dirty word.

The basic difference between those who advocate punishment on the various conventional grounds and those who reject it seems to be one of time orientation. The punishers are concerned with the past and its projection into the present. For them, it is a matter of just deserts. The offender committed an offense and deserves to be punished. This obviously has nothing to do with the offender's future behavior except for the disputed rationalization of deterrence. The nonpunishers—or rehabilitators, to give them a more affirmative name—are interested in the future. To them the past offenses are relevant only insofar as they uncovered the need for treatment. Future outcomes are the only respectable concern and criterion. They then conclude that punishment and treatment form a polar dichotomy, that they are incompatible. Actually, this conclusion in many cases has become a major article of faith which is no longer readily open to examination.

ARE PUNISHMENT AND REHABILITATION UNRELATED?

Granting that revenge is outmoded as public policy; granting that brutality has no place in the affairs of a civilized society; granting that punishment does not deter in the initial instance;

granting that the consequences of an offense are in no important way modified by punishing the offender, does it follow from these premises that punishment is truly irrelevant to rehabilitation? Certainly, this seems to be an issue well worth further exploration.

Is punishment inconsistent with the positive treatment of the offender? Without regarding it as an authoritative source of an answer to this question, but solely as an illustration of human thought on the subject, one may quote the Bible which says: "He that spareth the rod hateth his son, but he that loveth him chasteneth him betimes." Certainly a vast multitude of parents who love their children also punish them. In many of these cases, one may be reasonably certain, the motivation is not revenge but correction. There is ample testimony of more recent origin than Biblical times that parents, who fail to correct their children or who protect them from the commonly accepted consequences of their own acts, directly cause or allow to occur severe damage to the developing character structure in these children. The ability to deal effectively with the unending problems of living is developed early by confronting frustrating circumstances and learning how to overcome them or, failing this, how to tolerate them. It is probably not overstating the case to say that encountering frustration is a prerequisite to becoming a successful human being. It can be argued that there is a close parallel between rearing children and rehabilitating offenders. In each case, one begins with a relatively uncivilized individual and through the processes of learning, fosters the development of a system of values, attitudes, and ways of relating to and interacting with the environment so that he becomes an acceptable member of society. In this process, the trainee is sustained through the rigors of training by what might be called a positive relationship with the trainer. One might even call it love.

Perhaps because the offender is so often seen as having been deprived of love, a deprivation which is said to be at the source of his misbehavior, there may be a natural tendency on the part of some correction workers to attempt in some small measure to make it up to him. They bend over backwards to avoid any appearance of rejection. They maintain that to understand is to forgive, although not to condone. But by their very understanding and in the act of forgiving the transgressor, they run the risk of forgetting the transgression. At least it recedes into the background where little attention need be given to it. In the course of becoming a law-abiding person, the offender must do more than adopt the ways of the models given to him. He must also give up the kinds of behavior which are condemned as offensive to the law. Accordingly, this offensiveness must be stressed, not minimized or ignored.

Also, the distinction is often made between the offender and his offense. It is emphasized that it is the offense which is rejected, not the offender. If this distinction is made sufficiently clear and strong, it may well encourage the offender to regard his offense as something so apart from himself that he may feel little or no responsibility for it.

In reaction against the excesses of the past which were in many instances sustained by the doctrine of free will, determinism has become the new rationale. If anything, it is even less satisfactory than free will, but a synthesis seems possible. Broad limits of behavior are established for the individual, by the interaction of heredity and environment, but he has some degree of effective control over what he will do and how he will do it between these limits. To the extent that this is true, the individual retains a degree of responsibility for himself. To argue, as some do, that his control, itself, and the ways in which he exercises it are also determined and therefore cannot imply responsibility is a sophistry. Any act performed in the knowledge of the possible or likely consequences of that act renders the actor responsible. The question of moral or ethical culpability is a different although related matter. To deprive a person of such responsibility or to deny it to him is at least as degrading as to brutally mistreat him. In either case, he comes an object without volition, to be manipulated without regard for his own inherent dignity which, in fact, is denied. Responsibility, however, involves the acceptance of the consequences of the acts for which one is responsible.

ACCEPTANCE OF RESPONSIBILITY IS THE FOCAL ISSUE

This seems to be the crux of the whole matter. In the sense of this discussion, consequences are painful. Whether the pain results from a frown of disapproval, a scolding, a spanking, a fine, or a prison sentence is not material to this issue, although in other contexts it is of enormous practical importance. The avoidance of pain to the maximum degree possible is for most people, if not completely fundamental, at least a major motivating force. When one transgresses against the laws of nature, recognizing that technically this is really not possible, the consequences are immediate and unavoidable. This lesson is learned easily and well. No one seriously protests that he should not fall if he steps out of a window, however disinclined he is to reach the ground. On the other hand, many, if not most, people will try to avoid the consequences of their own actions when these consequences are ordained by man-made laws. It is equally true, however, that most people will generally obey the law because they feel it is right to do so and wrong to do otherwise. Avoiding the philosophical question of moral absolutes, this feeling of the wrongness of proscribed acts is held to derive from the internalization of social controls which originally were applied from the external environment to the child.

These controls may be positive or negative. Positive controls make conformance pleasurable in some derivative manner. Negative controls render nonconformity painful. Both kinds can be applied lovingly in the sense that the motivation of the controller is, in part at least, concern for the child. Both are universally used, but our immediate concern is with the negative type. If the child does not forego the forbidden act or fails to respond in the desired way, he is encouraged to do so by making him relatively less comfortable, in a word by inflicting pain. The pain may result from the temporary withholding or diminution of expressions of love. The controller may indicate grief or disappointment or displeasure. He may do so verbally or by physical action. The variety of means of exercising such negative controls is large.

Since this discussion might be construed as being in some way a defense of, or an apology for, brutality, a brief digression seems in order. Normally, as the child matures, certain relatively primitive modes of punishment cease to be appropriate. Spanking a child is effective in that it serves to attract and focus his attention on the conflict. Beating an older offender is too literal a translation of child-rearing practices. It does intolerable violence to the dignity of the human being and represents too high a price to pay for the social good desired. In addition, such techniques are very rarely necessary in dealing with offenders who have passed childhood. They have developed, in some measure, the capacity to substitute symbols for concrete referrants and can be reached through verbal or other symbolic representations of force. Too, they have developed wider horizons than the child and have formed attachments to a far wider variety of objects and activities of which they may be deprived.

To return to the matter of internalization of social controls, the child is said to take into his own personality structure the constellation of prohibition and consequent punishment for its violation as well as mandate and gratification resulting from compliance. This occurs as one result of identification with parents or other valued persons in the environment who are also the sources of the prohibitions and mandates which are internalized. Where originally the pain which followed misbehavior came from the environment, subsequently it comes from the conscience which stirs while the wrongdoing is still only incipient. At the risk of oversimplification, it may be said that many offenders have failed to develop adequate internal controls in this way and so are unable to behave appropriately when their impulses conflict with the law.

LIMITS AND SANCTIONS

Viewed from another angle, each person seems to be so constituted as to seek to know the permissible limits within which he may act. Very few today would seriously question the need for limits. Limits, however, must imply the concept of sanctions, to be invoked if the limits are violated. Sanctions are designed to increase the discomfort of the violator in some way. It is literally meaningless to consider a penalty as other than painful in some degree. No matter how the offender is viewed, the purpose of the limit setter in invoking sanctions is to cause pain. It is true that sometimes "this hurts me more than it does you," but the only pertinent pain is that which the offender experiences. It is necessary to clearly distinguish between the purpose, which is to cause pain, and the basic motivation, which is to bring about behavioral change in a desired direction.

It is also necessary to distinguish between the pain and the means by which it is induced. Pain is a subjective experience. There is no clear-cut relationship between the sanctions which are imposed upon the offender and the pain which he experiences. A scolding may cause anguish to one far greater than a prison sentence to another. The only acceptable reason for applying either is to bring about a desired change. The only appropriate degree of punishment is that which in turn produces the requisite degree of discomfort which, when experienced, creates the motivation to avoid future repetition of the offense-punishment-pain sequence.

Thus it appears that both from the point of view of stimulating learning to deal more effectively with reality and from that of fostering the development of inner controls of conscience, punishment, again defined as the imposition of appropriate penalties consequent upon wrongdoing, is justified as being one factor in creating the motivation for change which is basic to rehabilitation of the offender. In this view, there is no effort to let the punishment fit the crime nor to any major extent the offender. Rather it is designed to fit the desired outcome. One punishes in order to more effectively rehabilitate or educate, in full recognition of the fact that by itself punishment is not enough either.

THEORY INTO PRACTICE

At this point, one may well ask how these rather theoretical considerations may be related to practice. How does one deal with the flesh and blood law violator? There can be no general or definitive answer, but perhaps some illustrations will help.

John is in late adolescence. He has no prior record and his career to date has been undistinguished. He graduated from high school without major difficulty, although he did talk of quitting. His parents had to be quite firm to keep him in school. A weekend party, too much to drink, and an alert prowl-car crew landed him in jail for drunk-driving. Now he is sober, contrite, and scared. He has already been punished by the impersonal procedures of law enforcement and is experiencing much discomfort. If nothing more happens to him, he may well go home determined to sin no more. The likelihood is, however, that in a few weeks most of the pain of this experience will have been forgotten. He will probably emerge feeling that it was not too bad. His ability to refrain from this particular kind of law violation will not be much enhanced. Consolidation of the initial gain is necessary. The imposition of a moderate fine to be paid in weekly installments over the same period of several weeks will serve as a continuing and unpleasant reminder of the offense and its outcome. The punishment is prompt so that it is firmly related to the offense, and it continues long enough to permit attitudinal change. It is neither so severe nor so prolonged as to permit the gradual growth of a sense of grievance which first minimizes the guilt and finally justifies the offense. The amount of the fine is determined not by a schedule but by John's circumstances. It is intended to hurt but not cripple.

Bill follows John to the bench. He is charged with the same offense in much the same circumstances. Bill is a much more sensitive soul. He turns faint at the sight of blood and sheds surreptitious tears at sad movies. As far as was reasonably possible, he has been shielded from the more unpleasant facts of life. He is even more disturbed by his plight than John. He would like nothing more than to forget the nightmarish situation. He is sentenced to spend one or two Saturday nights viewing the outcome of drunk driving at the scenes of accidents, at the emergency hospitals, and at the morgue. Although this may seem almost sadistic, it will leave Bill with some badly needed scar tissue that will ache when there is a threat of wet weather.

Tom is the last of our trio. He drinks, too, but he is an old hand. He has what is delicately called a drinking problem. In fact he is a hopeless, sodden alcoholic who has an intimate and long-time acquaintance with the drunk tank. Beneath his frowsty surface, Tom is in agony. He suffers because he drinks and he drinks because he suffers. One way or another he hurts all of the time. To punish Tom is pointless and heartless. To inflict further pain on him would be without purpose or sense. He has inner controls, but they do not work well enough. He needs external support; something besides a lamp pole on which to lean. He illustrates the idea that punishment is no end in itself and that there are circumstances in which it is not appropriate.

SUMMARY

The attempt has been made to show that punishment for wrongdoing originated in the needs of the punisher. In the course of social development, increasingly great concern has been directed to the wrongdoer and his needs. One result of this shift in emphasis has been to place the entire concept of punishment in question and disrepute. This trend has developed to the point where the baby has become so confused with the bathwater that both are in danger of being discarded. It is suggested that punishment is a proper technique of social control when applied appropriately and in the right situations. The attitudes of correctional workers on either side of this question might well be reevaluated with profit to all.

NOTES AND REFERENCES

1. Throughout this essay, punishment is defined as the imposition of appropriate penalties consequent upon wrongdoing. The meaning of appropriate emerges from the discussion itself.

A New Prison Discipline—Implementing the Declaration of Principles of 1870

HOWARD B. GILL

Several times during recent years, an attempt has been made to revise the Declaration of Principles established by the National Prison Congress in 1870. Such changes as were made were insignificant. No one has ever extolled the revised version of 1930 or 1960. One might as well suggest a revision of the Declaration of Independence! New times call for new manifestos, not revisions of old declarations. What is needed today, 100 years later, is not a revised or a new Declaration of Principles, but a statement implementing the Declaration of Principles of 1870—a statement summarizing what that Declaration has produced through trial

NOTE: Reprinted from *Federal Probation,* 34 (2) , 1970.

and error over the past 100 years; a codification of progress achieved, an affirmation for the future. Let us call it a New Prison Discipline.

There are two types of discipline: One, a set of rules and regulations governing a group; the other, a way of life. There is a discipline in medicine, in religion, in education. So in corrections there is a discipline. It includes rules and regulations, but it is of much broader scope; it is a way of life.

PRISON DISCIPLINE: 1825-1925

Historically, the prison discipline recognized by prison workers for over 100 years was founded by Elam Lynds, the warden of Auburn Prison, about 1825. It was founded on the basic assumption that the prerequisite for reform was to "break the spirit of the criminal." It prevailed almost universally in the United States from 1825 until 1925. It still is standard operating procedure in some American prisons.

Specifically, this old prison discipline stood for some very concrete things:

1. *Hard labor.* Through productive work from "making little ones out of big ones" to constructive prison industries, or through nonproductive punitive labor such as the treadmill and the carrying of cannon shot from one end of the prison yard to the other.

2. *Deprivation.* Of everything except the bare essentials of existence.

3. *Monotony.* Of diet and drab daily routine.

4. *Uniformity.* The warden's proudest boast: "We treat every prisoner alike."

5. *Mass movement.* Mass living in cell blocks, mass eating, mass recreation, even mass bathing. In this monolithic type of program, the loss of individual personality was characteristic. One watched the dull gray line with its prison shuffle where the faces of men were as if shellacked with a single mask.

6. *Degradation.* To complete the loss of identity prisoners became numbers. Housed in monkey cages, dressed in shoddy, nondescript clothing, denied civil contacts even with guards

like the one who snarled: "Who the hell are you to wish me a Merry Christmas?" Degradation became complete.

7. *Subservience.* To rules, rules, rules—the petty whims of petty men.

8. *Corporal punishment.* Brutality and force prevailed. In Tennessee the paddle, in Colorado the whip, in Florida the sweat box, etc.

9. *Noncommunication.* Silence or solitary confinement; limited news, letters, visits, or contacts of any normal kind.

10. *Recreation.* At first none; later a desultory or perfunctory daily hour in the yard.

11. *No responsibility.* "No prisoner is going to tell me how to run my prison." Actually prisoners were relieved of every social, civic, domestic, economic, or even personal responsibility for the simplest daily routines.

12. *Isolation.* Often 16 hours a day. Psychologically, the admonition to "do your own time" with no thought for the other fellow only increased the egocentricity of the lone wolves.

13. *No "fraternization" with the guards.* The rule found in many prisons that guards must not talk with prisoners about their personal problems or their crimes prevented any attempt at solving the criminal problem.

14. *Reform by exhortation.*

THE OLD GUARD KNEW WHAT THEY WANTED

Now that psychology has come of age, we know that such a discipline denied every normal, basic need of the human personality and its corresponding opposite essential to a healthy and normal life. These included love and a proper comprehension of its opposite, hate; independence and the right kind of dependence; constructive use of imagination and truth; achievement and learning how to meet failure; identity and a decent humility which recognized the dignity of the individual; intimacy and its opposite, discrimination; creativity and constructive criticism; integration and concentration.

These 16 human needs are recognized today as basic in the making of a healthy personality. Yet the prison discipline which was current for 100 years prior to 1925 denied every one of these basic needs. More than this, such a discipline fostered every pathology which results from a malfunctioning of these needs, namely rejection, doubt, guilt, inferiority, inadequacy, diffusion, self-absorption, apathy, despair. Is it any wonder that men left prison worse than when they entered?

However, let us give the Old Guard credit. They knew what they wanted. They could tell you just what the "prison discipline" stood for. A young guard learned these concepts in order to be a "good prison officer." And anyone who violated these sacred rules was soon out of a job. There are still a few prison systems—in Arkansas and Mississippi—and in other isolated institutions, described by Dr. Karl Menninger in *The Crime of Punishment,* where such a prison discipline prevails.

"MODERN PENOLOGY": 1925-1970

During the past 50 years, however, several things have happened which are gradually changing all this.

1. The programs inaugurated at Auburn and Sing Sing prisons in New York and at the Navy prison in Portsmouth by Thomas Mott Osborne (1916-1920) showed plainly that prisoners knew more about what was going on in prisons than the warden and his officers. This broke the back of the "Old Guard."

2. The individual study of the offender inaugurated by Dr. William Healy in 1915 and followed up by Dr. Bernard Glueck, Dr. W. T. Root, Dr. W. J. Ellis, and Dr. Edgar Doll, resulting in the establishment of the so-called classification system, destroyed the basic tenet of the old prison discipline that "every prisoner should be treated alike." This was the coup de grace that finished the "Old Guard."

3. A new type of correctional institution for tractable prisoners which abandoned the massive, monolithic, monkey cages in favor of small-group cottages or dormitories in an open community, within or without walls, is producing profound changes in climate, personnel, and methods as well as structure. Institutions for women at Alderson, West Virginia, Dwight, Illinois, and elsewhere, and for men at Lorton, Virginia, Norfolk, Massachusetts, Annandale, New Jersey, and Algoa Farms, Missouri, led the way.

The concept of the "therapeutic community" where offenders learn to live like normal, responsible human beings has resulted. The Old Guard are not competent to administer a therapeutic community for offenders.

4. In 1913, Wisconsin, following informal experiments elsewhere, enacted the Huber Law which provided that misdemeanants might serve jail sentences by living in prison at night and working in the community by day. The law was almost forgotten for 50 years. Revived in the past 10 years, 20 states have enacted similar laws and one of the great movements in corrections got underway. Work release is becoming as important in modern corrections as the introduction of probation and parole was 100 years ago.

Since 1925, we have witnessed the development of "modern penology"—an attempt to replace the old prison discipline with "programs of rehabilitation"—social work and smug satisfaction, pious platitudes and programs, actually a period of conflict and confusion. The result is that we again have what Samuel L. Parsons, the Quaker superintendent of prisons for Virginia, described in 1826 as a "sickly and mistaken administration of the American penitentiary system."

It can be stated conservatively that over half of the major prisons and reformatories in the United States are just "sweat jails," institutions where prisoners dawdle at their work, engage in a variety of desultory social and educational activities, receive good medical care, and live under so-called programs of treatment which have little or no relation to the particular criminal problem of any one of them. This is called "bird-shot" penology. We fill the old blunderbuss full of a little work, a modicum of education, a bit of religion, some medical care if necessary, a good deal of recreation—rodeos, radios, baseball, bands, choral groups, and what not—and call it rehabilitation. This is better than what passes for treatment in a minority of our prisons where "machine-gun penology" still prevails, even if the old prison discipline no longer is acknowledged; but it is not good prison discipline.

The difficulty today is that we do not know specifically for what we stand in structure, in personnel, in method, or even in

our basic concepts. What is needed is not a restatement of fundamental principles, most of which are as applicable now as they
were 100 years ago, but rather a formulation of precise, operational, down-to-earth concepts by which we can guide the course
of twentieth-century corrections. At least it may give us a starting
point toward a new prison discipline.

Ten Basic Concepts

First, then, let us consider some basic concepts for such a discipline.

1. Prisoners go to prison as punishment and not for punishment.

2. The purpose of imprisonment is threefold: (a) to keep
prisoners in security, (b) to reduce criminality through problem-
solving, and (c) to adjust prisoners through acculturation to the
society to which they will return. These three words—security,
problem-solving, acculturation—open the doors to the new discipline.

3. Security must be assured and then assumed. Thus security
becomes the primary, but not the ultimate, aim of penology.

4. Treatment will begin with restitution to the victim whenever and so far as possible.

5. In the reduction of criminality, problem-solving must pre-
cede programming, and programming should be geared to the
significant problems affecting criminality in each case. All else is
secondary.

6. Since the crime committed is only one symptom of a basic
maladjustment, we shall not treat murder, robbery, rape, or trea-
son. Treatment for the reduction of criminality will deal with
one or more of the five areas of maladjustment, namely, the situ-
ational, the medical, the psychological or psychiatric, the antisocial or ethical, and/or the elementary custodial needs of shel-
ter, food, clothing, and well-being.

7. Programs of work, education, medical care, religion, recreation, and family welfare geared to solving significant problems
of criminality should also be designed to adjust the offender to
the society to which he will return, i.e. acculturation. Such a concept will revolutionize the structure and the methods of treat-

ment in prisons as well as the personnel. We shall stop erecting massive, medieval, monastic, monolithic, monkey-cages, magnificent monstrosities as prisons. We shall adopt small-group, community-type layouts which resemble as nearly as possible normal living in an American community; and we shall develop halfway houses and residential centers for offenders who can live and work satisfactorily under careful supervision in the community.

8. Treatment through problem-solving and acculturation must proceed whether or not causation can be established or dealt with. While it is helpful to know and understand causation, it is not necessary for treatment. However, causation should be explored as far as possible in environmental, physical, psychological, and characterological areas.

9. The function of the prison will be limited to safe-keeping, observation, diagnosis, planning, and training or treatment. Rehabilitation or readjustment will be conducted in the normal community, under normal conditions with all the attendant problems, influences, and responsibilities. This will inevitably lead to the following basic concept.

10. The establishment between the prison and parole of a program of partial or semirelease—what I have called "social servitude" or servitude in society as contrasted with penal servitude— under close daily supervision in the community similar to the Intermediate Plan of the Irish System (1850-1870), the Huber Law of Wisconsin (1913), and the work-release programs now in vogue in more than 20 states. This alone should reduce the present population of American prisons by 50 percent, remove the necessity for great expansion in prison building, help solve the prison labor problem, reduce the cost of keeping prisoners by millions of dollars, and insure realistic proof of satisfactory adjustment to community life, thus insuring a satisfactory parole program.

Operational Benchmarks

To implement these basic concepts, the following specific operational benchmarks will be essential.

1. Observation, diagnosis, planning and training of treatment will be based on recognized essentials: (a) posttrial and presen-

tence investigation and report, (b) individual case histories and institutional case records, (c) clinical examinations and tests, physical and psychological, and (d) clinical procedures such as counseling to secure change in attitude and action.

2. Prisoners will be classified primarily in five basic groups for treatment: (a) new prisoners, (b) tractable—those who desire to change and who respond to mutual trust, cooperation, and normal conditions and relationships, (c) intractable—those who do not desire to change or cooperate and who respond only to fear, force, and deprivation, (d) defective—those who are subnormal or abnormal, and (e) potential work-release prospects.

Each group will be housed either in separate institutions or in separate sections of the same institution. The indiscriminate mixing of these groups will be avoided in any sound treatment program.

3. Each of these five basic groups will be further classified for security as: (a) maximum custody—requiring close supervision, (b) medium custody—responsible within certain limits, and (c) minimum custody—free under general supervision.

4. Treatment of each of these five basic groups will follow well-defined lines: (a) orientation and preliminary problem-solving for new prisoners, (b) problem-solving and acculturation for tractable prisoners, (c) simple custodial care for intractable prisoners with severely limited privileges and programs, (d) custodial care and limited training under medical supervision for defective prisoners, and (e) treatment and supervision in the free community.

Thus shall we eliminate the "sweat jail."

5. Personnel will develop around five main groups of officers: (a) executive personnel, (b) administrative, fiscal, and clerical personnel, (c) professional and technical personnel—medical, industrial, educational, religious, social, recreational, psychiatric, legal—with advisory powers only as regards prisoners, (d) security personnel, especially trained to prevent and handle escapes, contraband, and disorder (such personnel will be the police of the prison community—patrol and inspect the grounds and buildings; conduct search and shakedowns; man the walls, towers, and

gates; and direct transportation; they will not undertake training or treatment of prisoners including daily routine or disciplinary matters), and (e) supervisors and others in direct contact with prisoners in living quarters and in work assignments, especially trained in correctional counseling. These officers will be responsible for training and treatment of prisoners, including daily routine and disciplinary matters, in cooperation with professional and technical personnel.

By thus establishing a clear distinction between the advisory powers of the professional and technical staff and the authority for security only of one part of the guard force and for treatment of another part of the guard force, the separation of power and responsibility in the treatment of prisoners and the violent conflict between security and treatment which plagues American prisons today can be resolved.

6. Institutional design and structure to implement the foregoing will include different types of institutions or sections of institutions, namely: (a) reception center or section for new prisoners, (b) close-confinement institution or section for intractable prisoners, (c) community-type institution or section for tractable prisoners, (d) custodial-hospital–type institution for defectives, and (e) halfway houses and residential centers for work-release prisoners.

7. The outside community itself must supplement such a prison discipline with the following: (a) supervised probation following suspended sentences, (b) supervised semirelease following a period of penal servitude as preparation for parole, as outlined above, (c) supervised parole, (d) volunteer sponsorship for probationers and ex-prisoners, (e) crime prevention under noncorrectional civilian direction, and (f) supplementary services in providing employment, medical care, education, family welfare, recreation, and religious counseling not available in correctional agencies.

8. A more elusive but essential element in implementing the basic concepts of a new prison discipline is the maintenance of an institutional climate conducive to securing the desired results. Experienced prison workers are fully aware of the importance

of climate in the proper functioning of an institution. Climate is something one feels, but it is dependent on very concrete conditions.

All that has been set forth thus far as essentials in the new prison discipline will contribute to the climate. Many things pertaining to structure, personnel, and methods produce climate. In American prisons today, three general types of climate may be noted: the custodial, the progressive, and the professional. The custodial offers the minimum essentials and a decent routine in a rather grim and barren climate. The progressive satisfies many normal needs with its programs of different activities but falls short of reducing criminality, as the recidivism rate shows. The professional seeks to reduce criminality through problem solving and acculturation. Security must be assured in each.

9. There are five important elements in producing a professional climate: (a) Small-group planning as applied to structure, to groupings of prisoners, and to treatment methods, as contrasted with the indiscriminate massing in all these areas, (b) one-to-one relationship in counseling and guidance (whether in individual or group treatment) which is the key to any effective influence on attitudes and behavior, (c) development of joint participation and joint responsibility in which both prisoners and the official personnel work together in a common effort to maintain the good life, (d) normalcy in relationships between officials and inmates in structure, in methods, in rules and regulations, (e) community contacts between the prison and the outside, and (f) professional training of prison guards-in-contact as treatment aids to front office. Space does not permit discussion of these six essentials, but their application to an institution program will produce a climate conducive to effective treatment.

10. Finally, such a new prison discipline is not the possession or the responsibility only of prison workers. It can only be established under a leadership which recognizes the whole correctional process as a coordinated unit, including the police, the courts, probation, prisons, parole, and the public through prevention. It anticipates a rebirth of the old concern of the law for the entire administration of the criminal law. Indeed, until this correction-

al process from prevention and police work through to parole is removed from executive-political control and put under the judicial branch of the government, we may not expect the most effective professional understanding or leadership in this field of government.

These basic concepts and these ten groups of benchmarks furnish the starting point for a new prison discipline. They are purposefully definite and precise. They are operational. They are down-to-earth proposals which can be tested in any prison. They offer guideposts for those who want to develop effective treatment for criminals. Moreover, they are an attempt to reflect and to summarize what the Declaration of Principles of 1870 has produced during the past 100 years—the New Prison Discipline of 1970.

SECTION VI

SOME INNOVATIONS IN CORRECTIONAL PRACTICE

THE viewpoints on treatment presented here are frankly pointed toward innovation. Admittedly, not all current trends are represented; the selection was made in the interest of providing extant examples of immediately applicable concepts. Furthermore, these are concepts growing out of lengthy practical experience. A majority of the authors in this section have had direct experience in the management of institutional treatment programs.

The fallacy of seeing the prevention of crime as solely a function of penal facilities is scored by Heyns. He reminds us that "society breeds its own delinquents through its inattention to their problems, through its materialistic values, its concept that the possession of things is the measure of success. . . ." The importance of attention to the causes of delinquency has infrequently been of sufficient concern. Heyns notes that advocates of the "get rough" policy err in thinking that they advocate a new approach. It never seems to strike them that the "generally approved juvenile court practices and the progressive programs in juvenile institutions and parole agencies did not burst full panoplied from the dome of some egghead."

Burke supports Heyns' concept with an example drawn from actual experience. The extreme irony with which he expresses his rejection of the attitudes of those who view punishment as the penal preogative is unlikely to be missed. His eminently readable and thought-provoking article is written, purportedly, by a talebearer who has no use for "coddling" as institutional policy.

Korn decries the fact that major innovations in corrections have "almost invariably been the work of inspired amateurs." He outlines some of the reasons that fundamental change is so difficult to achieve. Liberation from the past proceeds sluggishly; the tenacity with which dogma has clung, barnacle-like, to the hull of penology cripples innovative progress. Exclusion of the con-

284

sumer from the scene of corrections has allowed the correctional establishment to continue to bleat for funds for expensive alternatives rather than to institute drastically needed reforms within the system proper to shatter this impermeable shell of dogma. Too often, through removal from positions of effectiveness, by promotion to administrative cul-de-sacs or by lateral removal from points of influence, emasculation is the destiny of innovators.

A resource infrequently taken account of in ongoing programs is the talents of the offender himself. It was many years before the mental health field began to accept the notion that patients could contribute to the treatment of other patients. The acceptance of group treatment methods in other settings required abandonment of the notion that therapy took place only through the direct, one-to-one treatment performed by professional personnel. Cressey advocates use of the knowledge gained from social psychological theory in understanding how noncriminals become criminals to help them retrace the path. Just as noncriminals have been recruited to criminality through the influence of their associates, inmates who have adopted prosocial attitudes may be instrumental in inculcating these attitudes in others. His decades of experience as a theorist in criminology afford him rare insight into "criminal-ology." Cressey attributes the success of a number of programs to their requirement that the "reformee perform the role of the reformer." Beyond this stands the fact that we have learned since World War I, in both hospitals and correctional institutions, "that change in patients and prisoners depends more on the actions of attendants, guards, and other patients and prisoners than it does on the action of professional personnel." It is his belief that if we are to develop a group of "people changers," the probability is high that ex-prisoners will be among the most effective practitioners of the occupation.

Shah cautions against judging as effective all programs dubbed "treatment" or "rehabilitative." Precise definition and evaluation of the endeavors of those interested in reclaiming offenders is needed. The officer should be aware that he constitutes the essential human element in the correctional environment. From Shah's point of view, the line officer, as well as others, must be conversant with the principles of learning theory if he is to be an effective agent of change. He states that "The relatively tight structure of the institution and possibilities for controlling large elements of the total environment in an orderly fashion can greatly facilitate behavior modification."

The question of whether the "new penology" is fact or fiction is examined by Schnur. He pleads for attention to the specific goals of confinement and points out that the limited amount of time which "professionals" have available to spend with individual inmates makes it impossible to build a treatment program solely with these professionals. Institutional staffs must be comprised of "dedicated, persistent, sincere men who know what to look for and know the significance of what they see" if the new penology is to be attempted. From the author's point of view, it has "not been tried."

The "Treat-'Em-Rough" Boys Are Here Again

GARRETT HEYNS

It is gratifying to note the great concern evident throughout the nation with the "rising tide" of juvenile delinquency. Whether there is actually so great an upsurge in juvenile law violation as some assert is not something we need discuss here. Were there but a fraction of the number of delinquents we actually have, there would still be a grave problem confronting us. Ideally, one delinquent is one too many.

Of course, all thinking citizens should be worried about the situation. Aside from the unhappiness, the loss of property, the threat of physical harm, the waste of lives involved, there is the threat to our democracy, for the successful operation of our form of government depends upon the wholehearted, intelligent participation of all citizens. Democratic government, or for that matter, any government, cannot function properly if there is among its citizens large-scale disrespect for law and order, indifference to the rights of others, lack of conscientious attention to the duties of citizenship. Widespread delinquency constitutes

NOTE: Reprinted from *Federal Probation*, 31 (2) :6-10, 1967.

too ominous a threat for us to be indifferent to its presence or to be unconcerned with doing something about it.

TO SOME THE SOLUTION IS SIMPLE!

The concern about the situation is very apparent. Many people write about the problem and still more talk about it. The approaches and the solutions offered are many and varied. All over the nation, individuals, committees, institution staffs, jurists, and others are putting much time and effort into the study of the causes of delinquency and in programs dealing with treatment and prevention. There are also many self-appointed experts who belittle such efforts. To them, delinquency is not a complicated phenomenon and its treatment is relatively simple. Their plan of attack is probably best summed up in the phrase "get 'em young, treat 'em rough, tell 'em nothin'." To some the solution is absurdly simple, like that of the probate judge who told me some years ago that the way to prevent delinquency among juveniles was to remove all married women from the swing shift.

Evident in the discussion of the problem is a strong tendency to indict existing agencies involved in doing something with the delinquent. We have heard businessmen, civic leaders, and other prominent citizens lay the blame for the situation upon the courts for not being tough enough with the youngsters who come to their attention. They declare that judges are giving probation to delinquents who should be taken out of circulation; that paroling authorities are far too lenient. They demand that these miscreants be punished so that they may gain respect for law and authority.

One is tempted to reply to those who go about looking for a scapegoat that this approach partakes of the nature of passing the buck. Where do these youngsters who are brought to the attention of the authorities come from? Certainly the courts, the paroling authorities, and the institutions did not spawn them. They come to these agencies already disturbed. Surely no carefully reared boy or girl ever became involved in delinquent acts because he or she heard that the judge was a softy and the institutions easy. These critics should be reminded that society breeds its own delinquents through its inattention to their problems, through its materialistic values, its concept that the possession of things is the measure of success, the vast difference that lies between its preachments and its practices. They should be reminded that respect for authority should be fostered in the home and the community. Force may inculcate fear of authority, but it will not foster respect. This fact is somewhat forcefully, though a bit gruesomely, brought out in the couplet:

> "Thief ne'er felt the halter draw
> With good opinion of the law."

PUNISHMENT AND TREATMENT DO NOT COEXIST

Another fact of which the "treat-'em-rough" advocates should be reminded is that a program which emphasizes the punitive and one which stresses the corrective cannot go hand in hand. You cannot have a regimen which aims at severity and one that aims at understanding treatment in the same institution. The fact is, however, that whatever the cause and regardless of whatever agency may have failed, we have these delinquent children on our hands, and we will have to do something for them.

The view that the most effective way of handling the delinquent is to treat him severely, to punish him and his parents is by no means confined to some laymen and women. Witness the pronouncements and practice of a judge in one of our Western states who proclaimed, wherever he could make himself heard, that he has been very successful in reducing delinquency in his jurisdiction by such expediencies as publishing the names of the youths appearing before him and those of the children's parents, and conducting the case in court as though the offender were an adult, the press and interested public being admitted to the hearing.

Careful investigation in 1964 by the National Council on Crime and Delinquency of the judge's claims for the success of his program reveals no evidence to support them. Nonetheless, his assertions were given wide publicity and in many quarters accepted at face value. There was even editorial comment urging that juvenile courts generally follow this judge's practices. Recently one hears little of the judge; apparently the facts have caught up with him.

It is, however, alarming that one who had had little acquaintance with the problem of delinquency and with the treatment of delinquent boys and girls, and thus little upon which to base his recommendations and practices, should have received so wide an audience and as much approval as he did. People experienced with delinquent youngsters will disagree with his approach. Such persons know that most of these young violators could not care less about the threat of publicity—in fact, they rather welcome it. They carry the clippings around to show others of their kind. In one form or another they obtain the status they so strongly desire.

Nor is there good basis for the thought that parents will pay more attention to the conduct of their children if they know that their own names, too, will be published in case their progeny are apprehended in acts of delinquency. Those parents who care little about the habits and behavior of their children will pay little or no heed to the threat of publicity. They are themselves little inclined to respect law and order and have fostered no love for authority in the home. On the other hand, to publish the names of those definitely solicitous of the welfare of their children is cruel. Everyone knows that there are parents whose boy or girl has become wayward in spite of their every effort of care. They already feel bad when these youngsters are cited for delinquency; why make matters worse by attempting to hold them up to public scorn? This whole program is thoughtless and sadistic, and utterly unworthy of emulation.

One wonders whether the judge and those who hold his opinion are not thinking more of prevention than effective treatment for the boy or girl already in trouble, by stressing dire consequences so that nobody will dare be bad. However, as history teaches, a policy of scaring people has never been generally effective. Assuming, however, that it could be, where does it leave the youngster who has been involved in delinquency and has been brought to the attention of the authorities?

WE NEED TO ATTACK THE CAUSES
OF DELINQUENCY

Allied with the advocacy of the "treat-'em-rough" program is the thought many have that the rehabilitation of the delinquent and the prevention of delinquency are largely a matter of good police practice and speedy apprehension, followed, of course, by court action—hopefully severe. One hears this stress on speedy action by the police, coming even from high places. There is no doubt as to the desirability of quick and efficient police action, that immediate apprehension is vital to stopping depredations of already delinquent youth. However, those who talk about this matter speak as if this were the solution to the whole problem of delinquency. There seems to be no thought given here to the need of an attack upon the causes of delinquency. What made delinquents of those whom we are seeking speedily to apprehend? The fact that most of these delinquent and predelinquent children have no code to which they can relate conduct save the pragmatic one—do that with which you can get by—seems to have been forgotten. Those who might have influenced them have never taught them any other code. Right and wrong are meaningless terms to them. If, as is contended, the courts treat them too leniently and the institutions and parole authorities coddle them, it is still pertinent to ask whence come these delinquents and what forces foster them.

Let me repeat, good police practice is vital, but it must not be regarded as sufficient in itself as a solution to our problem. We have no quarrel with those who stress it, provided they realize that the question remains: What can be done for those who are now delinquent and those who will, in the ordinary course of events, become delinquents? This part of the problem seems not to have been considered.

At times it seems that the advocates of the get rough policy think they are proposing a new approach. The irony in the situation lies in the fact that this method has been tried for many weary centuries. Anyone who knows anything about the history of crime and punishment is quite aware of the fact that harsh treatment of the offender has been very much the order of the day until a few decades ago when a child guilty of violation of the law was treated as an adult and could be, and in many cases actually was, hanged for stealing. However, all of the harsh punishments, all of the hangings and maimings were ineffective in reducing crime. The harsh treatment of the delinquent was equally ineffective.

On the other hand, of recent origin is the program of attempting to rehabilitate a disturbed juvenile by making an effort to understand the nature of his problem; to get at the causes of his delinquency; through wise counseling to inculcate new ideals, aims, and interests; to develop a program of treatment fitted to his individual needs, to help him reintegrate into his family and community, if that be a fitting one, or to help him find a new favorable one, if that seems indicated. Modern juvenile court procedures have been with us less than 70 years. Institutions with adequate programs, child-guidance clinics, careful parole supervision, public school counselors and psychologists are agencies and services even younger than the juvenile court.

It is ironical that because workers in these fields have not learned to solve the problems of every disturbed boy or girl, the approach stands condemned, and we are importuned by the uninformed to return to a method that has a long history of failure.

PROGRESSIVE PROGRAMS TODAY ARE BASED ON YEARS OF TESTED EXPERIENCE

It should be borne in mind that most delinquent youngsters are rather badly disturbed when they come to the correctional agency, be it child-guidance clinic, court, or a juvenile institution. Hence the task of these agencies is a tremendous one. Let me stress further that it is not the primary function of the court or that of the juvenile agencies to prevent delinquency. It is their task to help the one already delinquent into acceptable behavior and in this way to prevent the repetition of delinquent acts on the part of their charges. Yet the tendency of many critics is to hold them responsible for conditions with which it is not their primary function to concern themselves.

It never seems to strike the advocates of harshness that the present generally approved juvenile court practices and the progressive programs in juvenile institutions and parole agencies did not burst full panoplied from the dome of some egghead. They do not seem to be aware of the fact that many, many years of experience, of thought and experiment, observation of successes and failures, led to changes which brought into practice the methods to which objection is made.

A study of the record of the many of the states with institutions having progressive programs for the treatment of delinquent boys and girls will bear out my contention that the "treat-'em-rough" practice did not work. Practically all of these institutions had gone through years of emphasis on custody and harsh treatment and had come to realize its failure. Contrast the record of those years with the experience since the programs have been changed and modern treatment methods have been introduced.

The situation, past and present, in the training schools of one of our states is illustrative. As late as 1948, harsh discipline, head shaving for violations of rules, the silent system, injection of nausea-producing drugs, and long periods of solitary confinement were the order of the day at the school for girls in that state. There were no counselors and very little of an educational program. Here was practiced the severity some advocate, yet an average of one third of the girls at the institution during the period were returnees from parole or escape. There is no record of those who ran away and were not returned. The same situation prevailed at the training school for boys during the period cited. There, too, harsh discipline was very much in vogue and corporal punishment was resorted to freely. During those years of a total of 557 residents, 351 had been returned from parole or escape. Again, there is no record of those who had made a successful getaway. It might be added that riots, accompanied by destruction of property, were frequent. One third of the boys in residence had been committed one or more times previously, some as many as six times.

Contrast this situation with that obtaining today in these same institutions where counselors, social workers, and psychologists are on the staff, where educational programs under competent teachers and humane treatment, are parts of the program. Today only 4 percent of all those inmates of institutions for juveniles have been committed before, and the recidivism rate of all those released on parole has dropped from better than 30 percent in 1958 to less than 15 percent, the present figure. This decrease in recidivism holds in spite of the fact that, meanwhile, the population in the institutions has increased.

HARSH TREATMENT AND REPRESSION SIMPLY DO NOT WORK

It is apparent from this comparison that an institution program devoted to harsh treatment and repression has availed not at all in the rehabilitation of the inmates.

One sad point in regard to the contention of the "treat-'em-rough" advocates that progressive practices do not work is the fact that these practices have never been adequately implemented.

A large number of the juvenile courts throughout the nation are sadly lacking in staff to carry out a realistic program. There is no diagnostic service available to the judge; probation staff is insufficient in number and untrained to supervise adequately those youngsters whom the judge places on probation. Despite all of its interests in sound procedures, the court is not able to do what it would like to do—what seems to be indicated in each case. Frequently the only recourse is commitment to an institution, which in many cases is neither necessary nor desirable. Institutional commitment should never be the only recourse; it should be one of the many dispositions available to the court which the judge can choose when he has adequate diagnostic services at his command.

Notwithstanding, it is true that a large percentage of juveniles sent to institutions would not have been sent there if the court had sufficient staff and the citizens of the area had recognized their responsibilities and had been willing to help community programs to assist the delinquent to become a law-abiding citizen. Communities, courts, institutions, and paroling authorities all lack sufficient staff to carry out efficient treatment programs. This fact is responsible for lack of success. When citizens really become sufficiently concerned to want to see something done and are willing to pay for it, present-day programs will have startling success. A decade ago, 40 to 50 percent of the "graduates" of state juvenile correctional institutions were coming back after getting into new difficulties, or progressing to state reformatories or prisons. Today, about 85 percent of the youngsters treated in state institutions with progressive programs are able to make good on parole and lead respectable lives. And, the average gets better every year, wherever the treatment program grows in extent and intensity. Despite this fact, there are those who would want to see the return of a program that has never been successful.

What concerns the workers in the field of corrections is that they do not yet know all they would like to know about the problems and needs of wayward youngsters and the causes of delinquency. They still have too large a percentage of failures, even though the success ratio is mounting wherever the program has a chance to operate as it should.

CITIZENS TEND TO BE APATHETIC TOWARD BOTH PREVENTION AND CORRECTIVE TREATMENT

What troubles these workers still more is the constant flow of boys and girls coming to them—new recruits with whom correctional agencies have never before been involved. Institution heads bid farewell to their residents who are leaving on parole and know that they will never again encounter in the institution the majority of those who leave. At the same time, they will see enter the doors a greater number than those who are leaving. The game cannot be won that way.

The difficulty is that the program of prevention is not getting underway as it should, due largely to citizen apathy and unwillingness to pay the costs. Efforts at prevention are sporadic; persons and agencies engaged in the work do not communicate and cooperate as they should; public interest rises when there is a local wave of juvenile lawlessness, and ebbs as soon as the situation seems in hand, without giving any thought to the fact that public indifference and lack of program will inevitably lead to another "wave."

It would be helpful if those who face the wailing wall and weep about the low moral state of our youth, those who go about looking for someone to blame, some scapegoat upon whom they can heap opprobrium, could become interested in themselves doing something about prevention. For there are contributions which all can make as individuals. Citizens must cease relying exclusively on agencies (such as churches, police and law enforcement personnel, Boy Scouts and Girl Scouts, YMCA and YWCA, etc.) to carry on the work of delinquency prevention. Each, as an individual, must be helpful.

Delinquents are bred in society and not in courts and institutions. What do citizens do about raising the moral tone of the community, arousing in fellow citizens the need of practicing the ethics we preach to the youth, removing temptations, providing for child-guidance clinics and for counselors in school programs, establishing proper recreational facilities? If a citizen cannot become an influence in the many agencies that exist to help those with problems, he can at least support them. Let each citizen become a factor in the life of the boy or girl who needs help and has no one to whom he or she can go. Those who work with youth agree that what has been lacking in the lives of children who go astray is association with an honest, upright man or woman to whom they can relate. With a general interest on the part of citizens in the problem of delinquency and a willingness to contribute to the program in whatever way they can, a tremendous impact can be made on the problem. So, let us get going.

And let us quit blaming others and yelling "get rough."

To blame all of delinquency upon an approach that has had neither the time nor the facilities fully to demonstrate what can be done is certainly the height of folly when it comes to constructive thinking about a tragically serious problem.

"We've Got One of Those Coddling Prisons"

JOHN C. BURKE

Do you know what? I'm just an ordinary citizen, but I'm upset because a fellow Jones stole my new 3,000 dollar car in Milwaukee, wrapped it around a tree out in Oklahoma, and then got as far as California before he was apprehended. The county spent

NOTE: Reprinted from *Federal Probation*, 20 (4) :34-36, 1956.

about 300 dollars returning him. The county fed him in the county jail and absorbed the court costs. He was sent to prison up at Waupun with a one- to three-year sentence. He had it coming!

Do you know what? I figured after his sentence, "That will teach him." That will show him he can't go around stealing cars. He'll get punished!

Do you know what? I guess I was all wrong. We've got one of those "coddling prisons." Know what the prison did with him? I found out and I'll tell you. Right off the bat the chaplain got to feeling sorry for him, and the guy played the chaplain for a sucker. He hadn't been to church for years, but to make a good impression he started going to church. Not only that, but the chaplain fixed it so he could get out of work every Tuesday and Thursday afternoons for an hour to practice with the choir. Some punishment, eh?

Do you know what? This guy Jones is a smart cookie! He gave the educational director a song and dance about being a good carpenter except that he was poor with figures. He tells a lot of guff about having quit school in the seventh grade and now feeling awful sorry, and hoping he can study arithmetic and maybe even learn to read blueprints while he is in the clink. The educational director went for his story in a big way—so then the guy takes off two half-days a week and goes to school. When he isn't singing or going to school he works with the carpenter and repair crew. Hard life, isn't it?

Do you know what? You haven't heard the half of it yet! I kept checking. This bird got to playing softball while in prison. All the big lug ever did on the outside was to play cards down in the cheapest joint in town. So the prison punishes him by letting him play softball two nights a week and every Saturday and Sunday. I'm not a revengeful guy, but I was almost happy when I heard he got hit in the kisser with a ball and got two teeth knocked out. Know what happened? They have a couple dentists up there and I'll be darned if he didn't get to see one the next day—without a previous appointment. The way I heard it the doc says, "Jones, your teeth are a mess. It isn't only that two have been knocked out, but the rest are all shot, and what you need is a set of dentures." (Here is where I discovered the guy was being paid for his work at the prison.) No foolin', he was getting 35 cents a day. They made him pay for the materials for the new teeth, but what the heck—that only amounted to around 35 dollars. And me, who never stole a car, paid over 100 dollars for a set just last week. I figured I'd heard everything, but . . .

Do you know what? He gets the new teeth, has a checkup by the prison doctor, and then the officials call him in and ask, "Jones, how would you like to be sent to one of our forestry camps up in the northern part of the state?" How would he like to serve his time at a forestry camp up in Wisconsin's famous summer resort country? What a question! Don't leave me now. This isn't a fairy tale. I'm giving you the straight dope. It's the truth. See what I mean . . . "coddling" em!?

Do you know what? He went to that camp located over 200 miles from the prison. What's the place like? Man—that you should see! It's a new concrete block building with all modern conveniences—even inside plumbing. It's in a big state forest and built just back from the shore of a bend in the famous Flambeau River. Even Jones is shocked when he sees it. He never saw anything more pretty. There's no fences around it, the doors are never locked, there's no watchdogs, there's no guns, and only three civilians work there to supervise this camp of 50 prisoners. At night one civilian hangs around all night, but he goes to bed at 10 o'clock. One "con" stays up all night as night watchman! Maybe part of his job is to keep the public from coming in and stealing prison property!

Do you know what? Like I said before, when Jones was home in Milwaukee and out of work, or on vacation or having a day off, about all he did was play cards in the cheapest joint in town. So he isn't interested in fishing or swimming in that beautiful river that has plenty of fish—that is, at first he isn't. But, son of a gun, he sees other guys sitting around at night tying flies and talking about the big one that got away and, sure enough, he gradually gets interested. So now his punishment includes fishing up in Wisconsin's river and lake country. See what I mean!

Do you know what? For awhile he is in his glory! He seems to be really enjoying himself as he serves his time. But he starts to get irritable. He seems to be worring about something. He's in a bad way. So the superintendent of the camp has him into his office for a little visit. Jones really gives him a story. His wife hasn't been writing regularly; the last letter he got, his wife said she was worried about their two boys because she couldn't handle them—they needed a father around. She was getting sick of trying to make ends meet on the money the county was giving her and, well, she was just about fed up with it all. The camp superintendent doesn't know the guy, so he falls for the sob story. He doesn't know that when the guy was home he never took his two boys anywhere. When they wanted him to take them to a ball game or go fishing, he couldn't be bothered—he was too busy— he had to go down to Sloppy Joe's for a beer and a game of cards. This superintendent didn't realize that Jones never took his wife anywhere. So . . .

Do you know what? This camp superintendent writes a letter to the warden and tells all about Jones and his worries about his family. This old buck of a warden has been warden of the same prison for about 18 years, and was a probation and parole officer for about 7 years before that; but with all his experience he is still pretty gullible. So he grabs the phone and calls the head of the prison's social service department, and wants to know from him when he plans to visit the camp. It just happens he's leaving for the camp in a couple days, so the warden writes the camp superintendent and tells him to tell Jones to "keep his shirt on" and don't worry, because the social worker will see him in a couple days. So he does go up and see Jones and several other prisoners. This social worker is a pretty sharp fellow but he gets taken in some also, I suspect. Well, anyway, he tells Jones he will find out about the family. Well, sir, the day he gets back from the camp a field worker from the Milwaukee office of the probation and parole bureau is at the prison seeing several men who will be going out on parole soon. So the social worker tells him all about Jones, and the guy says he will go see Mrs. Jones and the two boys and see what the pitch is. He has a good visit with them and tells them how well Jones is getting along and how anxious he is to get home to them. By the time he leaves, the wife has promised to write Jones and the two boys figure they better put in a note also and maybe find out if dad really is getting to be a good fisherman. So this probation and parole officer sends a note to the prison about his visit.

Do you know what? The next day the social worker and the warden are chewing the fat about this and that and the problem of Jones is mentioned. Wouldn't you know it? The warden says he is going up to the camp and while he is there he will see Jones. The way I get it, Jones is "tickled pink" after the warden gives him the dope. But this warden, he doesn't stop there. He gets to asking Jones about when he is up for parole and what his plans are. You see, they don't only coddle them in prison, but they want to get them out before they finish their sentence.

Do you know what? You might have known it! Sure as anything, along comes the parole board in a couple months and paroles him. They listen to all this guff about how Jones is back interested in and practicing his religion, how he has studied like a trooper and has the math and blueprint reading to go with his carpentry, how he's learned to be interested in wholesome recreation—and, by golly, they read some of the letters he has been getting from his wife and the kids, and they figure the family situation looks good right now.

Do you know what? Here this no-account Jones steals my car, smashes it all to pieces, gets a three-year sentence, spends one year in the main prison and six months in a nice forestry camp where he can fish and swim and enjoy life, and he's out on the street on parole in half of three years. Oh well—he'll be back! He won't stay out of trouble. If they'd "punished" him like prisons should he might have "learned his lesson," but after this "coddling" business he will figure it's a joke.

Do you know what? Of all the things to happen! I go to work this morning on that construction job over on Fifteenth Street and who do you suppose is the new carpenter working next to me, building forms. It's Jones! I'm fit to be tied. But I figure—oh, well, I might as well make the best of it. He won't last. I get charitable-like and after work suggest we stop in at the corner tavern and have a beer. Was I taken back when he said, "Gosh, thanks, but I can't tonight. I'm going over to try out for a neighborhood softball team." That rascal makes the team, too, and it's a sight for sore eyes to see him out there playing, with his wife all dolled up sitting on the sidelines cheering. But those two boys—they're the ones you should watch. They're as happy and proud as all get-out. Who are the happiest kids for 50 miles around when, in the last half of the last inning, the opposition is up to bat, with Jones' team one run ahead, with the bases full and two out and the heavy hitter up, and he hits what should be a double —only it isn't, because Jones leaps in the air to catch the ball and save the game? Hell, man! Even I cheered! Maybe Jones is an "ex-con," but I was proud of him tonight.

Do you know what? The boys tell me Jones has gone high-hat on them. He hasn't been over to Sloppy Joe's for a game of cards since he got home a year ago. I'll tell you another thing. That Jones, with the experience and training he got in carpentry at the prison, is one darn good carpenter. It will be hard to keep him from being a foreman pretty soon. I guess I'm getting to be a "coddler" myself. Don't tell anyone, but last Saturday night my wife and I had the Joneses over for supper. I didn't even lock the car before they came. "They're good people."

Do you know what? We invited the Joneses and their kids to join us and our kids on a picnic next weekend. They turned us down. Know why? Maybe you guessed it. I got a sneaking notion it was coming when one of my kids came home and said he'd learned how to tie flies over at Jones' house. The Joneses have gone on vacation. Pa, ma, and the two boys loaded their old car (paid for—not stolen) full of fishing junk, and by now they must be halfway along on their trip up north to spend a week at a cottage not over ten miles from the prison forestry camp where, thank goodness, Jones was so well "coddled."

Correctional Innovation and the Dilemma of Change-from-Within

RICHARD R. KORN

INTRODUCTION

Why is fundamental change so difficult to achieve in corrections? Technological improvements have been made. New hopes have been proclaimed. In other fields, knowledge has been the

NOTE: Reprinted from *Canadian Journal of Corrections*, 10:449-457, 1968.

handmaiden of progress. Why is it that those with the most knowledge and authority are the most pessimistic about basic innovation? Why is it that those with the most experience are the most hesitant about applying the results of experimentation?

The correctional historian must be disquieted by the fact that the major advances in his field have almost invariably been the work of inspired amateurs. The revolutionary transformation of the blood-drenched penal codes of eighteenth-century Europe was set in motion by a treatise from the pen of a young Italian economist. Probation was the invention of a compassionate Boston shoemaker of the last century. These breakthroughs were achieved in the teeth of authoritative dogma by intrepid amateurs long ago.

Nevertheless, the conflict between creativity and penal dogma seems just as severe today—in an age which everywhere else celebrates its liberation from the past. It would almost seem as if corrections has succeeded in reducing science to its tool rather than elevating it to its physician—and this is no small achievement in a field where performance lags so far behind promise. The glamor cast by science over the role of the expert has had a costly fallout in corrections: it has tended to burn out the seedground from which the best inspirations have sprung. It has given the professional an almost invincible argument against his former rival. The creative enthusiasm of the amateur may now be discredited as a mark of naiveté by those whose experience with futility has convinced them of the responsibility of drastic change. If this is even partly the case, we may well be in the grip of a self-fulfilling prophecy in which the pessimism of the expert is itself the principal barrier to progress.

THE EXCLUSION OF THE LAYMAN FROM LAW ENFORCEMENT AND CORRECTION

In all modern countries, the socially necessary task of dealing with intolerable deviants has been assigned to specialized government agencies. Once a function performed by indigenous societal groups such as the family, the clan, and the small community, the responsibility for coping with the offender has been yielded up by the citizens to a tiny minority of "expert" functionaries whose work is walled from public scrutiny and increasingly remote from public participation.

This arrangement reflects a division of labor which has wrought prodigious benefits in other spheres. The participation of the ordinary citizen can now be dispensed with in virtually every field outside of his own vocational specialty. The urban dweller can safely delegate the responsibility for providing everything required for his physical existence to specialists he has never seen but whose dependable efficiency has earned them the unquestioned right to his patronage.

Nevertheless, the grant of his franchise is neither exclusive nor irrevocable. Though he may be incapable of comprehending the processes by which his material needs are satisfied, the customer can still exercise some control over the final products. The claims of the manufacturers must still survive the test of the open marketplace. The entrepreneurs know they can keep their franchises only if their skills and resources are adequate to meet the consumer's needs at prices he is willing to pay.

But it is becoming increasingly apparent that the same kind of specialization which has worked prodigies in overcoming the problems of physical existence has worked few comparable wonders in solving the dilemmas of social existence. It seems more and more clear that the civic conscience cannot safely be delegated to a minority of moral entrepreneurs and that the participation of the private citizen cannot be dispensed with in dealing with the problems presented by the deviance of other citizens. If the failure of specialization merely reflected an insufficient number of specialists, the situation might be restored by an enormous increase in social technicians. If the difficulty stems from the fact that the human personality resists processing by the same kinds of impersonal manipulations which were adequate for exploiting the physical environment, the problem bites deeper than technology. Moreover, if the problems manifested by social deviance reflect fundamental disruptions in the fabric of social relations as a whole, they will yield only to measures which involve the fabric as a whole. In this eventuality, the notion that deviance can be contained by specialists who limit their manipulations exclusively to the deviants themselves may well be illusory.

Indeed, the notion itself may be a symptom of the same causes which produced the deviance in the first place, in which case we confront a remedy which may be little more than a disguised manifestation of the disease.

In any event, the claim that the participation of ordinary citizens is unnecessary will no longer wash. The need for their participation is increasingly voiced by law enforcement and correctional functionaries themselves. However, acknowledgment of a need is one thing; the sharing of functions and powers is another. By and large, official recognition of the need for citizen participation has not been followed up by the organizational accommodations which make significant collaboration feasible.

Though complex, some of the reasons for the gap between acknowledgment and accommodation seem clear enough. Unlike the typical business enterprise, neither the law enforcement nor the correctional agency is directly dependent on the patronage of the customer—in this case, the taxpayer. An inefficient business will ordinarily fail to survive superior competition on the open market. Government agencies which provide law enforcement and correctional services have few, if any, serious competitors. Like the armed forces, they are essentially monopolies performing functions considered indispensable, and the fact that their services are unavailable elsewhere merely reinforces the belief in their indispensability. In many ways, the law enforcement and correctional monopolies enjoy an even more immune position than their military counterpart.

In recent times the overwhelming majority of military personnel are ordinary citizens who will return to civilian life immediately after their term of service. As participating consumers of military life, the citizen-soldiers have personally experienced the services they purchased as taxpayers. They have at least a chance, as voters, to act on the personal appraisals they make.

The immediate client of the law enforcement or correctional agency is not the ordinary citizen—at least, not the ordinary citizen in good repute. The typical consumer of these services did not elect to be served; nor is he in a good position to influence other citizens with his appraisal. The ordinary citizen in good standing has only two general sources of information about law enforcement and correction. His logical informants are the functionaries appointed by his elected officials. His only other knowledgeable sources are the correctional clients themselves, the offenders. Whatever misgivings he might have about the credibility of his politicians and their appointees, the citizen may find more reason to repose confidence in them than in their clients, who have already violated his trust in the act of offending.

This favored situation cannot help but impose a strain on the candor of correctional functionaries. Administering a public monopoly screened from close public scrutiny and wielding powers exclusively granted on grounds of their exclusive expertise, these functionaries may feel greater pressure to conceal their problems than to share them. Even the elected officials to whom they must report are essentially no different from the laymen who elected them in their direct knowledge of correctional procedures and problems. These officials too must turn to the correctional administrator for guidance and direction in penal matters.

If correctly drawn, the picture now takes on some of the features of the classical double-bind. The correctional administrator was assigned his exclusive franchise because the public believed his skills and resources were adequate to the task without direct public participation. Should the correctional administrator suddenly discover that his resources are inadequate and that massive citizen participation is, in fact, indispensible, the grounds of his exclusive grant would be instantly cut away. At this point, public confidence is transformed from an advantage into a trap. The administrator now finds he has been cut off from an indispensible resource. He has good reason to expect that a candid acknowledgment of this might well result in the loss of his exclusive franchise or, worse, by his replacement by others who might be less candid.

If this picture is even approximately correct, it seems clear that some way must be found to relieve the correctional administrator and his workers of the self-defeating pretension of exclusive competence. It is hard to see how this burden can be lifted without the most sympathetic assistance of those who are already aware of the problem.

Where is this help to be found? Who outside of the insulated circle of the correctional establishment has the requisite understanding and the incentive to share it? If the service in question were one offered by private enterprise, the answer would be immediate. There is one group of persons who knows more about the product than the vendor does, particularly if the vendor himself does not use it. When the nonusing vendor wishes to improve his product, he most diligently and painstakingly polls the consumers. Should the success of the product depend upon their skill in using it, the vendor requires even more than their educated advice; he requires their willing cooperation.

We are now brought face to face with another major dilemma of correction.

THE EXCLUSION OF THE CORRECTIONAL CONSUMER FROM CORRECTIONAL PLANNING

In spite of all that has been said in favor of citizen participation in correction, the fact remains that the penal establishment has, for better or worse, done without his services for many years. But there is one other category of person whose participation is indispensible beyond argument. An enlightened penal policy which no longer relies on the destruction or disablement of the offender has no alternative but to seek his cooperation. If the scope of this cooperation is limited to passive conformity to rules the inmate has no part in making, there is reason to suspect that the resulting gains will be similarly limited. Current rates of recidivism suggest that the gains are rather severely limited.

After his release, the offender will be required to do his own planning. If he values self-determination as much as the rest of us do, he will seek to follow ways of his own making. Like the rest of us who demand the rights of free navigation, he will encounter the perils of free navigation.

The one inarguable criterion of the success of a correctional policy is the behavior of the offender after his release. It would seem to follow that the ideal design for correctional living would be that which most accurately anticipates the problems the offender will encounter after release. It would also seem to follow that merely passive conformity under duress and constant close surveillance would least anticipate his probable behavior and the conditions of his situation on the street.[1]

In the end, a correctional policy must stand or fall not on what the correctional officials do but on what the released offender does. It follows that the key to the success of any program which does not succeed in reducing inmates to mindless robot rests, for better or worse, in the inmates' hands.

SOME MISSED OPPORTUNITIES OF CONTEMPORARY CORRECTION

In common with other men, the offender needs to believe he can be an agent in his own life. Like other men, he struggles to fashion the rough materials of the general human condition into a personal fate he can say he made.

As a criminal, he tried to build his lot by theft: his materials were acquired at the expense of others. His achievements, if he had any, were constructed out of the calamities of other men. His continued activity would pose a continual danger; his success would, and does, constitute a social disaster.

After his release, he will return to open society. If he has experienced little or nothing to move him to new ways of dealing with others, there is a high likelihood that he will resume his interrupted career.

In order to learn and to agree to new and acceptable ways of dealing with his fellow citizens, he must have contact with them. This contact cannot be that of a slave and a master, a child and a parent, a schoolboy and a teacher. He may force himself to accept these forms of relationship while in confinement, but only at the risk of danger to his personal integrity. Unless confinement has destroyed his self-respect, he surely will not accept them once he is free.

The relationships he urgently needs are those he can build on when he is released, and he requires experiences with them before he is released. What he needs are opportunities to prove to himself and others that he can be accepted for his usefulness to himself and to others and that he will be appreciated for his usefulness, as other men are. Again, he needs to learn these things before he is released; trying to learn them after may be too difficult or too late.

One does not learn these things from a relationship with a prison psychologist, or from a prison guard, or from a sermon by the prison chaplain, or from a book out of the prison library. One learns these things by experiencing them in a context of total and demanding authenticity. This is why correction so urgently needs the participation of the ordinary citizen in a new, dynamic, and authentic way.

But an authentic human relationship between responsible adults is necessarily a reciprocal one. It is not a relationship between a benefactor and a client or dependent, ultimately demeaning to both. The fact that the offender needs the ordinary citizen is clear. Is it equally clear to his fellow citizens that they need him? Under present conditions it is not clear at all.

Under existing arrangements, the ordinary citizen has no particular reason to believe in the convict's potential usefulness to anyone. As a criminal on the loose, he was a costly menace; as a convict supported by the citizens' taxes, he is a costly burden. The citizen has had to pay a double price: one for the criminal's crimes; the other for his keep. The cost of keeping men in fortified human warehouses is not small. If the layman has precious little reason to feel kindly toward the criminal as a public menace, he has equally little reason to respect him as the recipient of a public dole.

Under these conditions, it is not difficult to understand why the terms "convict" and "ex-convict" carry so damaging a stigma. For all of his remoteness from the scene, the citizen can still grasp the essentially parasitical condition of the prisoner's life, and the citizen's resentment at having to pay the bill for it may spring from a sounder intuitive basis than many penologists realize. One can more easily respect an enemy than the recipient of one's grudging and unreciprocated charity. (The fact that the image of the gangster has always stimulated greater respect, if not appeal, than the image of the convict is something that correctional authorities might well ponder about.)

Self-respect is contingent on respect from others. If the offender is to receive the respect of the law-abiding, he must earn it. Notoriously, the role of "good convict" has not given him an opportunity to earn it. On the other hand, on those tragically rare occasions when prisoners are permitted to make a genuine contribution to the welfare of the community, the responses of the citizenry have been invariably warm. It almost seems as if the citizens, in some stumbling, intuitive manner, had found an opportunity to overcome their resentment against the criminal and were grateful for it. An act of genuine human service on the part of the criminal had accomplished what no amount of retribution, however severe, had been able to accomplish: it had discharged the anger of the community and restored the offender, at least psychologically, to membership in it.

These opportunities come rarely; invariably their import is missed by a correctional establishment preoccupied with the weightier business of "protecting" the community from dangerous felons. The fact that an ounce of genuine restitution by the offender can do what a pound of revenge by the victim can never do for the victim himself has not yet been grasped by correctional theorists at large, though it has been demonstrated on a thousand accidental occasions. The fact that there are numberless rejects of society now wasting their lives in prisons who would be grateful for a chance to restore themselves—even by the most dangerous and self-sacrificial forms of restitution—has not yet been put together with the first fact, namely, that society would be equally grateful for the chance to be relieved of the burden of its resentment and the opportunity to have its rejects restored to it.

Taken together, these two facts constitute the most profound hopes of correction and represent its most grievously missed opportunity.

The reason why this and other opportunities have been missed deserves urgent study by the community. In recent years, the public has spent millions in a search for alternatives to the prison. Many experiments have been funded; a few have been strikingly successful. None have been implemented on any large scale, and none have brought about a basic change. An expanding correctional establishment continues to call for funds to develop alternatives. The citizenry might well ask to know why the already proven alternatives have not been implemented.

What is the typical fate of a successful innovation in correction? What is the typical fate of the innovator? Like the modern church, the modern correctional establishment no longer burns its heretics; its methods are more subtle and businesslike. Instead of neutralizing them by martyring them, it subverts their efforts by rewarding or diverting them. Modern bureaucracy has discovered that its bureaucratic "yes" can be infinitely more effective than its "no."

To cite some cases in point: the founder of one of the most promising innovations in recent years, a halfway house program for serious delinquents who might otherwise be incarcerated, was rewarded, first, by promotion to the wardenship of the state's archaic prison and, finally, by appointment to the post of commissioner of all the institutions of the state. He is now fully occupied in administering several of the programs his innovation might have replaced. Although his reward reflects a well-merited recognition of his earlier achievement, his present preoccupation with administering traditional prisons and mental hospitals makes about as much sense as rewarding the developer of an antismog device by putting him in charge of all the old-fashioned blast furnaces in the area. During his tenure, only a handful of new halfway houses have been built. However, a massive expansion of the state's reformatory system is now underway.

A few years ago, another outstanding innovator launched a program which trained and employed adult felons as correctional therapists. A grand total of 18 men went through the whole program; two years later, 16 were still usefully employed in the community and a few had made correction their career. The creator of this program is no longer employed in his state's correctional service. He is now hard at work developing another promising innovation under other auspices. After permitting him to demonstrate the success of his "new careers" program, the state abandoned it. This case illustrates another technique of neutralization. The innovator is eased from the center to the periphery of influence and given a harmless new toy with which to occupy himself.

The basic reason these projects were abandoned is that they offered a genuine alternative to present practices: it was their success, not their failure, that doomed them. In its primordial wisdom, the establishment sensed that an implementation of the new ideas would require a root and branch transformation of penal policy. A program of social reconciliation through restitution and service was threatening to replace the old ideology of social alienation through segregation and suffering. In neutralizing the new idea, the establishment confirmed the old observation, "There is nothing more embarrassing to the Bishop than a saint in the neighborhood."[2]

Instead of providing bridges on which the offender and his future fellow citizens can meet and deal with each other under ideally mediated conditions of mutual facilitation and service, the penal establishment continues to lend itself to its ancient task of perpetuating their mutual isolation and abetting their mutual alienation.

Instead of providing new opportunities for constructive and responsible self-determination, under ideal conditions of guidance and correction, the penal establishment, on the whole, continues to deny its wards the right to practice the decision-making skills they will be called on to exercise when they are required to fend for themselves on the street.

It is not to be wondered at that prisoners reject a situation which has essentially rejected them. The spontaneous human response to a denial of autonomy is subversion. Refusing to commit themselves to a program they had no part in and which they cannot trust because it refuses to trust them, the collectivity of exiles, thrown back upon their own resources, create an underground program of their own. The overriding purpose of this program is to enable them to reassert the autonomy which the official program has denied them, but the assertion of autonomy in a situation which forbids it is explicitly illegal. It follows, in the nature of the case, that the representative custodial situation gives the offender no alternative to the loss of his autonomy but that of continuing his career of law violation while in the correctional institution. The convicts have a word for the program they create for themselves. They call it a school of crime.

CONCLUSION

This inquiry began with the question, Why is fundamental innovation so difficult to achieve in correction? Why is an establishment committed to the reformation of others unable to reform itself?

In seeking to account for this, we cited three general causes: the invalid attribution of exclusive expertise, the exclusion of the ordinary citizens' indispensable contribution, and the exclusion of the offender's meaningful participation in his own rehabilitation. The end result has been that those most dependent on one another for the success of each have been isolated or alienated from each other. The same causes which prevent correction from achieving its mission prevent it from reforming itself.

Like the ancient kingdom of China which has always absorbed its conquerors, correction has always neutralized the individual efforts of those seeking to change it. The thought stimulates sober reflection about the doctrine of gradualism. The force required to move a massive rock from a roadway cannot be divided. Each of 10,000 men singly pitting his strength against it day after day will not be able to move it. The huge inertia of the obstacle, which might yield to the concentrated strength of ten, will absorb the isolated strengths of 10,000. The roadblock will remain, to be pointed out by succeeding generations of the defeated as a monument to the futility of human effort.

NOTES AND REFERENCES

1. After watching his prisoners marching to their assignments according to a precisely clocked schedule, a warden remarked, "How can I teach them to be punctual when I never let them be late?"
2. I am indebted to another innovator, Professor Charles Slack of Harvard, for using this phrase in a similar context.

Social Psychological Foundations for Using Criminals in the Rehabilitation of Criminals

DONALD R. CRESSEY

Social psychological theory has broad and significant implications for the use of criminals in the rehabilitation of criminals. However, the implications of general social psychological theory or of social psychological theories of criminal conduct have not been spelled out and have not been explicitly utilized in attempts to change criminals into noncriminals. Such theory has enabled us to learn a great deal about the processes by which men move from the status of "noncriminal" to the status of "criminal." We ought to use the same theory and the knowledge gained by means of it in attempts to move men from the status of "criminal" to the status of "noncriminal." Its use would be of great theoretical significance, for each attempt to change criminals could be an experimental test of hypotheses derived from theory, and each such test would lead to improvement of theory.

On practical grounds, correctional agencies need theory enabling them to make maximum use of the personnel available to act as rehabilitation agents. By and large, correctional leaders of the last quarter century have subscribed to a psychiatric theory of rehabilitation—a set of theory which, unfortunately, can be implemented only by a highly educated, "professionally trained" person; they often conclude, therefore, that rehabilitation work attempted by persons not trained on the university postgraduate level is both ineffective and potentially dangerous. Despite this conclusion, there are not now and never will be enough similarly trained persons to man our rehabilitation agencies. As an alternative to louder and more desperate pleas for greater number of psychiatrists and social workers, there should be developed rehabilitation theory acknowledging the fact that highly educated personnel are not available to change criminals into noncriminals.

There is no shortage, in the United States or elsewhere, of av-

NOTE: Reprinted from *Journal of Research in Crime and Delinquency*, 2 (2) :49-59, 1965.

erage, run-of-the-mill, but mature and moral men and women of the sort making up the majority of the personnel in factories, businesses, and prisons—men and women with at most a high-school education. With increasing automation, more and more personnel of this kind will be leaving "production" occupations and will be available for "service" occupations, including that of rehabilitating criminals. The first important task in rehabilitation criminology is recognition of the availability of this tremendous manpower force. The second task, and the most difficult and crucial task that criminologists will face during the remainder of this century, is development of sound rehabilitation theory and procedures which will enable correctional agencies to utilize this reservoir of men.

Wardens and other agency administrators could then implement such a rehabilitation theory by creating an organization made up principally of men who have been trained in trade school to be skilled correctional technicians and whose occupational titles could properly be "people changers." If we have learned one thing about mental hospitals and correctional institutions since World War II, it is that change in patients and prisoners depends more on the actions of attendants, guards, and other patients and prisoners than it does on the actions of professional personnel. In the manpower pool that could readily supply the people changers, we need a copious supply of convicted persons being discharged from probation, prison, and parole each year, and of persons who are ex-convicts even if they are still under the supervision of a correctional agency. If we develop a theory on which to base a "people-changer" occupation calling for skills somewhat comparable to those of automobile mechanics and television repairmen, the probability is high that ex-criminals will be among the most effective practitioners of the occupation. There is a basis in social psychological theory for the belief that ex-criminals can be highly effective agents of change and, further, that as they act as agents of change they themselves become the targets of change, thus insuring their own rehabilitation. Still to be accomplished is the difficult task of showing how general social psychological theory and criminological theory can be transformed into a theory of correction, and the difficult task of transforming the new theory of correction into a program of action.

"SYMBOLIC INTERACTION" THEORY AND CRIME CAUSATION

Sutherland's theory of differential association places great emphasis upon the kinds of variables that must be considered as fundamental if one is to explain delinquent and criminal behavior.[1] One can best appreciate the "individual conduct" part of this theory, in contrast to the "epidemiological" part if he views it as a set of directives about the kinds of things that ought to be included in a theory of criminality, rather than as an actual statement of theory.[2] The variables identified as important to delinquency and criminality are the same variables considered in social psychology's general "symbolic interaction" theory as the elements basic in any kind of social behavior—verbalizations ("symbolizations") in the form of norms, values, definitions, attitudes, rationalizations, rules, etc. Moreover, the theory of differential association also directs us, as does general "symbolic interaction" theory, to a concern for the fact that the process of receiving a behavior pattern is greatly affected by the nature of the relationship between donor and receiver. In short, the theory implies that in attempts to explain delinquent and criminal conduct, we should stop looking for emotional disturbances and personality traits, which are secondary variables, and start looking at the verbalizations of groups in which individuals participate, which are primary variables.

In telling us to look at people's words ("symbols") when we try to explain why most people are noncriminals and only a small proportion are criminals, Sutherland early aligned himself with a group of social scientists called, for convenience, "symbolic interactionists." The ideas of this group are quite different from the psychiatric view that "personality" is an outgrowth of the effect that the "restrictions" necessary to social order have on the individual's expressions of his own pristine needs. The "symbolic interactionists" view "social organization" and "personality" as two facets of the same thing.[3] The person or personality is seen as a part of the kinds of social relationships and values in which he participates; he obtains his essence from the rituals, values, norms, rules, schedules, customs, and regulations of various kinds which surround him; he is not separable from the social relationships in which he lives. The person behaves according to the rules (which are sometimes contradictory) of the social organizations in which he participates; he cannot behave any other way. This is to say that criminal or noncriminal behavior is—like other behaviors, attitudes, beliefs, and values which a person exhibits— the property of groups, not of individuals. Criminal and delinquent behavior is not just a product of an individual's contacts with certain kinds of groups; it is in a very real sense "owned" by groups rather than by individuals, just as a language is owned by a collectivity rather than by any individual.

"Participation" in "social relationships" and in "social organization" is, of course, the subject matter of all anthropology, sociology, and social psychology. Nevertheless, "participation" in "social organization" is rather meaningless as an explanatory principle when it stands alone. As I have pointed out elsewhere, "[such concepts] serve only to indicate in a general way, to oversimplify, and to dramatize social interactions which are so confused, entangled, complicated, and subtle that even the participants are unable to describe clearly their own involvements."[4] Sutherland's criminological principle, like more general symbolic interactionist theory, tells us what to look for after we have moved toward consideration of the specific effects that "participation in social relationships" has on individual conduct. What Sutherland says we should study if we are going to establish a theory for explaining criminal conduct is, in a word, words. Values, attitudes, norms, rationalizations, and rules are all composed of symbols ("verbalizations"), and these verbalizations, of course, are learned from others, as was pointed out years ago by symbolic interaction theorists like Mead, Dewey, Cooley, Baldwin, Whorf, Langer, and others.

In simplified form, symbolic interactionists theory tells us that cultures and subcultures consist of collections of behaviors contained in the use of words in prescribed ways. These words make it "proper" to behave in a certain way toward an object designated by the word "cat," and "improper" to behave in this same way toward an object designated by the word "hammer." They also make it "wrong" or "illegal" to behave in other ways. It is highly relevant to a theory of criminal behavior and to a theory of correction that words also make it "all right" to behave in some situations in a manner which also is "wrong" or "illegal."

Verbalizations, it should be emphasized, are not invented by a person on the spur of the moment. They exist as group definitions of what is appropriate; they necessarily are learned from persons who have had prior experience with them. In our culture, for example, there are many ideologies, contained in words, which sanction crime. To give some easy examples: "Honesty is the best policy, but business is business." "It is all right to steal a loaf of bread when you are starving." "All people steal when they get into a tight spot." "Some of our most respectable citizens got their start in life by using other people's money temporarily."

An anthropologist has given us an excellent example, from another culture, of the highly significant effect that words have in the production of individual conduct of the kind likely to be labeled "deviant," if not "criminal":

> The Burmese are Buddhist, hence must not take the life of animals. Fishermen are threatened with dire punishment for their murderous occupation, but they find a loophole by not literally killing the fish. "These are merely put on the bank to dry, after their long soaking in the river, and if they are foolish and ill-judged enough to die while undergoing the process, it is their own fault." . . . When so convenient a theory had once been expounded, it naturally became an apology of the whole guild of fishermen.[5]

Other examples of the significant influence words have on individual conduct can be found in my study of criminal violators of financial trust,[6] in which I noted that the embezzler defines the relationship between an unsharable financial problem and an illegal solution to that problem (embezzlement) in words, supplied by his culture, that enable him to look upon his embezzlement as something other than embezzlement. Suppose that a bank clerk with no significant history of criminality finds himself with an unsharable financial problem and an opportunity to solve that problem by stealing from his company. Suppose, further, that you said to him, "Jack, steal the money from your boss." The chances are that in response to these words, he would simply look at you in horror, just as he would if you suggested that he solve his problem by sticking a pistol into the face of an attendant at the corner gas station. But suppose you said, "Jack, steal the money from your company." That would probably bring about less of a horror reaction,[7] but still Jack would feel honest and trusted men "just don't do such things." However, if you suggest that he surreptitiously "borrow" some money from the bank, you would be helping him over a tremendous hurdle, for honest and trusted men do "borrow." As a matter of fact, the idea of "borrowing" is used by some embezzlers as a verbalization that adjusts the two contradictory roles involved, the role of an honest man and the role of a crook, and hence is one of a number of verbalizations that make embezzlement possible.

A great deal of additional evidence supporting the importance of verbalizations in both criminal and noncriminal conduct is found in the literature, but it has not been systematically collected and published. Here are a few examples:

1. Lindesmith reported that if a person habituated to drugs talks to himself in certain ways, he will become an addict, while if he talks to himself in other ways, he will avoid addiction entirely. Lindesmith's most general conclusion was that persons can become addicts only if certain kinds of verbalizations are available to them.[8]

2. Becker's studies of marijuana addicts consistently showed that perception of the effect of marijuana is determined by the kinds of words given to smokers by users.[9]

3. Lane found that differences in the white-collar crime rate among New England shoe manufacturing firms was determined by the verbalizations available in local communities. For example, 7 per cent of the firms in one town violated the laws, while in another town 44 per cent violated. Lane concluded that at least one of the reasons for the differences is "the difference in attitude toward the law, the government, and the morality of illegality."[10]

4. Similarly, Clinard analyzed violations of O.P.A. regulations during World War II and concluded that businessmen violated

the regulations because they did not "believe in" them; they possessed verbalizations which made the criminal law seem irrelevant.[11]

5. In a study of delinquents, Sykes and Matza, following up the idea suggested in *Other People's Money,* concluded that since all youths accept conventional values to some degree, they must "neutralize" these conventional values before they can commit delinquencies. As illustrations of the "techniques of neutralization" used by delinquents, Sykes and Matza cite use of verbalizations which blame parents or misfortune for one's theft, define the victim as worthless, justify offenses as a duty toward one's friends, and note the faults of those who condemn delinquency.[12]

In a recent discussion of the research on social class and childhood personality, Sewell, who might be called a general "symbolic interaction" theorist, stressed the importance of attitudes and values (verbalizations), in contrast to emotional traits:

> It now seems clear that scientific concern with the relations between social class and personality has perhaps been too much focused on global aspects of personality and possibly too much on early socialization. Therefore, it is suggested that the more promising direction for future research will come from a shift in emphasis, toward greater concern with those particular aspects of personality which are most likely to be directly influenced by the positions of the child's family in the social stratification system, such as attitudes, values, and aspirations, rather than with deeper personality characteristics.[13]

The trend noted by Sewell in general social psychological research has been noted by Glaser in criminological research and thinking. Since criminology must get at least the general direction of its theory from the behavioral sciences, it is not surprising to find it following the general trends in theory. Glaser summarized the theoretical position in criminology as follows:

> The process of rationalization reconciles crime or delinquency with conventionality; it permits a person to maintain a favorable conception of himself while acting in ways which others see as inconsistent with a favorable self-conception. In this analysis of motivation by the verbal representation of the world with which a person justifies his behavior, sociologists are converging with many psychologists. This

seems to be an individualistic analysis of behavior, but the so-called "symbolic interactionist's" viewpoint is gaining acceptance, and it sees individual human thought as essentially a social interaction process: the individual "talks to himself" in thinking and reacts to his own words and gestures in "working himself" into an emotional state in much the same manner as he does in discussion or in emotional interaction with others.[14]

"SYMBOLIC INTERACTION" THEORY AND THE PROBLEM OF CHANGING CRIMINALS

If social conduct is a function of verbalization learned from membership groups and reference groups, then attempts to change it should concentrate on methods for avoiding certain verbalizations and acquiring others. Theory indicates that men conceive of themselves as a type (e.g. "criminal") when they have intimate associates who conceive of themselves as that type and when they are officially handled as if they were members of that type. Both processes have verbalizations as their content. This observation has enabled us to start working on a consistent set of "rehabilitation theory" which holds that a person can be stopped from conceiving of himself as one type (e.g. "criminal") and stimulated to conceive of himself as another type (e.g. "square John") by isolating him from persons who conceive of themselves as the first type and refraining from handling him as if he were a member of that type, while at the same time surrounding him with intimate associates who think of themselves as the second type and officially handling him as if he were a member of the second type. The basic idea here is that a new set of attitudes, values, rationalizations, definitions, etc., must be substituted for the set that he has been using in performing the social conduct said to be undesirable, illegal, or immoral. The new set of verbalizations must be concerned with the fact that criminal conduct is wrong.

The infrequency of crime in our society cannot be accounted for by lack of opportunities for learning illegitimate skills or by fear of the risk attending the commission of criminal acts. The opportunity to acquire the skills of the criminal is great, and the probability of being arrested for a crime committed is low. Why, then, do more people not commit crime? Toby, who asked this question, has answered that people have learned that criminal conduct is wrong, indecent, or immoral. He points out that the tremendous amount of conforming behavior in any society can be understood only if we can see that individuals possess self-conceptions which make it impossible for them to engage in criminal or delinquent conduct without arousing feelings of guilt and shame that are incompatible with the self-conceptions.[15] "Guilt" and "shame" are contained in the verbalizations that make up a culture. In changing criminals, the basic problem is one of insuring that these criminals become active members of intimate groups whose verbalizations produce "guilt" and "shame" when criminal acts are performed or even contemplated. Stated negatively, the problem is one of insuring that persons do not learn to behave according to verbalizations which make crime psychologically possible.[16]

However, implementation of this basic idea is not as simple as it seems. First of all, our attempts to change a criminal's conduct might merely reinforce his use of the myriad verbalizations that have made and are making him act as he does. Or, he might be changed into a different kind of criminal. At a minimum, then, we must learn more about the process of social interaction in correctional settings, where the criminal whose change is being attempted is sometimes given words that make his criminality worse or that substitute one form of criminality for another.

USING CRIMINALS TO REFORM CRIMINALS

"Symbolic interaction" theory supports the idea that criminals can be used effectively to introduce "guilt" and "shame" into the psychological make-up of those who would commit crime and to avoid production of further criminality or a different form of criminality, among the population whose change is sought. In the first place, criminals who have committed crimes and delinquencies by means of certain verbalizations, and who have rejected these verbalizations in favor of verbalizations making crime psychologically difficult or even impossible, should be more effective in changing criminals' self-conceptions than would men who have never had close familiarity with the procriminal verbalizations. In the second place, criminals used as agents of change should be more efficient than noncriminals in avoiding the presentation of the verbalizations appropriate to a new kind of criminality or deviancy.

There are two approaches to the problem of expecting criminals to present anticriminal verbalizations to other criminals. In the first approach, the criminal-turned-reformer is viewed as the agent of change; in the second, he is viewed as the target of change.

The literature on group therapy reports many examples of groups in which the subjects served as effective agents of change. Opinion is almost unanimous that group therapy is an effective technique for treating mental patients and that its principal contribution has been reduction of social isolation and egocentricity among the subjects.[17] Arguments in favor of group therapy for criminals are less frequent; they tend to be organized around the "emotional disturbances" theory of criminality, rather than around symbolic interaction theory. One principal argument centers on the criminal's ability to establish rapport with other criminals.[18] Another centers on the function of therapy in reducing isolation and egocentricity among criminals.[19] As I pointed out some ten years ago, neither of these is actually an argument for the effectiveness of group therapy in changing criminals.[20]

From the standpoint of the theory sketched out above, group therapy for criminals ought to be effective to the degree that the criminal-as-an-agent-of-change prevents criminals from using the "techniques of neutralization"—the verbalizations—which he, himself, used in perpetrating offenses and to the degree that new anticriminal verbalizations are substituted. In one experiment with group therapy for female offenders, the old verbalizations were not prevented; the result was that, in the words of the therapist, "the participants would not accept the proposition that the source of their predicament was not 'bad luck' or a 'bad judge.' "[21] Another report said that delinquents "were convinced that everyone is dishonest, that even the police, the government, and the judges took bribes. Thus, they sought to convince themselves that they were not different from anyone else. . . . They needed persons with socially acceptable standards and conduct with whom they could identify."[22] Theoretically, at least, the degree of rapport is increased if these "persons with socially acceptable standards and conduct" are themselves criminals-turned-reformers, rather than professional reformers such as social workers and prison guards. Just as men are relatively unaffected by radio and television dramatizations, they are unaffected by verbalizations presented by men they cannot understand and do not respect. On a general level, Festinger and his co-workers have provided extensive documentation of the principle that the persons who are to be changed and the persons doing the changing must have a strong sense of belonging to the same group.[23]

The implications of the social psychological ideas discussed above seem even clearer in connection with making the criminal "rehabilitator" the target of change. The basic notion here is that as a person tries to change others, he necessarily must use the verbalizations appropriate to the behavior he is trying to create in those others. In an earlier article, I named this process "retroflexive reformation," for in attempting to change others, the criminal almost automatically identifies himself with other persons engaging in reformation and, accordingly, with persons whose behavior is controlled by noncriminal and anticriminal verbalizations. When this is the case, he is by definition a member of law-abiding groups, the objective of reformation programs. At the same time, he is alienated from his previous procriminal groups, in the sense that he loses the verbalizations which enable him to assign high status to men whose conduct has been considered "all right" even if "illegal" and "criminal."

It is my hypothesis that such success as has been experienced by Alcoholics Anonymous, Synanon, and even "official" programs like institutional group therapy and group counseling programs is attributable to the requirement that the reformee perform the role of the reformer, thus enabling him to gain experience in the role which the group has identified as desirable.

> The most effective mechanism for exerting group pressure on members will be found in groups so organized that criminals are induced to join with noncriminals for the purpose of changing other criminals. A group in which criminal A joins with some noncriminals to change criminal B is probably most effective in changing criminal A, not B; in order to change criminal B, criminal A must necessarily share the values of the anticriminal members.[25]

This notion proposes that the same mechanisms which produce criminality be utilized in attempts to change criminals into non-criminals. The criminal has learned that he can gain desired status in one or more groups by participation in the use of verbalizations that enable him to perform in a manner our law defines as "criminal." Now he must learn that he can "make out" in a group by participating in verbalizations conducive to noncriminality. Further, this learning must be reinforced by arranging for him to be an "elite," one who knows the proper verbalizations and therefore the modes of conduct, and who, furthermore, attempts to enforce his conceptions of right conduct among those beneath him in the status system. When these two things occur, he becomes more than a passive noncriminal; he becomes an active reformer of criminals, a true "square."

We now turn to the problem of avoiding the presentation, in the rehabilitation process, of verbalizations that inadvertently make criminals worse. In recent years, sociologists and social psychologists have displayed increasing concern for this problem, as reflected in the large number of studies of the detailed operations of rehabilitation organizations like mental hospitals and prisons. So far as criminology is concerned, the problem seems to have been first identified in 1938 by Tannenbaum, who wrote *Crime and the Community* with the help of two famous "symbolic interactionists," John Dewey and Thorsten Veblen. Tannenbaum's basic idea was that officially separating the delinquent child from his group for special handling amounts to a "dramatization of evil" that plays a greater role in making him a criminal than any other experience: "The process of making the criminal is a process of tagging, defining, identifying, segregating, describing, emphasizing, making conscious and self-conscious; it becomes a way of stimulating, suggesting, emphasizing, and evoking the very traits that are complained of."[26] This notion has been discussed more recently by Merton as "the self-fulfilling prophecy,"[27] and in 1951, Lemert gave the name "secondary deviation" to the outcome of the process.[28] The important point is that in attempting to correct what Lemert calls "primary deviation," we sometimes give the deviants words which make their problems worse.

It is possible to carry this notion of "dramatization of evil" and "secondary deviation" so far that it can be erroneously deduced that the police and other official instrumentalities of the state are more important than informal interaction in producing criminality and other forms of deviancy. There seems to be a current tendency among social scientists to view police, prison workers, and parole officers as "bad guys" that are producing criminality, while the crooks and other carriers of crooked values are the "good guys." This is absurd. Nevertheless, the current focus on both secondary deviation and primary deviation places our scientific concern exactly where, according to symbolic interaction theory, it needs to be placed—on the subcultures made up of verbalizations which inadvertently, but nevertheless inexorably, are presented to persons who adopt them and who, in adopting them, become criminals. To take a simple example from outside the field of criminology, speech experts have found that stutterers often are people whose parents have dealt with them severely in order to get them to speak correctly.[29] Similarly, others have shown that the male homosexual is often a person who has been stigmatized for effeminacy or who applies a verbalization like "queer" to himself when he recognizes in himself erotic responses to other males.[30]

Recent studies have indicated that the physician's attention plays a considerable part in bringing on the very symptoms which it is designed to diagnose. For example, Scheff points out that a false diagnosis of illness (made because the physician is obligated to suspect illness even when the evidence is not clear) often incapacitates the person being diagnosed:

> Perhaps the combination of a physician determined to find disease signs, if they are to be found, and the suggestible patient searching for subjective symptoms among the many amorphous and usually unattended bodily impulses, is often sufficient to unearth a disease which changes the patient's status from well to sick and may also have effects on his familial and occupational status. . . . It can be argued that when a person is in a confused and suggestible state, when he organizes his feelings and behavior by using the sick role, and when his choice of roles is validated by physician and/or others, he is "hooked" and will proceed on a career of chronic illness.[31]

Consistently, a physician reports the case of a woman who began to suffer the symptoms of heart trouble only after she was informed that a routine chest x-ray revealed that she had an enlarged heart.[32]

From these observations in areas other than criminology, it may safely be concluded that official action by rehabilitators of criminals is important to producing a "vicious circle" of the kind described by Toby, "When an individual commits one crime, forces are set in motion which increase the probability of his committing others. When he uses alcohol to help himself cope with an unpleasant social situation, the reactions of his friends, employers, and relatives may be such as to give him additional reason to drink."[33]

While the problem of "secondary deviation" is by no means solved when criminals are used as agents for changing other criminals or themselves, symbolic interaction theory hints that there might be an essential difference between situations in which "secondary deviation verbalizations" are provided by professional agents of change and those in which such verbalizations making secondary deviation appropriate; he is at the same time presenting verbalizations making it possible to move out of the secondary deviant's role. This is not true when the noncriminal, and especially a "professional" rehabilitator, presents the verbalizations. For example, I might easily be able to show a man signs that will lead him to a conception of himself as a homosexual, with resultant secondary deviation; but an ex-homosexual can show the same man the same signs, together with other signs (exemplified in his own case) that mark the road to abandoning both the primary deviation and the secondary deviation. Or, to take an easier example, in presenting anticriminal verbalizations to a criminal, I might inadvertently convince him that the life of a square is undesirable because there is no way for a square John to get his kicks; a criminal, however, could show the subject that there is a kick in just being square.

In this connection, Volkman and Cressey have observed that addicts who go through withdrawal distress at Synanon, a self-help organization made up of ex-addicts, universally report that the withdrawal sickness is not as severe as it is in involuntary organizations such as jails and mental hospitals.[34] The suggestion from theory is that much of the sickness ordinarily accompanying withdrawal distress is brought about by close familiarity with verbalizations making it appropriate to become sick when opiates are withdrawn. At Synanon these verbalizations are not available. A newcomer learns that sickness is not important to men and women who have themselves gone through withdrawal distress. He kicks on a sofa in the center of the large living room, not in a special isolation room or other quarantine room where, in effect, someone would tell him that he is "supposed to" get sick. In one sense, however, Synanon members do force newcomers into a "sick role," for a large part of the reception process is devoted to convincing newcomers that only crazy people would go around sticking needles in their arms. The important point, however, is that this "sick role" is not the one that addicts experience when drugs are withdrawn in a jail or hospital. It is a role that is learned at the same time a new "non-sick role" is being learned; the learning process is facilitated by the fact that the teachers are themselves persons who have learned the new "non-sick role." We have heard the following verbalizations, and many similar ones, made to new addicts at Synanon.[35] None of the comments could reasonably have been made by a rehabilitation official or a "professional" therapist. Each of them provides a route out of both addiction and the special sick role expected of newcomers to the organization:

> It's OK, boy. We've all been through it before.
> For once you're with people like us. You've got everything to gain here and nothing to lose.
> You think you're tough. Listen, we've got guys in here who could run circles around you, so quit your bullshit.
> You're one of us now, so keep your eyes open, your mouth shut, and try to listen for a while. Maybe you'll learn a few things.
> Hang tough, baby. We won't let you die.

SUMMARY AND CONCLUSIONS

The theory of differential association and the more general "symbolic interaction theory" suggest that whether criminals are viewed as agents of change or targets of change when they are used as rehabilitators of other criminals, the concern must be for the fact that criminal conduct is wrong. "Guilt" and "shame" are contained in the verbalizations that make up a culture, and the problem of changing criminals is a problem of insuring that criminals become active members of intimate groups whose verbalizations make all criminality as guilt-producing, shameful, repulsive, and impossible as, say, cannibalism. Stated negatively, the problem is one of insuring that persons do not behave according to verbalizations which make criminality psychologically possible. Since reformed criminals have learned both to feel guilt and not to feel not guilty when they contemplate participation in crimes, they are elite carriers of anticriminal verbalizations and can be used effectively in the effort to prevent crime and reform criminals.

NOTES AND REFERENCES

1. Sutherland, E. H. and Cressey, D. R.: *Principles of Criminology,* 6th ed. New York, Lippincott, 1960, pp. 74-80. See also Cohen, A. K., Lindesmith, A. R., and Schuessler, K. F. (Eds.): *The Sutherland Papers,* Bloomington, Indiana University Press, 1956.

2. Cressey, D. R.: Epidemiology and individual conduct: A case from criminology. *Pacific Sociological Review,* Fall, 1960, pp. 47-58.

3. See Stanton, A. H. and Schwartz, M. S.: *The Mental Hospital: A Study of Institutional Participation in Psychiatric Illness and Treatment.* New York, Basic Books, 1954, pp. 37-38.

4. Cressey, D. R. (Ed.): *The Prison.* New York, Holt, Rinehart, and Winston, 1961, pp. 2-4.

5. Lowie, R. H.: *An Introduction to Cultural Anthropology,* enlarged ed. New York, Rinehart, 1940, p. 379.

6. Cressey, D. R.: *Other People's Money: A Study in the Social Psychology of Embezzlement.* Glencoe, Free Press, 1953.

7. Smigel, E. O.: Public attitudes toward stealing as related to the size of the victim organization. *American Sociological Review,* June, 1956, pp. 320-37.

8. Lindesmith, A. R.: *Opiate Addiction.* Bloomington, Principia Press, 1947.

9. Becker, H. S.: Becoming a marijuana user. *American Journal of Sociology,* November, 1953, pp. 235-43; and Marijuana use and social control. *Social Problems,* Summer, 1955, pp. 35-44.

10. Lane, R. E.: Why businessmen violate the law. *Journal of Criminal Law and Criminology,* July-August, 1953, pp. 151-65.
11. Clinard, M. B.: Criminological theories of violations of wartime regulations. *American Journal of Sociology,* June, 1946, pp. 258-70; and *The Black Market.* New York, Rinehart, 1952.
12. Sykes, G. and Matza, D.: Techniques of neutralization: A theory of delinquency. *American Sociological Review,* December, 1957, pp. 664-70.
13. Sewell, W. H.: Social class and childhood personality. *Sociometry,* December, 1961, pp. 340-56.
14. Glaser, D.: The sociological approach to crime and correction. *Law and Contemporary Problems,* Autumn, 1958, pp. 683-702.
15. Toby, J.: Criminal Motivation. *British Journal of Criminology,* April, 1962, pp. 317-36.
16. See Reckless, W. C., Dinitz, S., and Murray, E.: Self concept as an insulator against delinquency. *American Sociological Review,* December, 1956, pp. 744-46; Reckless, W. C., Dinitz, S., and Kay, B.: The self component in potential delinquency and potential nondelinquency. *American Sociological Review,* October, 1957, pp. 566-70; Lively, E. L., Dinitz, S., and Reckless, W. C.: Self concept as a predictor of juvenile delinquency. *American Journal of Orthopsychiatry,* January, 1962, pp. 159-68; and Dinitz, S., Scarpitti, F. R., and Reckless, W. C.: Delinquency vulnerability: A cross group and longitudinal analysis. *American Sociological Review,* August, 1962, pp. 515-17.
17. Clinard, M. B.: The group approach to social reintegration. *American Sociological Review,* April, 1949, pp. 257-62.
18. Bixby, F. L. and McCorkle, L. W.: Applying the principles of group therapy in correctional institutions. *Federal Probation,* December, 1952, pp. 22-27.
19. McCorkle, L. W.: Group therapy in the treatment of offenders. *Federal Probation,* December, 1952, pp. 22-27.
20. Cressey, D. R.: Contradictory theories in correctional group therapy programs. *Federal Probation,* June, 1954, pp. 20-26.
21. Fidler, J. W.: Possibility of group therapy with female offenders. *International Journal of Group Psychotherapy,* November, 1951, pp. 330-36.
22. Gersten, C.: An experimental evaluation of group therapy with juvenile delinquents. *International Journal of Group Psychotherapy,* November, 1951, pp. 311-18.

23. Festinger, L. *et al.: Theory and Experiment in Social Communication: Collected Papers.* Ann Arbor, Institute for Social Research, 1951.

24. Cressey, D. R.: Changing criminals: The application of the theory of differential association. *American Journal of Sociology,* September, 1955, pp. 116-20.

25. *Ibid.*

26. Tannenbaum, F.: *Crime and the Community.* Boston, Ginn, 1938, p. 21.

27. Merton, R. K.: *Social Theory and Social Structure,* rev. ed. (Glencoe, Free Press, 1957, pp. 421-36.

28. Lemert, E. M.: *Social Pathology.* New York, McGraw-Hill, 1951, pp. 75-76.

29. Johnson, W.: The Indians have no word for it: Stuttering in children. *Quarterly Journal of Speech,* October, 1944, pp. 330-37.

30. Fry, C. C.: *Mental Health in College.* New York, Commonwealth Fund, 1942, pp. 139-40, 146-48; and Leshan, L.: A case of schizophrenia, paranoid type. *Etc.,* July, 1949, pp. 169-73.

31. Scheff, T. J.: Decision rules, types of error, and their consequences in medical diagnosis. *Behavioral Science,* April, 1963, pp. 97-107.

32. Gardiner-Hill, H.: *Clinical Involvements.* London, Butterworth, 1958, p. 158.

33. Toby, *supra* note 15.

34. Volkman, R. and Cressey, D. R.: Differential association and the rehabilitation of drug addicts. *American Journal of Sociology,* September, 1963, pp. 129-42.

35. *Ibid.*

Treatment of Offenders: Some Behavioral Concepts, Principles, and Approaches

SALEEM A. SHAH

Psychological laboratories have been conducting systematic and controlled research on behavior and principles of learning for many years. After considerable experimental vertification, these principles, in recent years, have been applied to a variety of clinical and other situations with rather encouraging and promising results. This presentation outlines some of these relatively new

NOTE: Reprinted from *Federal Probation,* 30 (2) :29-38, 1966.

developments and scientific principles, particularly as they apply to work with offenders. Space will not allow any detailed discussion of the many principles and techniques, nor of the complexities involved in their precise application. However, the several studies listed in the references will provide further information.

The term "offender" is used here to include both adults and juveniles in trouble with the law. "Treatment" is used broadly to describe various methods, including psychotherapy and counseling, designed to change the behavior of offenders. The particular concepts and principles discussed are related to individual therapy situations, treatment approaches within institutional settings, and also in terms of the relevance of such concepts and analysis to broad community structure and practice.

To begin with, a behavioral approach to treatment requires that we deal with clear, explicit, and observable aspects of behavior which lend themselves to objective study and evaluation. It has to be borne in mind that labeling a procedure as "treatment" does not necessarily make it therapeutic. Nor, for that matter, do programs labeled "rehabilitative" necessarily result in rehabilitation. It is essential that the therapeutic and rehabilitative endeavors be defined precisely and that careful evaluation be a basic part of all such programs. Without such evaluative research, crucial feedback about the efficacy of our programs would be lacking, and we may continue using methods having little actual value.

The problems of delinquency and crime have assumed such magnitude, and the shortage of skilled manpower has become so acute, that there is urgent need for more innovative and efficient treatment approaches. It is not enough to know that certain methods, in many instances, are of value. More precise knowledge is required to assess the actual cost and overall efficacy of various approaches; to determine the most efficient and desirable combinations of types of treatment, types of problems, and the variety of circumstances and settings in which specific treatments are best conducted. In addition, a body of systematic knowledge has to be developed which can be utilized in making our techniques more exact and effective and in the training of a broad range of needed personnel. Obviously, that knowledge and those particular skills should be taught which, on the basis of objective evaluation, are found to be both useful and efficient in modifying deviant behavior.

SOME BEHAVIORAL CONCEPTS

Human behavior, in large measure, is shaped by learning. Various patterns of behavior are produced by particular personal histories. Recent advances in learning theory offer some very useful ideas as to the role of various experiences in the development of complex behavioral patterns and characteristics. In short, behavior increasingly is being subjected to scientific analysis and study and the results of such study are shedding much light on problems pertaining to habilitation, rehabilitation, and treatment endeavors with offenders and others.

While there is indeed much therapeutic interest in background of the individual to know how a particular pattern of behavior may have been learned, the concern in behavior may have been learned, the concern in behavioral approaches is even more with the specific variables that may *currently* maintain and otherwise influence such behavior. There is mounting evidence that in a variety of cases, marked behavioral changes may indeed be accomplished without engaging in long-term intensive study of the childhood and without developing "insights" regarding the problem. This does not imply, however, that insight and understanding may not be useful and desirable to the extent that they relate to behavior modification. Nor can it be denied that there are many serious and long-standing problems which require special and prolonged treatment efforts. But it is becoming evident that treatment designed to modify specific aspects of behavior need not as often be such a long and expensive process.

A behavioral approach to the treatment of offenders would view the goal as involving cessation of antisocial activities, and the bringing about of more constructive personal and social functioning. To accomplish this, a variety of techniques and approaches may be used. Therapeutic methods which utilize various principles and procedures derived from learning theory and which seek specific modifications in behavior have been labeled behavior therapy.

Behavior may be seen as *involving a relationship between an individual and a particular environment.* Behavior is neither fixed nor absolute, and rarely does it involve only the individual. For example, we do not behave on the job as we do in church, at a party, or in the privacy of our homes. It is not surprising that certain persons who are described as highly impulsive and erratic in the community may be described as "model inmates" within the penal institution. Such common observations concerning the variability of behavior are surprising only if one views behavior as a somewhat fixed and absolute quality of the individual. Such conceptualizations, and attempts to predict behavior without considering the eliciting, stimulating, provoking, and controlling characteristics of particular environments would appear to be both inadequate and erroneous.

Since behavior may be seen as an interaction between an individual and a particular environment, treatment efforts may be directed at the individual and also to alterations of the environment. In contrast to the concern of most traditional psychotherapies with inferred intrapsychic processes, behavioral approaches have engaged in considerable research and empirical study to see how changes in environmental variables and consequences can bring about changes in the individual's behavior. This brings us to a discussion of operant behavior.

There is a broad range of behavior which has the characteristic of being influenced by its consequences. Particular consequences tend to bring about rather predictable changes in the rate, frequency, and other characteristics of the behavior. For example, if Johnny's whining results in obtaining mother's attention, then this consequence may tend to maintain or even increase the whining behavior. On the other hand, if the effect of the whining behavior on mother is to provoke immediate punishment by her, then this consequence may decrease that behavior. However, it may well be that mother's attention by itself, be it positive or negative, is rewarding in some way to Johnny. In such case, the punishment may have no effect on the whining. But very possibly the absence of any response, i.e. ignoring the whining, may then lead to the decrease and probable elimination of that behavior. This latter process is referred to as *extinction.* Thus, differing consequences tend to have varying effects on the particular behavior.

Much of our behavior is influenced in rather complex fashion by the consequences we experience. Unpleasant or negative consequences tend to decrease the particular behavior, whereas positive or pleasant consequences tend to maintain or even increase that behavior. Behavior which has the above characteristic, i.e. of being influenced by its consequences, is referred to as *operant behavior*.

A vast amount of research has been conducted over the past decade or more to determine how, to what degree, and under what set of circumstances behavior can be influenced and modified by certain consequences. Such investigations suggest that our social environment plays a major role in shaping and maintaining various patterns of behavior—both deviant and adaptive.

The consequences to which behavior is exposed may be of two broad kinds: reinforcing or aversive. While the common terms reward and punishment often may be used to convey the general sense of reinforcing and aversive consequences, respectively, the technical terms will be explained here in view of their more precise meaning.

For an event to be defined as reinforcing, it must meet two specific criteria: (a) it must be made contingent upon a particular response, i.e. it will not occur unless the specified behavior occurs and (b) it maintains or increases the response that produced it. A worker being rewarded with a bonus for good work is an example of positive reinforcement.

There is another form of reinforcement in which some aversive or punishing stimuli are removed, contingent upon a particular response. An example of this would be a situation where a person is given back his driver's permit after he satisfactorily completes a driver training course or other similar requirement. However, in this instance, the rewarding situation is referred to as negative reinforcement.

The removal of positive reinforcement, when made contingent upon a particular response, defines one form of aversive consequence or punishment. An example of this would be when a worker loses a bonus because of deterioration in his work. The other form of punishment is where an aversive consequence, when contingent upon a particular response, tends to decrease or eliminate that response; for example, when a worker's pay is docked because he comes late to work.

It can also be arranged that a response which hitherto produced a consequence now no longer produces it. Such a cessation of any consequence, i.e. having the response achieve no effect on the environment, is referred to as extinction.

It is very important to remember that for a consequence (reinforcing or punishing) to be effective, it should follow rather closely the response or behavior to be influenced. There is a general principle in operant procedures which states that, other things being equal, *behavior is as shapeable as the consequences are immediate.* Thus the desired effects of a reinforcement may indeed be lost if the element of timing and related aspects are not taken into consideration.

Reinforcement contingencies, i.e. rewards and punishments as defined above, may have very diverse effects, depending upon such factors as the intensity and timing of the consequences, the certainty of the punishment or reinforcement, the nature and strength of the particular response being influenced, the schedule or sequence of the reinforcement, and other aspects. Failure to consider, or to even be aware of, these several critical factors may well thwart the effectiveness of the otherwise sound reinforcement principles. This situation may then lead to erroneous beliefs regarding the value or effectiveness of the principles involved.

The aforementioned terms are defined in relation to the actual and resulting behavior. Thus, even though a parent or a court may mete out "punishment" in an effort to remove the occurrence of some undesirable behavior, if the behavior shows no change, then the procedure could not be termed punishment, as this word is used in operant terminology. Even though the intention of the parent or judge may clearly have been to punish, the particular consequence may not have been punishing to the individual. It may even be, in many instances, that what a parent views as being "punishment," e.g. scolding, may actually be in some fashion reinforcing to the child. Hence the particular behavior will be maintained rather than diminished, while ostensibly being punished.

Since terms such as "punishment" have popular, philosophical, technical, and other usage, and since discussion of such matters often involves both empirical and ideological aspects, it should be emphasized that the discussion here is in terms of certain technical principles and involves various considerations that are empirical rather than philosophical or ideological. Both empirical and ideological aspects are, in fact, important and must be evaluated in their proper place. However, discussions which confuse empirical and ideological considerations can rarely lead to clarification of the issues involved.

The above has been a rather brief explanation of some basic reinforcement contingencies. There are, as indicated earlier, many different rates and schedules of reinforcement which have different applications and produce very diverse and characteristic effects upon behavior. In addition, there are several other variables involved in the operant paradigm and all of these have to be considered very carefully when seeking to influence behavior.

THE "SHAPING" OF BEHAVIOR

A general principle which has long been used by skillful teachers, coaches, parents, therapists, and others, in modifying or shaping behavior, involves making slow and gradual changes, starting with the individual's existing level of performance. Experimental psychologists have made careful studies of this important process and refer to it as the method of "successive approximation." The technical term simply means that successive approaches to the criterion behavior or goal are systematically reinforced.

In making precise use of this method, one starts with the existing level of skill, or lack of it, and then proceeds in such small and graduated steps that the chances of failure at each step are almost eliminated and success made almost a certainty. Each appropriate or correct move toward the goal is provided external, or extrinsic, reinforcements (praise, approval, prizes, candy, good grades, etc.). Such progress may also generate internal or intrinsic reinforcements for the individual, that is, the pleasure, satisfaction, and feeling of pride at having been right, knowing the answer, making visible progress, etc.

All too often, for example, therapeutic efforts with offenders may fail because therapists require but fail to obtain the necessary degree of interest and motivation from the individuals. Fairly often, the very real difficulties presented by the offenders' poor motivation for treatment may further be compounded by the equally poor motivation of some therapists to treat them. The reluctance of many therapists to treat offenders may, in large measure, be related to the absence of the reinforcements provided by therapeutic successes.

Educational and therapeutic techniques have to be adjusted to meet the needs of particular individuals with their existing handicaps and the process started at the available level of functioning. Therapists, counselors, teachers, and others have to accept lack of interest, motivation, proper attitudes, etc., as a basic and integral part of the problem presented by such persons. What is required is that we develop approaches and techniques designed specifically to bypass and overcome such obstacles.

EXPERIMENTER-SUBJECT APPROACH TO THERAPY

Schwitzgebel[1] conducted a study with 40 rather confirmed delinquents. The average number of arrests in the group was 8.2, the average age at first arrest, 13.5 years, and average length of incarceration, 15.1 months. These delinquents were sought out and offered part-time jobs talking into a tape recorder about anything they wished. A reinforcement procedure was initiated—using an hourly rate of pay, cokes, food, subway tokens, bonuses, etc.—by means of which attendance in the project gradually became dependable and also prompt. After two months of employment in the project, the subjects typically began to value the relationship with the project and the experimenter as much or even more than their small salary. That is, the conditioned reinforcement provided by the money was gradually changed and broadened to include generalized social reinforcements, i.e. the attention and interest of the experimenter and the relationship with him. Termination of the job with the project came gradually and as the boys began to take part-time jobs in the community. Three years after termination of the employment of the experimental group, an extensive followup showed a statistically significant reduction in number of arrests and the number of months of incarceration, as compared with a control group.

Schwitzgebel's study is an interesting example of novel and imaginative methods coupled with useful procedures (viz. operant conditioning) to influence the behavior of hard-core delinquents. It would not be difficult to envision the situation had these delinquents been approached in the usual fashion and referred to a typical psychiatric clinic for outpatient therapy. Chances are that the majority would not even have shown up for the first visit, let alone continue for any length of time in the treatment program. The careful utilization of extrinsic motivation, or pressure from probation or parole officers or related sources, frequently may have a desirable influence in terms of participation in a treatment program. Schwitzgebel used extrinsic reinforcements in the form of hourly pay rates and other such incentives.

ENVIRONMENTAL FACTORS AFFECTING THERAPY

To the extent that such community contacts with patients are typically very limited in time and few controls are possible over the many factors influencing the individual's behavior, treatment results may not be very satisfactory. It may well be in many cases that the 1, 2, or even 3 hours a week spent in therapy cannot match or surpass the influence of the peer group, family, and other environmental constraints present in the neighborhood during the remainder of the week. However, to the extent that the therapist is aware of these other variables, that certain key members of the person's social environment can be included in the therapeutic effort, and also if systematic use can be made of efficacious techniques, the treatment results may indeed be markedly improved.

In dealing with persons seriously handicapped in terms of social-personal skills and controls, or because of the possible threat posed to the community, the treatment and rehabilitation program may at times best be conducted in an institutional setting.

The relatively tight structure of the institution and possibilities for controlling large elements of the total environment in an orderly fashion can greatly facilitate behavior modification. Many studies which have utilized the environmental controls readily available within mental hospitals, residential treatment centers, etc., illustrate the effectiveness with which operant and related procedures can be applied in such settings.

OTHER APPROACHES TO BEHAVIOR THERAPY

In addition to the use of operant methods, which are derived in large measure from learning theories formulated by B. F. Skinner and his associates, other forms of behavior therapy have applied learning principles derived from Hullian theory and classical or respondent conditioning. Wolpe[2] is the foremost exponent of a number of rather efficient therapeutic techniques based upon Hullian principles. These techniques have already been applied to a variety of neurotic disorders, sexual deviations, and several other types of behavior disorders. More recently, even broader applications of these methods have been attempted. The results of these therapeutic techniques compare most favorably in terms of cost and overall efficiency with traditional intensive techniques. In view of the above advantages, and the additional important fact that behavior therapy uses concepts which are more explicitly formulated, amenable to verification, and also have much research to support their findings, these methods have gained considerable importance in the past few years. However, it should be emphasized that no claim has been made that all types of disorders may be treated effectively through such methods, nor that these are the only useful therapeutic methods currently available.

BEHAVIORAL DEFICIENCIES AS RELATED TO SOCIAL MALADJUSTMENT

Most of the traditional therapeutic approaches view behavior problems in terms of various "inner" or "intrapsychic" processes assumed to bring about the deviant manifestations. What has been given little attention is that many offenders, particularly those with marked social, personal, cultural, and educational deprivations, are remarkably lacking in skills which the middle-class person takes almost for granted. For example, frequently there are glaring deficits in these offenders' behavior in regard to correct speech and language proficiency, manner of approaching job and other interviews, culturally acceptable means of expressing anger and hostility, and numerous other aspects of social and interpersonal skills. Similarly, the lack of adequate education and necessary vocational training among many such persons makes suitable adjustment in a complex and demanding society a very real and at times an insurmountable problem.

It is known, for example, that a variety of deprivations experienced in regard to early interpersonal relationships, environmental stimulation, and exposure to a variety of educational and other such situations, etc., tend to bring about a degree of functional retardation in children from very impoverished backgrounds. Such children, even though possessing average capacity, are often a year or more behind in educational and social development, even when starting in first grade. Lacking the skills essential to function adequately in the usual classroom setting and further lacking the kind of experiences which develop educational interest, motivation, and high achievement drive, many of these youngsters may keep falling behind and eventually end up as voluntary or involuntary "dropouts." With serious educational, vocational, and attitudinal handicaps, these individuals are poorly equipped to function well in the community. The choice of employment for such persons is also very limited and lies generally in a disappearing section of unskilled physical labor. In the absence of socially rewarding capabilities, many such handicapped persons may turn to a variety of deviant means for achieving those reinforcements which otherwise are difficult to obtain or are even quite unattainable. Unquestionably, numerous other factors also enter into the development of such complex and multidetermined problems.

One of the treatment tasks, then, is to provide specially constructed environments for such individuals so that they may be able to obtain at least some response for their limited behavioral repertoires. Using "successive approximation" and related methods and by offering specialized training and education, the competence and capabilities may gradually be improved to desirable levels.

PROGRAMMED INSTRUCTION AS A THERAPEUTIC TOOL

A procedure closely related to the method of "successive approximation" is programmed instruction. In programmed instruction, one again starts at the existing level of skill possessed by the student, and then there is a systematic presentation of small bits of subject matter proceeding in such a fashion that success is maximized and failure and errors minimized. Such methods, often typified by "teaching machines," have been found to be very useful in producing educational achievement in delinquents, offenders, and others. The individual can work at his own speed and without the aversive reactions and consequences often experienced in the classroom setting. Even more important, the experience of success, i.e. of being "right" and knowing the answer, provides very valuable intrinsic reinforcement.

On the basis of some recent research, it may be hypothesized that the importance of any change in behavior lies in the effect which it produces upon the reactions of the social culture. If, for example, a small decrease in the deviant behavior is immediately followed by approval of the peer group, parents, teachers, or others, this should accelerate the learning of new behavior. This is, as the child becomes less of a brat, i.e. more likeable, the environment provides an increase in positive social reinforcements. As these new behavior patterns are learned, they should in turn lead to even greater positive reactions from the environment. Under these circumstances, the changes in behavior could be dramatic, even though the focus of the treatment effort was rather limited. Needless to say, since a number of variables and conditions are involved in the above types of changes and precise control of them is an ideal seldom actually attained, it is not surprising that when dealing with more complicated and long-standing problems of adults, such rapid and dramatic changes are infrequent. However, the theoretical analysis and explanation of the above findings do suggest ideas for increasing generalization effects and developing more efficient treatment approaches and therapeutic environments.

APPLICATIONS IN INSTITUTIONAL SETTINGS

Operant approaches to behavior modification have been applied in a number of situations: with hospitalized mental patients, autistic children, retarded children, the physically handicapped, and also with offenders. While the settings and problems have been quite varied, the same general principles have been applied. The precise forms of behavior to be modified have differed, as have the kinds of environmental controls and reinforcements available and the degree and kind of problem to be treated.

In work with seriously disturbed mental patients, it has been found that the greatest difficulty is with patients in whom, probably because of their long-term hospitalization, many behavior patterns have been distinguished. Those patients may do little more than just eat and sleep.

Such findings have the implication that whenever the behavior pattern is seriously restricted or extinguished, such as in some forms of long-term institutionalization, it may make it extremely difficult for the individual to then learn to adapt to the normal community environment. Certainly it seems true of many recidivist offenders that long and repeated incarceration and the lack of appropriate programs to develop and support social and vocational repertoires make the behavioral deficits even more pronounced. Often, then, such offenders may come to experience adjustment in the free community as distinctly threatening and may some times see it as actually being somewhat more aversive and punishing than even incarceration.

The Draper Project

For the past four years, Dr. John M. McKee[3] has been using programmed instruction and related procedures in an educational experiment at Draper Correctional Center in Alabama. In marked contrast to the passive and disinterested groups of offenders often seen in the regular classroom situation, the programmed instruction approach has brought about a marked degree of interest, effort, and actual educational achievement. Twenty-two students retook the California Achievement Test and registered an average gain of three grades. The average total time of association in the program of this group was 5.5 months. Also, a large number of students have passed the GED (General Educational Development) examination; not a single student who has taken this examination has yet failed. Seven "graduates" of the program are actually enrolled in colleges in the community. A Service Corps consisting of inmate counselors has been developed, and many inmates have been trained to assist in the project in various capacities. Other offenders have been trained to write new "programs" for the teaching machines. A couple of the "graduates," ex-inmates, have been hired to work in the project and are rendering valuable service.

In addition to the obvious achievements in the educational and vocational areas, many other changes have also been noted. There has been approximately a 45 percent reduction in disciplinary actions since the project got underway, the inmates in the program see themselves as "students" and tend to behave as such, and a variety of related social and attitudinal changes have also been observed.

McKee is currently programming courses on "Holding a Successful Job Interview," "How to Succeed on Parole," "Changing Spoken English Habits," and "Steps to Good Grooming." Work has also been started on an experimental project to develop and evaluate the effectiveness of a programmed course aimed at providing ethical instruction.

Needless to say, all this has not been accomplished simply by using "teaching machines." Other related operant principles have been utilized, close educational supervision and counseling have been provided for the students, various incentives and reinforcements have been made available, and efforts have been made to modify the institutional milieu. In addition, this program is giving very careful attention to developing and providing close parole supervision and job placement services, and obtaining regular follow-up information to evaluate the actual progress and adjustment of the released inmates.

The Draper program's particular concern with careful and thorough parole planning and supervision and related services points up a most crucial issue. It goes without saying that the best efforts of the correctional institution can very easily be thwarted and undone if the community fails to provide the essential services and facilities so urgently needed by released offenders during their readjustment to the free society. In the absence of such programs and without the community's active support in the rehabilitation process, the time, money, and efforts expended in correctional programs will simply have been wasted.

The National Training School Project

The other project I should like to describe is the one being conducted locally at the National Training School for Boys. This project has utilized operant procedures to develop educational achievement.[4] Within the six-month period allowed for the initial demonstration project, and working three hours a day in this special unit, all 15 juveniles in the program showed marked academic achievement. The average achievement in the six-month period was almost two grades. Harold Cohen, the project director, instituted very precise operant procedures, especially designed the learning environment, and used very detailed and rather precise measures of almost all conceivable behavior of the boys while in the project. Educational work, i.e. working on the "teaching machines" and taking related course work, was reinforced by a point system. The points thus earned could be used to purchase a variety of things, e.g. use of a comfortably appointed lounge, cokes, food, clothing, and even items from a Sears catalog (one point being equal to a cent). The boys were not compelled to study; however, a variety of external (extrinsic) reinforcements were obviously available to them if they did engage in such educational behavior. Very quickly the performance and motivation of the boys showed progress and they began to put in hours of very consistent and diligent work on the teaching machines. As the behavior of the boys improved, the "payoffs" in points were systematically varied and other positive reinforcements also made available. After a while, some of the boys were willing to pay for additional courses of instruction offered, for special tutoring, and to rent space for "private" offices, and even used a bank which gave interest on the deposits.

In this project, too, it was noted that the improvements in educational behaviors and skills generalized to various other areas of functioning. The social behavior and general manner of the subjects indicated marked improvements, about two-thirds of the boys from the project moved up to the honor cottage in the institution, and there were no disciplinary problems at all in the project.

The use of "teaching machines" was only one of several operant principles applied in a methodical fashion to elicit and reinforce certain desired behaviors while curbing and controlling the manifestation of deviant behaviors.

PRECISE USE OF A POINT SYSTEM

The use of a point system to influence behavior is, of course, nothing new. However, the procedures used in this project in regard to the points have several different and distinctive features. The point system in this research was used very precisely as a convenient means for providing extrinsic reinforcements and as a rather basic and essential part of a more complex application of operant principles.

Various aspects of the physical environment in the project were carefully designed by Cohen to have rather specific effects on the behavior of the boys. This was also true of the particular manner in which the point system was used. The points could only be earned by the individual's satisfactory performance in educational work, and a careful record of the points earned and spent by each person was kept by the project staff. Thus, points could not be given away, loaned, borrowed, begged, or stolen; they could only be earned and be used by the person working for them. Since the behavior upon which the points were contingent was rather precise and could objectively be measured, viz. sections of programmed courses, objective test scores, etc., only the desired educational behaviors were reinforced. No matter how manipulative the individual or how extremely skilled at "conning," the environmental constraints were such that these behaviors simply did not work in that environment and obtained no response whatsoever. Thus, these and related behaviors were rarely even attempted in the project.

Cohen[5] is now starting a new project with 30 boys, this time using an entire cottage, where he will again utilize a system of external reinforcers (among them the use of points), and will devise a simulated "real-world" economy to improve academic, vocational, and acceptable social behaviors of the inmates. Another objective of this new project is to seek additional means of parole evaluation, which are similar in measurement to behaviors typically required for the individual's self-maintenance in the community. For example, the requirement for parole, as generally envisioned at this point, may be that an individual (a) has reached a specific academic grade, (b) has acquired a vocational skill at a particular level, and (c) has demonstrated for six months an ability to work a minimum of 40 hours a week to earn enough funds (in points) to support himself in terms of housing, food, clothing, and certain social behaviors.

The above project promises to be one of the most fascinating and remarkable pieces of innovative research in the correctional field utilizing scientific principles of behavior modification. As indicated earlier, there is built right into the project a vast amount of objective measurement and close and careful evaluation at each and every stage.

ENVIRONMENTAL FACTORS AND SOCIAL DEVIANCE

We can hope that in the not-too-distant future it may be possible to apply some of the above and related insights to make a fairly precise analysis of the functional relationships between various community practices and particular social problems, that is, to determine the effects of certain structures and practices upon the occurrence and frequency of various offenses and other social problems. It is already evident that the structure and inadequacies of various aspects of our economic, social, and educational systems, particularly in terms of their inability to assist many who have severe social and behavior handicaps, undoubtedly help to produce a variety of social and human problems. In particular, current educational facilities, programs, and approaches seem in the main ill-equipped to deal with the many acute problems manifested in part by the numerous underachievers, school dropouts, and the number of youngsters ill-prepared to adapt satisfactorily to the increasingly complex culture. Whether we have to face the expected consequences of having to rear children in child institutions, or the thousands on welfare and relief rolls who do not seem to benefit much from programs aimed at making them self-sufficient, or the many others who spend large periods of their lives in penal and correctional institutions, in all of this and much else the entire community and the country has to pay the price for deficiencies in the social structure and system.

To take a more specific aspect of the relationship between social and environmental factors and deviant behavior, it seems evident that the form and frequency of certain criminal acts bears some connection to the environmental structure and opportunities provided. Thus the relative ease with which checks may be obtained and also cashed in the United States is undoubtedly related to the frequency of bad checks and various related offenses. The relative ease with which cars may be broken into and be started without use of ignition keys clearly affects the frequency of offenses involving "joy-riding" and automobile theft. Similarly, the facility with which firearms may be obtained by almost all segments of the population would appear to have a definite bearing on the numerous offenses involving such weapons.

It seems obvious that certain changes in community practices, the requirement that the vast technological skills available in the country be utilized more adequately in the manufacturing of automobiles with better door locks and less vulnerable ignition systems, the enactment of other appropriate legislation, etc., could do much to influence the frequency of certain law violations and other undesirable social situations.

Then, again, sociologists have for years been pointing to the strong social class and other biases operating within the entire structure of our system of legislation, laws, law enforcement, and related practices. It seems a lot easier, for example, to pass laws meting out severe penalties for offenses like housebreaking than for more dangerous offenses—but involving a less restricted sample of offenders—as in the case of drunk driving. In these and many similar situations, a variety of biases, prevailing cultural attitudes in the more vocal, organized, or influential segments of the population, and factors pertaining to social and political power may effectively thwart needed legislation and other social actions.

Such an analysis could go on and on. The important point is that behavior is indeed a function of individuals and the social environment. As such, programs of treatment, habilitation, and rehabilitation should not be confined only to the deviant individuals and more immediate situations, but should devote increasing attention to modifications of the social environment. Such changes could, in turn, affect the behavior of large segments of the community and thus be distinctly appropriate as broad-based and efficient approaches for coping with the complex phenomena of crime and related social problems.

CONCLUSION

In conclusion, it should be emphasized that the behavioral principles and approaches described here are by no means the only useful methods available, nor are they totally new. Many of the principles described have been used over the years by experienced and skilled therapists, teachers, and others. What is new, however, are the developments in the experimental analysis of behavior, the variety of controlled research concerning these and other techniques for the modification of behavior, and the systematic formulation of such findings into testable and scientific theory. Such research and related technological developments are designed to provide precise and accurate information which may be added to the body of scientific knowledge about human behavior.

It is crucial that we subject our treatment and rehabilitation program to careful and objective evaluation and begin to use a more rigorous approach in such endeavors. The enormity of the task at hand indicates that we can no longer afford the dubious luxury of "flying by the seat of our pants," so to speak. Furthermore, there is a compelling need for conscientious reexamination of the relevance and efficacy of some of our traditional roles and concepts and of the practices that follow from them. Such efforts should enable us to devise more efficient treatment methods and more appropriate strategies for the training and deployment of our manpower resources. To do this, we will have to forsake some of our traditional shibboleths and sacred cows which fail to stand the test of relevancy to present needs and evaluative research.

NOTES AND REFERENCES

1. Schwitzgebel, R. and Kolb, D. A.: Inducing change in adolescent delinquents. *Behavior Research and Therapy,* March, 1964; and Schwitzgebel, R.: *Streetcorner Research: An Experimental Approach to Juvenile Delinquency.* Cambridge, Harvard University Press, 1964. See also Schwitzgebel, R.: A new approach to understanding delinquency. *Federal Probation,* March, 1960.
2. Wolpe, J.: *Psychotherapy by Reciprocal Inhibition.* Stanford: Stanford University Press, 1958.
3. McKee, J. M.: Programmed instruction as a therapeutic tool. Paper read at American Psychological Association meetings, Philadelphia, 1963; and The Draper experiment: A programmed learning project. In Ofiesh, G. D. and Meierhenry, W. C. (Eds.): *Trends in Programmed Instruction.* Washington, National Education Association, 1964.
4. Cohen, H. L., Filipczak, J. A. and Bis, J. S.: Case project. *Progress Report,* August, 1965 (mimeographed).
5. Cohen, H. L.: Case II-model. Jefferson Hall, National Training School for Boys (mimeographed).

The New Penology: Fact or Fiction?

ALFRED C. SCHNUR

In state and federal prisons and reformatories, 26,938 persons are employed full time. They are responsible for 161,587 inmates. For every six inmates, there is one employee. Prison personnel can be arranged in several functional groupings. The vast majority, 17,280, are hired to keep prisoners in prison; others, "to keep 'em busy, keep 'em fed, or to keep 'em reasonably well." A few, 1,337, are there to get them ready to go out and stay out.

NOTE: Reprinted from *The Journal of Criminal Law, Criminology and Police Science,* 49:331-334, 1958.

More people, however, are employed to shuffle papers than to implement the new penology.

What is the goal of the new penology? It is to get men ready, as rapidly and economically as possible, to go out and stay out by returning them to society, as useful, law-abiding, self-supporting, self-sufficient, independent citizens who will not contribute to the commission of crime by others—men who obey the law because they want to and not because they are afraid not to. What kinds of professional people, and how many, have been hired to implement the new penology and achieve its goals? Not many!

Twenty-three full-time psychiatrists are employed to treat the 161,587 prisoners. Each psychiatrist is responsible for 7,026 inmates. If full-time employment for a psychiatrist meant an eight-hour day and a 160-hour month, it would mean that there is not more than 82 seconds of psychiatric help available for each inmate during a whole month. Little psychiatric time in prison, however, is focused on life after prison. Instead, however, it is focused on keeping things in reasonable order for the prison administration and on readying a man for transfer to a mental institution.

If the 67 psychologists and psychometrists distributed their time evenly, each inmate could secure about four minutes of their time monthly for individual attention. The 96 institutional parole officers would have about six minutes for each man each month. Less than ten minutes a month could be afforded each prisoner by the 155 chaplains. The 257 employees responsible for individual casework services have less than 16 minutes for each man. Not over 45 minutes are available from the 739 academic, vocational, and trade teachers.[1] Inmates who consume more than 80 minutes of service in one month from the whole classification, training and treatment staff are taking more than their fair share.

This time analysis assumes that the professional training and treatment staff take no coffee breaks or vacations; that they are never sick; that they are not involved in classification committee meetings, institutional meetings, or staff conferences; that they never attend professional meetings; that they are not snowed under by paperwork; that they need not plan their work; that they are not used to pacify the inmate population for the administration's peace of mind or to front for the institution in placating politicians; and that they are not sent out on public relations missions to inform the public—or to beguile it.

Half of the law violators who enter prison today will be back on the streets before 22 months have passed. It is appalling to realize that the average (median) prisoner will have had but 30 hours of treatment time allocated to him during the time that he was withdrawn from society to make him safe for return to society. One cannot avoid concluding from this that such rehabilitation as does occur must be largely the consequence of a prisoner's do-it-yourself project. It should come as no surprise that so many men return to crime following such "lavish" treatment programs. It is, indeed, remarkable that there are not more recidivists.

Men like James V. Bennett, Director of the Federal Bureau of Prisons, and J. Edgar Hoover, former Director of the Federal Bureau of Investigation, have cited evidence that should alert the public to penology's batting average. Mr. Bennett called attention to several carefully made samplings that indicate that "at least 55 to 60 percent of the prisoners leaving prison today will return within five years." In some places, he continued, "the recidivist rate exceeds 70 percent."[2] Mr. Hoover pointed out that 70 percent of the fingerprints of arrested persons received by the FBI's Identification Division are of persons who have records of previous arrests. Hoover directed attention also to the 63.8 percent repeaters among the men received in federal prisons for sentences of more than one year in 1954.[3]

These figures serve to document the statement that the majority of the men leaving prison are not refraining from crime. Although it is not the purpose of this paper to assign responsibility for this fact, it is manifestly clear that the new penology cannot be charged with responsibility for it. Very few practitioners of the new penology have got inside the prison gates, and of this few, some are obliged to leave to maintain their integrity or to avoid dry rot. The new penology has not yet really been drafted into the war against crime. The distribution of treatment personnel to implement the new penology is uneven. Institutions where treatment personnel are concentrated serve as beacon lights to those of us who feel the new penology should be tried. We take heart that this is an indication that someday diagnosis and therapy will supplant blame and punishment in the management of law violators.

For the new penology to function effectively, more than the mere addition of treatment personnel is required. The new penology should be staffed by dedicated, persistent, sincere men who know what to look for and know the significance of what they see. The legal stage, also, needs to be properly set. Archiac judicial predestination in sentencing should be replaced by the absolute indeterminate sentence. Eventually, too, the ignorance now at work on the American crime problem should be retired through the establishment of a correctional accounting system and the use of its findings. Ignorance should be put on shorter hours at once through the use of what has already been discovered through research in human behavior and corrections.

Ignorance is credited with much of the blame for the floundering and ineffectiveness in the field of corrections. Mr. Richard A. McGee, Director of the California Department of Corrections, has made a significant statement in this regard.

> Ideas and principles form the essential foundation of a system, but it is impossible to have ideas without facts about which to have ideas. It is therefore essential that an agency of the state government be set up to collect, analyze and publicize information about crime and delinquency. . . . The job is tedious, it is difficult, it is expensive, but undoubtedly much of the floundering in the correctional field has its genesis in the fact that we have too many theories and not enough information. No matter what a good fact-finding agency may cost, it cannot possibly cost more than it is worth.[4]

No reasonable man could quarrel with the statements of Mr. McGee. To secure maximum efficiency in the administration of justice and attain the objectives of the new penology, there is no question that much research is undoubtedly needed. Very little has been done to determine correction's batting average by evaluating the effectiveness of what is done to, for, and with the arrested law violator. If a business knew as little about the performance of its product and the explanation for its performance after it reached the market as corrections knows about the performance of its graduates and the reasons for their performance, the business would surely fail. Products that had to be taken in for repairs as often as correctional graduates are returned for more rehabilitation would soon be off the market.

However, corrections must also face the fact that very little of the correctional research that has been conducted is being utilized in practice. Although no reasonable man can quarrel with the need for research identified by Mr. McGee, any reasonable man should quarrel with the failure to apply what is now known. Dr. Thomas Sellin once said

> . . . progress in penology moves on leaden feet. . . ."[5] If penology does not get the lead out of its feet, a moratorium on research could safely be declared for several decades at least without researchers' needing to have any fear that the practice of penology would catch up with them. There is no immediate prospect that the chasm between practice and theory will be bridged. The present relationship between correctional theory and correctional practice is well illustrated by the story about an eager salesman who was high pressuring a farmer to buy a book on scientific agronomy. He was squelched by the farmer's retort, "Shucks, Son, I ain't farming half as good as I know how to now."[6]

A material increase in the attainment of the objectives of the new penology could be brought about through the immediate application of contemporary correctional knowledge to the control of recurrent crime. This would reduce some of the present inefficiency and vagueness of hunch, whim, intuition, informal experience, and anecdote in the treatment of law violators. For maximum efficiency, however, a continuous correctional accounting system should be established. Crime control and correctional treatment should have an efficiency that cannot be excelled.

Little real progress can be expected in providing maximum protection at minimum cost from crime's toll in personal violence and property loss until the importance of securing facts regarding the crime problem and its management is realized and the means are provided for securing and using them. Sound programs cannot be developed and operated in any line of endeavor without sound and relevant facts. There should be no doubt that the present methods of handling the crime problem are in urgent need of improvement to reduce the needless exposure of people to criminal violence. Many remedies have been proposed and no doubt will continue to be proposed to solve particular portions of the crime problem by individuals and groups who are especially conscious of certain aspects of the problem. By themselves, certain remedies may be warranted for certain immediate purposes but the piecemeal adoption of ideas in response to dramatic instances merely serves to prolong the short-sighted, unintegrated, uncoordinated, discontinuous procedures that characterize much of America's approach to the crime problem. With facts, the merits of various contemplated reforms can be properly gauged and adopted or rejected intelligently. Without sufficient evidence, impulsive decisions may be made. This could mean that things will be done which are neither effective nor economic in solving the crime problem.

Effective administration of correctional policy requires the consideration of the results of past management and the conditions of present management, whether working in the present or planning the future. With the information that a correctional accounting system can provide, members of legislatures and all other persons concerned with the crime problem will be more able to use present facilities effectively and to plan for the future with sound knowledge of the present and the past. When new ideas are proposed, they will be more able to know what is involved and what the idea is worth. More adequate evaluation of proposed legislation will be facilitated.

A correctional accounting system would promote better protection for the people from law violators and greater efficiency in the expenditure of money for correctional purposes by making knowledge of experience with law violators from arrest to release more readily available and usable. Correctional accounting will help the personnel concerned with crime control to recognize and demonstrate the need for altering, developing, and planning correctional programs.

If correctional administrators are to fulfill their responsibilities of reducing the crime potential of men through treatment, they must know the possible effects any one of the treatment techniques now available may have upon the men under their jurisdiction. For treatment personnel to function effectively, the research personnel should make for them a series of evaluative studies of all the techniques used in the treatment of arrested law violators. Research based upon prearrest factors and upon manipulative and nonmanipulative postarrest, treatment, and postrelease factors would assist the correction personnel in answering questions basic to their work and in fulfilling their responsibility to the people.

Basic research would provide more adequate bases for treatment. Grounds for determining what can be done in the current treatment situation with the available means could be established. Questioning of current techniques which retard reformation or assist but little would be stimulated. With decrease in posttreatment recidivism as the criterion for change, increased reformation would be secured through abandoning useless treatment techniques, reorganizing current procedures, and experimenting with new methods.

Through the development of prognostic instruments in connection with the work of the correctional accounting system, administrators would have additional help in selecting the most efficient treatment techniques for a given man. An additional basis for determining that further treatment will no longer contribute to adjustment would be provided. Such research will contribute to the day when those concerned with the treatment of law violators can prescribe treatment with knowledge of the expected effects of all the available techniques upon them. From among those procedures, the ones that will help the offender the most can be chosen. This could be accomplished by identifying for him those methods that have minimized the recidivism of men like him in the past. Correctional authorities could act more according to calculation and less according to hunch and whim.

Because there are so few practitioners of the new penology staffing our correctional services, because the legal framework for the administration of criminal justice is archaic, because the knowledge already revealed by research in human behavior and corrections is not being utilized, and because correctional accounting systems are not in operation, my answer to the question posed by the title of this paper: "The New Penology—Fact or Fiction ?" is: "I don't know. It has not been tried!"

NOTES AND REFERENCES

1. Federal Bureau of Prisons, *National Prisoner Statistics: Prisoners in State and Federal Institutions, 1950,* 1954. Tables 42 and 43. Also correspondence with James A. McCafferty, Criminologist, Federal Bureau of Prisons.
2. Bennett, James V.: Evaluating a prison. *Annals of the American Academy of Political and Social Science,* 293:10, May, 1954.
3. Hoover, J. Edgar: The Challenge of Crime Control. In *National Probation and Parole Association, Parole in Principle and Practice; A Manual and Report.* New York, The Association, 1957, p. 45.
4. McGee, Richard A.: Planning a State Correctional System, *National Probation and Parole Association Yearbook,* 1947.
5. Sellin, Thorsten: Foreword, *Annals of the American Academy of Political and Social Sciences,* 293:vii, May, 1954.
6. Turnbladh, Will C.: Substitutes for imprisonment. *Annals of the American Academy of Political and Social Sciences,* 293: 117, May, 1954.